# Casino Gambling

# Casino Gambling
## Why You Win, Why You Lose

By

## Russell T. Barnhart

*A Brandywine Press Book*

E. P. Dutton

New York

This book was edited and produced by
*The Brandywine Press, Inc.*
Clarkson N. Potter, President

Printed and bound in Great Britain by Cox & Wyman Ltd.

Published, 1978, in the United States by E. P. Dutton, a
Division of Sequoia-Elsevier Publishing Company, Inc.,
New York, and simultaneously in Canada by Clarke, Irwin
& Company Limited, Toronto and Vancouver

Library of Congress Catalog Card Number: 77–14552

ISBN: 0–87690–270–0

10 9 8 7 6 5 4 3 2 1
First Edition

# Contents

*'Chance favors the prepared mind.'*

——Louis Pasteur

# Introduction

Why have I written this book?

Although it should interest people who want just intellectual knowledge of games of chance, the book is aimed primarily at people who actually intend to gamble.

The contents of the book may be divided into five sections though not necessarily consecutive:

(1) The first section gives the correct and up-to-date *rules* and *procedures* of Monte Carlo (single zero) roulette, American (double zero) roulette, craps, blackjack, Nevada baccarat, baccara chemin-de-fer, baccara-en-banque, slot machines, bingo, keno, trente-et-quarante, and boule.

*N.B.* What little information is presently available to the public oftentimes gives, even for the commonest games, either erroneous, out-of-date, or inadequate rules and procedures – or sometimes none at all. Without knowledge or correct rules and procedures it's obvious that a person can't either stand or sit down and gamble. Or if he does, he'll either lose money or possibly be publicly rebuked.

In addition for each bet at each game I give the accurate percentage – if any – the casino has over the player. Again what little information is presently available to the public on this matter is oftentimes, even for the commonest games, either erroneous, out-of-date, or non-existent.

(2) The second section takes up and answers, in *simple arithmetic*, what I consider the most important mathematical questions about gambling. These are the probability of *winning* and *losing streaks* or of *breaking even*, either *by the end* of a gambling session or *during its actual course*.

Then there is the probability at any game of *winning* or *losing consecutive times in a row*, i.e. the theory of *runs*, which are, of course, the most prominent winning and losing streaks. In particular I discuss the unfortunate probability of a player's running out of capital *before* a winning streak *even begins* – which indicates, of course, how much capital a gambler should bring to the table.

*N.B.* How winning and losing streaks fluctuate, following simple, easy-to-understand mathematical laws, has never been applied to casino games of chance and presented to the public.

(3) The third section presents the results of the Hartman sample of *50,000 consecutive roulette spins* from an *actual* Monte-Carlo roulette table. To illustrate the theories of winning and losing streaks etc. in Section (2) above I break down the Hartman sample into gambling sessions of varying lengths from as small as 100 spins – equal, say, to gambling at the tables at *craps*, *blackjack*, *roulette*, etc. for an hour and a half – to a gambling session as large as 50,000 spins – equal to gambling for almost three months without ever stopping even to eat or sleep. On the one hand I analyze an arbitrarily selected single number – to illustrate the *fluctuations* of the type known to gamblers as a *long shot* – and on the other I analyze an even-money chance, the red – to illustrate the *fluctuations* of the opposite type of bet known as a *short shot*.

*N.B.* One or two mathematicians refer to results of 'random-number tables' or 'theoretical computer read-outs,' but I question whether these terms or their results mean anything to the average reader or gambler. No one has ever taken an actual large gambling sample and analyzed it, either for mathematicians or for gamblers. The illustrative results of the Hartman sample from a *real gambling game* form the core of this book. To accomplish my analysis required 500 sheets of graph paper and blinding work over many months. By analogy the reader may imagine someone's opening the telephone directory of any large city, copying out the first 50,000 telephone numbers, and analyzing the latter from eight independent standpoints.

(4) The fourth section devotes itself to describing and analyzing various staking systems, a subject about which a lot of useless chatter, both *pro* and *con*, has been expended. *Every* gambler adopts *some sort* of staking system – even if it's only betting one dollar a time on the even-money chances of, say, craps, blackjack, roulette, chemin-de-fer, or baccara. I have listed the results of the Hartman sample in such a way and to such an extent that any gambler, whether for a short or long shot, may try out *easily* any gambling system he wants. As some staking systems are much better than others, their consideration is important.

(5) The fifth section is the *conclusion*, in which I draw together whatever threads are necessary.

*N.B.* In my book I don't waste either my time or the reader's giving lectures – mathematical, moral, or of any other type. I assume the reader is an adult, has an interest in the theory of gambling, has perhaps the intention of actually going and gambling at the tables, and can add two and two. That's all.

For the more mathematically inclined reader I provide an appendix of brief references, notes, and discussion.

I hope that the information in my book will be informative and help clear up various unsolved questions. Good luck!

New York, 1977. Russell T. Barnhart

# Casino Gambling

# CHAPTER I

# Heads or Tails?

Peter and Paul are two inveterate, indeed obsessed gamblers who appear frequently in mathematical textbooks tossing a coin for heads or tails, Peter wagering on heads, Paul on tails. The two gamblers never stop, never sleep, never eat. They've been tossing now for over at least two hundred years and their tosses, or *trials*, as mathematicians define a gambling event such as the outcome of a throw of a pair of dice, spin of a roulette wheel, hand of cards, etc. must now number in the billions. What may the results of their efforts teach us?

The first question we should like answered is as follows: were we to divide their games into various sample lengths – one of 2 tosses, 6 tosses, 10 tosses ... 100 tosses ... and as many as 100,000 tosses, in terms of *units of money* (dollars, pounds, francs, marks, lira, etc.), signified by the letter $z$, what would be, say, Peter's *average* win or loss (called a plus or minus *digression*) *at the end* of a specific number of trials, signified by the letter $n$?

For from 2 to 100,000 trials the answers are listed in Table 1, which is easy to interpret. At the end of 10 trials Peter will have either won or lost on an average 3.26 units. At the end of 100 trials he will have either won or lost on an average 8.00 units. And at the end of 1,000 trials he will have either won or lost on an average 25.28 units.

Table 1 also corroborates the mathematical rule known as the Law of Large Numbers: as the value of $n$, the number of trials, increases, the average plus or minus absolute digression (from an even number of wins for both Peter and Paul) *increases* simultaneously and in proportion to the square root of $n$.

TABLE 1

| n | z |
|---|---|
| 2 | 2.00 |
| 6 | 2.73 |
| 10 | 3.26 |
| 18 | 4.12 |
| 36 | 4.80 |
| 100 | 8.00 |
| 1000 | 25.28 |
| 10000 | 80.00 |
| 100000 | 252.80 |

In relation to the Law of Large Numbers there is one digression which has particular significance, the digression of zero *at the end* of n trials. Such a digression means that Peter and Paul have each broken even, i.e. whatever the value of n the number of heads (H) exactly equals the number of tails (T). Mathematicians call such an equalization at the end of n trials a *return to equilibrium*. We should remember that every time a gambler places a bet at a gambling game, be it at blackjack, craps, roulette, or anything else, he is perforce playing, *consciously or not*, either *for* or *against* a return to equilibrium, depending on the staking system he is using. After the initial trial no other alternatives exist. In a later chapter we shall discover that, interestingly enough, the mathematical basis for at least two famous gambling systems is simply a return to equilibrium at the end of n trials.

As we examine Peter's and Paul's game, let us remember that for Peter the probability of tossing heads at any designated trial is 1/2, represented by the letter $p$, and by the same token for Paul the probability of tossing tails at any designated trial is also 1/2, represented by the letter $q$. Henceforth we shall always assume that we are backing the fortunes of Peter.

TABLE 2

$p=q=1/2$

| n | eq |
|---|---|
| 2 | 0.50000 |
| 4 | 0.37500 |
| 6 | 0.31250 |
| 8 | 0.27344 |
| 10 | 0.24610 |
| 12 | 0.22559 |
| 14 | 0.20947 |
| 16 | 0.19638 |
| 18 | 0.18547 |
| 20 | 0.17620 |
| 22 | 0.16819 |
| 24 | 0.16112 |
| 30 | 0.14447 |
| 40 | 0.12537 |
| 50 | 0.11228 |

In Table 2 we list the probability *eq* of a return to equilibrium for various selected values of n – from the 2nd through the 1,000,000th trial. As we may note from Table 2, in accordance with the mentioned Law of Large numbers, as n increases in value, the probability of a return to equilibrium constantly *decreases*. In other words if, for example, Peter is losing, the more he gambles the likelihood becomes smaller and smaller that he will ever break even, oh sad to say.

| | |
|---|---|
| 60 | 0.10256 |
| 70 | 0.09503 |
| 80 | 0.08893 |
| 90 | 0.08387 |
| 100 | 0.07958 |
| 200 | 0.05635 |
| 300 | 0.04603 |
| 400 | 0.03987 |
| 500 | 0.03566 |
| 600 | 0.03256 |
| 700 | 0.03015 |
| 800 | 0.02820 |
| 900 | 0.02659 |
| 1000 | 0.02523 |
| 2000 | 0.01784 |
| 5000 | 0.01128 |
| 10000 | 0.00798 |
| 100000 | 0.00252 |
| 1000000 | 0.00079 |

We might visualize the probability of a return to equilibrium as occurring along a magnetic line. Magnets do pull objects (say, Peter) towards themselves. But the *farther* away an object gets (see $z$ column, Table 1, p. 2), the *weaker* is its pull. Finally the pull becomes so weak that, for all practical gambling purposes, it ceases to affect the outcome of Peter's bet.

One of the most prevalent delusions among gamblers – it's even known as the Gambler's Fallacy – is that the longer they gamble (i.e. as the value of $n$ increases) the larger becomes the probability *eq* of their breaking even. As we have shown by the figures in Tables 1 and 2, the reverse is true: the longer Peter gambles, the smaller the likelihood that he will ever break even.

Table 2 (p. 2) gives us the probability *eq* of the average number of returns to equilibrium *at the end* of $n$ trials. This brings us to the question of how often, if at all, Peter is likely on average to break even *during the course* of a game. How often on average will he weave back and forth across the line of equilibrium before terminating his game at the $n$th trial? Table 3 lists the average number of returns to equilibrium *during* a game of $n$ trials. The reader will immediately observe that, as $n$ increases, the returns to equilibrium become *relatively* fewer and fewer, i.e. the ratio (or relative proportion) of the number of returns to the number of trials gradually decreases. Thus, for example, during 200 trials there are roughly 10 returns. But if we roughly double the number of returns to 21, the corresponding number of trials must be increased not to 400 but to *800*, i.e. it

TABLE 3

| $n$ | average number of returns |
|---|---|
| 2 | 0.5000 |
| 4 | 0.8750 |
| 6 | 1.1875 |
| 8 | 1.4609 |
| 10 | 1.7070 |
| 12 | 1.9326 |
| 20 | 2.5240 |
| 50 | 4.6140 |
| 100 | 6.9780 |
| 200 | 10.3130 |
| 500 | 16.8390 |
| 800 | 21.7270 |
| 1000 | 24.2300 |
| 5000 | 55.5300 |
| 10000 | 78.7800 |

3

| | |
|---|---|
| 50000 | 178.9000 |
| 100000 | 251.2000 |
| 500000 | 564.3000 |
| 1000000 | 796.8000 |

must be increased not twice but *four* times! The rule is in accord with the Law of Large Numbers: the average number of returns to equilibrium during $n$ trials increases only (approximately) as the square root of $n$.

For gamblers the relatively slow rate of increase of returns to equilibrium is portentous enough, for if the average number of returns to equilibrium is becoming smaller and smaller, then obviously the length of the average plus and minus digression is becoming longer and longer (as shown in Table 1, p. 2). And in the case of the average minus or losing digression, this is bad news, but better that we find it out now than at the tables.

TABLE 4

| exactly | $n=20$ |
|---|---|
| 0 | 0.176 |
| 1 | 0.176 |
| 2 | 0.167 |
| 3 | 0.148 |
| 4 | 0.122 |
| 5 | 0.092 |
| 6 | 0.061 |
| 7 | 0.035 |
| 8 | 0.016 |
| 9 | 0.005 |
| 10 | 0.001 |
| | 0.999 |

During any game the minimal number of returns is obviously $0$ or none, and the maximal number is obviously $n/2$. Let's say Peter and Paul toss a coin 20 times (i.e. $n$ equals 20). What are the probabilities of exactly 0 returns to equilibrium, 1 return, 2 returns, 3 returns ... or the maximum of 10 returns (every other toss)? Table 4 lists all $n/2 = 20/2 = 10$ probabilities. We see how dangerous is a staking system based on any returns to equilibrium at all. For example, if we sum the probabilities of 0, 1, and 2 returns, i.e. $0.176 + 0.176 + 0.167 = 0.519$, we find that in a large number of games, each 20 trials long, *as many as 51.9 per cent of the games*, or roughly *half*, will have *only* 2 or fewer returns to equilibrium.

A similar addition of the values in Table 4 (p. 4) results in Table 5A and 5B. What if a gambler is using a staking system, for example, which requires 2 (or fewer) returns to equilibrium during his game of 20 trials? We have already calculated the favorable probability of occurrence as 0.519, and we note this value as the third one listed in Table 5A. Thus the letter P, defined here as the probability of $z$ *or fewer* returns during $n$ trials, heads the probability column of Table 5A, while the complementary letter Q, defined here as the probability of *more than* $z$ returns during $n$ trials, heads the probability column of Table 5B. As P plus Q (like

4

$p$ plus $q$) must axiomatically always equal 1 (signifying certainty, with O, at the other extreme, signifying impossibility), the reader will note that any P value in Table 5A added to its opposite or complementary number in Table 5B always sums to 1.

Tables 5A and 5B again point up the danger of a gambler using any staking system requiring *even one* return to equilibrium during a game of $n$ trials. Table 5A (p. 5) shows that the probability of 0 (or fewer) returns during the game is 'only' 0.176 and across the way in the Q column of Table 5B (p. 5) we see that the complementary probability of 1 (or more) returns is 0.824. Let us phrase it differently. These figures mean that a gambler using any staking system requiring *only one* return to equilibrium during 20 trials will win 82.4 per cent of the time – but it is self-evident that he stands to lose perhaps a substantial sum of money (especially if he be progressively increasing his stake) during the other 17.6 per cent of the time. And let us remember: the occurrence of that 17.6 per cent loss is inevitable from the practical standpoint. The optimist will say that the 82.4 per cent will come *first*, thereby allowing him to build up capital to carry him over the 17.6 per cent: arbitrarily I side with the pessimist.

| TABLE 5A | | TABLE 5B | | |
|---|---|---|---|---|
| z or fewer | n=20 P | more than z | n=20 Q | Probability Q that: |
| 0 | 0.176 | 0 | 0.824 | 1 (or more) returns will occur: |
| 1 | 0.352 | 1 | 0.648 | 2 |
| 2 | 0.519 | 2 | 0.481 | 3 |
| 3 | 0.667 | 3 | 0.333 | 4 |
| 4 | 0.789 | 4 | 0.211 | 5 |
| 5 | 0.881 | 5 | 0.119 | 6 |
| 6 | 0.942 | 6 | 0.058 | 7 |
| 7 | 0.977 | 7 | 0.023 | 8 |
| 8 | 0.993 | 8 | 0.007 | 9 |
| 9 | 0.998 | 9 | 0.002 | 10 |
| 10 | 1.000 | 10 | 0.000 | etc |

The reader may easily draw more conclusions by pairing other complementary values of P and Q from Tables 5A and 5B (p. 5). Of these values it is interesting to note that when a gambler's requirement of returns *increases* from only 3 to 4 the probability of success *drops* from 0.481 to 0.333, or from roughly a half to as little as a third.

Because gamblers frequently spend an hour or less at their favorite casino game – be it craps, blackjack, or roulette – Table 6 (p. 6) lists the Q probabilities of some typical values of $z$ returns applying to a game of 100 trials. It should be remembered that to calculate the complementary values of the absent P probabilities one needs only to subtract from 1 the Q values of Table 6 (p. 6).

Let us say that again a gambler's staking system requires that he break even *only once* (or more) during the game of 100 trials. Table 6 shows that he will win 92.04 per cent of the time (or games) and go broke 1−92.04 per cent=7.96 per cent of the time (or games).

TABLE 6

| more than z | n=100 Q | Probability Q that: |
|---|---|---|
| 0 | 0.9204 | 1 (or more) returns will occur: |
| 1 | 0.8431 | 2 |
| 2 | 0.7557 | 3 |
| 3 | 0.6817 | 4 |
| 4 | 0.6107 | 5 |
| 5 | 0.5338 | 6 |
| 6 | 0.4708 | 10 |
| 10 | 0.2462 | 11 |
| 11 | 0.2082 | 15 |
| 15 | 0.0819 | 20 |
| 20 | 0.0189 | 25 |
| 25 | 0.0027 | 30 |
| 30 | 0.0003 | etc. |

Another example. Let us say a gambler requires 4 (or more) returns to equilibrium. He will win 68.17 per cent of the time and go broke 1−68.17 per cent = 31.83 per cent of the time. Notice that the win–lose fifty-fifty point in a game of 100 trials comes at about 5 returns.

But what of a really big game? For this we have recourse to a simple graph of black dots constituting the entire history of a coin-tossing game 10,000 trials long, reported and analyzed by the late Professor William Feller.[1] Of the three lines comprising Table

[1] *An Introduction to Probability Theory and Its Applications*, by William Feller (1906–70), Vol. 1 (Third Edition), N.Y., 1968, p. 87.

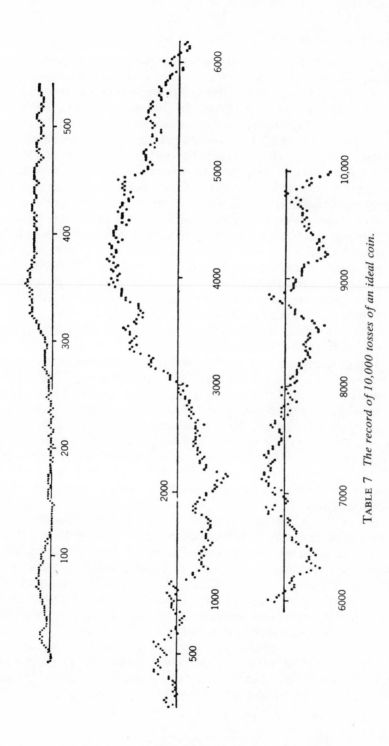

TABLE 7  *The record of 10,000 tosses of an ideal coin.*

7 (p. 7) the upper one, the 1st line, is merely a duplication – an enlargement of the first 550 trials, each black dot or *particle*, to use Professor Feller's term, signifying 2 trials (whether plus or minus). The two lower lines of particles, the 2nd and 3rd lines, constitute the history in its entirety, each particle signifying 20 trials. Hence the upper graph, the 1st line, is compressed into the initial portion of the 2nd line up to and slightly beyond the 500th trial mark. The 2nd and 3rd lines again constitute equilibrium, and the numbers 500, 1,000, 2,000, 3,000 . . . 10,000 the increasing values of *n*, the number of trials.

When the particle is above the line of equilibrium Peter is winning, i.e. experiencing a plus digression. Conversely when the particle is below the line, he is losing, i.e. experiencing a minus digression.[1] Thus, for example, around the 9,800th trial (unmarked on the graph) Peter is just barely above the line, having suffered a minus digression for roughly the previous 1,000 trials. Unfortunately for the remainder of the game he experiences another minus digression, the particle at the 10,000th trial ending considerably below the line.

The graph illustrates clearly how very *infrequent* is the occurrence of returns to equilibrium during a typical game. In particular from roughly the 3,000th trial to the 6,000 (ending the 2nd line approximately), a sequence of 3,000 trials comprising almost *one third* of the whole game, *there does not occur a single return!* From the 3,000th trial to roughly the 4,100th, on the 2nd line, Peter encounters the most favorable plus digression of the game, but from the 4,100th trial to the 6,000th (near end of 2nd line) an adverse digression unfortunately sets in, and he loses back all his previous gains.

One of the important lessons of the graph is that of the danger of calculating in terms of a theoretical *average* number of returns rather than, as we did in Tables 5 and 6 (pp. 5 and 6), their *probability*. Although our topic at hand pertains to returns to equilibrium, this warning applies to all averages. The danger lies in assuming that the result of any *particular* game will *probably* be *close* to the theoretical average. In actual fact such a result will *probably* be more or less *distant* from the average.

During 10,000 trials, for example, the average number of returns to equilibrium is 79 as we saw in Table 3 (p. 3). How many returns, we ask, occur in the particular game represented by Table

[1] For the plus and minus average digressions, see Table 1 (p. 2).

8

7 (p. 7)? Before stating Professor Feller's answer it should be noted that one may legitimately read his graph either forwards or backwards, because each trial is physically, and therefore mathematically, independent of its immediate predecessor and successor. To read the graph first forward as one game, then backward as another, obviously endows it with double utility. When one reads the graph of Table 7 (p. 7) forward, there occur, according to Professor Feller, 140 returns. When one reads the graph backward (the line of equilibrium in this case originating at the last particle from the standpoint of the first game), there occur only 14 returns.[1] Now both these numbers – 140 and 14 – are quite distant from our theoretical average of 79 returns, for $140-79 = 61$ too many returns and $79-14 = 64$ too few returns.

How probable are these divergences in the case of a particular game of 10,000 trials? There are two questions.

First, what is the probability of 14 (or fewer) returns to equilibrium during 10,000 tosses of a coin? The answer is P = *0.124* (and $1-P= Q = 0.876$).

Second, what is the probability of more than 140 returns to equilibrium during 10,000 tosses of a coin? The answer is (P = 0.843) = $1-P = Q = 0.157$.

What do these two almost identical probabilities signify for a player? This question should be answered from two standpoints.

From the purely *mathematical* standpoint we see that neither probability is so small as one might expect on the basis of hasty conjecture. The probability 0.157 indicates that in a large number of games, each 10,000 trials long, as many as from 1 to 2 games out of every 15 (roughly 15.7 per cent of the total) will contain more than 140 returns. The probability 0.124 indicates that in the same number of games of the same length, again as many as from 1 to 2 games out of every 12 (roughly 12.4 per cent of the total) will contain 14 or fewer returns. Concerning the latter answer in particular Professor Feller comments: 'Thus, contrary to intuition, finding only 14 equalizations is not surprising at all.'

The content of the foregoing paragraph answers our preceding question of whether 140 and 14 returns to equilibrium are

[1] This horizontal line of equilibrium of the second game passes below every single particle until striking that representing very roughly the 2,200th trial from the standpoint of the first game's trial marks. Hence in terms of the second game's calibration this means that the first return to equilibrium does not occur until the 8,800th trial!

9

respectively excessive or deficient, given that the theoretical *average* is 79: from the standpoint of their *probability* we see that they are not.

From the *gambling* standpoint, however, the two answers – 140 and 14 – must also be viewed in their proportional relation to the number of trials. Thus the fraction 140/10,000 indicates a proportion of about 1 return for every 72 trials and 14/10,000 only 1 return for as many as 715 trials! These proportions bring us to the question of the *location* or *distribution* of $z$ returns (whether 14, 140, 79, or whatever) during a game of $n$ trials. Will the $z$ returns tend to cluster somewhere – say at the beginning, middle, or end of the game – or will they tend to string themselves out more or less equidistantly? The question is answered by a cursory examination of the 550 trials comprising the 1st line of Table 7 (p. 7). We observe that from roughly the 10th to the 110th trial there does not occur a *single* return to equilibrium, whereas from very roughly the 110th to the 270th trial there occur *many* returns; and finally from very roughly the 270th to the 550th trial, again there does not occur a *single* return. Thus we see that in the 1st line (and similarly in the 2nd and 3rd lines, the reader will note) *there is an exceedingly strong tendency for the returns to cluster*. Is this distributional tendency typical of all games, not just the one analyzed by Professor Feller? The answer is definitely yes. It is obvious that knowledge of this 'feast or famine' distribution of returns may be of great value to players – especially to those whose systems are based on the delusory assumption that returns, whether few or many in number, tend to be strung out equidistantly. As we shall see anon, even a simple, ostensibly safe system, if based even partially on this illusion, may eventuate too easily in a large loss.

If the two proportions of returns to trials at all surprised the reader, he should feel better to know that many professional mathematicians themselves found the proportions quite difficult to believe. To quote Professor Feller: 'Sampling of expert opinion has revealed that even trained statisticians feel that 140 equalizations in 10,000 tosses of a coin is a surprisingly small number, and 14 appears quite out of bounds.'[1]

In analyzing the probability of $z$ returns to equilibrium during $n$ trials we made $n$ equal to 20 and then 100. Comparable to Table 5 (p.5) for the selected values of P and Q, Table 8 lists under $z$ the number of returns to equilibrium during 10,000 trials.

[1] See Feller, *op. cit.* (1st edition, 1950), p. 85.

TABLE 8

$n = 10,000$

| P | Q | z |
|------|------|-----|
| 0.10 | 0.90 | 11 |
| 0.20 | 0.80 | 17 |
| 0.33 | 0.67 | 44 |
| 0.50 | 0.50 | 66 |
| 0.67 | 0.33 | 95 |
| 0.80 | 0.20 | 127 |
| 0.90 | 0.10 | 163 |
| 0.99 | 0.01 | 256 |

Naturally the numbers in the $z$ column are substantially larger than those in Table 6 (p. 6). Thus Table 6 indicates, for example, that the median number of returns during 100 trials is 5, while Table 8 indicates that the median number during 10,000 trials is 66. But to obtain this roughly *13 fold* increase in the number of *returns* we have been obliged to increase *20 fold* the number of trials. This implies, of course, that the average length of a digression (whether plus or minus) between returns has increased as the square root of the number of trials, a statement only reminding us that, whatever be our superficial topic, we are always dealing at base with the Law of Large Numbers.

Our discussion should point up strongly how infrequent, or improbable, may be a return to equilibrium, and by the same token how long may be a plus or minus digression (a winning or losing streak).

11

# CHAPTER II

# Winning and Losing Streaks

Peter and Paul are still at it: night and day they toss that coin, heads (H) favoring Peter, tails (T) favoring Paul.

In the first chapter we examined fundamentals of a return to equilibrium both *at the end* of $n$ trials and *during $n$* trials. We noted that a return to equilibrium may also be called a digression of 0 units.

In the present chapter we turn to the subject of a *plus* (or *winning*) digression and its unfortunate counterpart a *minus* (or *losing*) digression. Again $p=q=1/2$, with $p$ presenting Peter's probability in a *single* toss of winning ($q$ of his losing, i.e. of Paul's winning). Henceforth we shall always espouse Peter's cause.

When Peter is ahead of Paul *at the end* of $n$ trials, he says he *has been* in a 'winning streak'. When Peter is similarly behind, he says he *has been* in a 'losing streak'.

From Table 1 (p. 2) we listed, among other digressions, Peter's *plus* or *minus average* digression of $z$ units *at the end* of 100 trials. From Table 1 (p. 2) we note that *at the end* of 100 trials the value of the *average* digression is 8.00 units, won or lost. But *at the end* of 100 trials what is the *probability* of winning or losing these 8.00 units – as well as that of winning or losing anywhere from the minimum 0 units (equilibrium) to as much as 50 units? Unless otherwise specified, we assume Peter bets only 1 unit on every toss or trial.

The answer to our questions may be found in the four columns of Table 9 (p. 13), which is headed, as the reader will observe, by the two letters $P$ and $Q$, plus these two letters divided by number 2, i.e. $P/2$ and $Q/2$. Now let us examine the significance of the table from the standpoint of each of its columns.

## TABLE 9

$$n = 100, p = q = 1/2$$

| z | P | Q | P/2 | Q/2 |
|---|---|---|-----|-----|
| 0 | 0.0795 | 0.9205 | 0.0398 | 0.4602 |
| 2 | 0.2335 | 0.7665 | 0.1168 | 0.3833 |
| 4 | 0.3793 | 0.6207 | 0.1897 | 0.3104 |
| 6 | 0.5116 | 0.4884 | 0.2558 | 0.2442 |
| 8 | 0.6270 | 0.3730 | 0.3135 | 0.1865 |
| 10 | 0.7238 | 0.2762 | 0.3619 | 0.1381 |
| 12 | 0.8018 | 0.1982 | 0.4009 | 0.0991 |
| 14 | 0.8624 | 0.1376 | 0.4312 | 0.0688 |
| 16 | 0.9076 | 0.0924 | 0.4538 | 0.0462 |
| 18 | 0.9400 | 0.0600 | 0.4700 | 0.0300 |
| 20 | 0.9623 | 0.377 | 0.4812 | 0.0189 |
| 22 | 0.9772 | 0.0228 | 0.4886 | 0.0114 |
| 24 | 0.9866 | 0.0134 | 0.4933 | 0.0067 |
| 26 | 0.9924 | 0.0076 | 0.4962 | 0.0038 |
| 28 | 0.9959 | 0.0041 | 0.4980 | 0.0021 |
| 30 | 0.9978 | 0.0022 | 0.4989 | 0.0011 |
| 40 | 0.9999507 | 0.0000493 | 0.4999754 | 0.0000247 |
| 50 | 0.9999995 | 0.0000004 | 0.4999998 | 0.0000002 |

Definitions for above table: $z$ signifies the number of units (won or lost) *at the end* of 100 trials; P the probability of *either* winning *or* losing $z$ or fewer units; P/2 the probability of *specifically* winning or *specifically* losing $z$ or fewer units; and by the same token Q the probability of *either* winning *or* losing more than $z$ units.

Of the four columns, the righthand one, Q/2, comprises the answers that most interest gamblers. Thus *at the end* of 100 trials Peter will have a probability of 0.1865 of specifically winning (losing) more than 8 units (these being the average number as we recall from Table 1, p. 2). Peter has also the relatively small probability of 0.0189 of specifically winning (losing) more than 20 units, of only 0.0021 of specifically winning (losing) more than 28 units, and of only 0.0000002 of specifically winning (losing) more than 50 units. (As the last entries of Table 9, p. [13], portend, the probabilities of winning or losing more than 50 units at the end of 100 trials are insignificant.)

A gambler might object, however, stating: 'Yes, but I've often shot craps for just 100 throws and won (lost) a hell of a lot more money than $50.00!' To which I must naturally reply: 'Most

13

certainly, but were you always betting *only $1.00* per throw like Peter?' This leads me to add that the probability values of Table 9 (p. 13) apply *without change* to any amount won or lost *depending on your basic or average bet.* Instead of Peter's betting only 1 unit per trial let us say he bets 10 per trial. Just multiply all the unit figures in the $z$ column by 10, and the rest of the table applies, as mentioned, without change. Thus if we look again down the fourth or Q/2 column, Peter has a probability of 0.1381 of winning (losing) more than 100 units at the end of 100 trials, one of just 0.0011 of winning (losing) more than 300 units at the end of 100 trials, and one of only 0.0000002 of winning (losing) more than 500 units at the end of 100 trials.

Want to go for $100 a stake? See your banker, and the best of luck!

Now we remember that in the case of a return to equilibrium we studied first the fluctuations *at the end* of n trials, secondly those *during n* trials. Let us proceed to do the same with plus and minus digressions.

When Peter is ahead of Paul *during n* trials, he says he *is* in a 'winning streak'. When Peter is similarly behind, he says he is in a 'losing streak'. (Compare this to the wording of the fourth paragraph of this chapter.)

Many a player loses his entire capital of $z$ units sometime during a game and perforce abandons play, only to watch with frustration as a highly profitable digression favors the remaining players at the table. Thus at roulette a gambler wagers without success on a particular number until the expenditure of his last unit. Then looking on as an impoverished bystander he observes his number appear several times within a short period. At craps another player, using a progressive staking system, loses a substantial sum during the first three-quarters of the game. Then forced to abandon his system and reduced to meager flat stakes, during the last quarter he wins a sum paltry in comparison to what he lost. And finally at blackjack another player, ruined by the many low-value cards (which disfavor a player) during, say, the first two-thirds of the game, rises from his chair only to watch enviously as the other players, with larger capitals, win hand after hand from the final emergence of the high-value cards (which favor a player).

The foregoing may be summed up by saying that mathematically the average plus or minus digression *during* a game is invariably *larger* and therefore *more probable* than that *at the end* of a game.

How much larger and how much more probable? Let us examine first one, then the other.

Table 10 below lists the average plus or minus digression pertinent to selected values of *n* from 2 to 100,000. As the reader will recognize, the table is actually Table 1 (p. 2) to which we now add the *z-during* column on the right.[1] Table 10 is easily read. Whereas at the end of 100 trials the average plus or minus digression is 8.00 units, that during the course of the game is 13.00 units. Whereas at the end of 1,000 trials the average gain or loss is 25.28 units, that during the course of the game is 41.08 units. Whereas at the end of 50,000 trials the average plus or minus digression is 178.44 units, that during the course of the game is 290.00 units (two figures to be compared to the average 'gain' or loss at the end of the 50,000 spins of the Hartman Sample, to be examined anon). And so forth for any number of trials in an even-money game in which $p=q=1/2$.

TABLE 10

| n | at end z | during z |
|---|---|---|
| 2 | 2.00 | 3.25 |
| 6 | 2.73 | 4.44 |
| 10 | 3.26 | 5.30 |
| 18 | 4.12 | 6.70 |
| 36 | 4.80 | 7.80 |
| 100 | 8.00 | 13.00 |
| 1000 | 25.28 | 41.08 |
| 10000 | 80.00 | 130.00 |
| 50000 | 178.44 | 290.00 |
| 100000 | 252.80 | 410.80 |

Now we come to the second part of our question. What is the *probability* of a digression of *z* units *during* the course of *n* trials? The answer is easy. The probability of a gain (loss) of *z* units *during* a game is *exactly double* that of a gain (loss) of *z* units *at the end* of the same game.[2]

This simple theorem allows us to refer again to Table 9 (p. 13): if Q/2 be the probability of a gain (loss) of more than *z* units *at the end* of *n* trials, then Q itself is the probability of a gain (loss) of more than *z* units *during the course of n* trials. In the case of Table 9 (p. 13) the number of trials, of course, is 100.

Hence for examples of the theorem we need not resort to any computations.

Thus if the probability of winning (losing) more than 10 units at

[1] When $p=q=1/2$, the average digression during *n* trials is always 1.625 times larger than that at the end of *n* trials.

[2] This theorem is valid for all values of *p* and *q* assuming a mathematically fair game.

15

the end of 100 trials is $Q/2=0.1381$, that during 100 trials is $Q=0.2762$. If the probability of winning (losing) more than 20 units at the end of 100 trials is $Q/2=0.0189$, that during 100 trials is $Q=0.0377$. And if the probability of winning (losing) more than 28 units at the end of 100 trials is $Q/2=0.0021$, that during 100 trials is $Q=0.0041$ (disregarding the triviality of rounding off final digits).

The theorems relating *during* to *at end* digressions were formulated by the late French mathematician Louis Bachelier (1870–1946) in his *Traité sur le Calcul des Probabilités*, Paris, 1912, Chapt., 10, Sec. 337, pp. 225–26. It is self-evident that Bachelier's theories may be of considerable intellectual help to gamblers.

# CHAPTER III

# The Bank's Percentage

Although most gamblers know that the Bank or casino has some slight mathematical advantage over them on each trial, few players know with any exactitude either the extent of this advantage or its adverse effect on their game.

Rule: In a mathematically *fair* game the *positive* expectation *equals* the *negative* expectation.

As the positive expectation is represented algebraically by $pb$ and the negative expectation by $qa$, then these two quantities will be equal if the game be mathematically fair. Thus to verify the mathematical fairness (or unfairness) of a game one substitutes in the following equation:

$$pb=qa$$

Let us take two examples, the first a coin-tossing game, the second a dice-throwing game.

Peter and Paul toss a coin, the former betting on heads, the latter on tails. Let $p$ signify the favorable probability of the occurrence of H in a single trial, and $b$ the number of units Peter wins from Paul if H occur; let $q$ signify the unfavorable probability of the occurrence of T in a single trial, and $a$ the constant or average number of units Peter bets on each trial. As always in a coin-tossing game, $p=q=1/2$; and if Peter bet 1 unit per trial, then $a=1$; and whenever he wins, Paul pays him off at 1-to-1 odds, i.e. the pay-off odds to 1 in a single trial are $b$, i.e. $b=1$. Hence we have . . .

$$(1/2)(1)=(1/2)(1), \ 1/2=1/2$$

As both sides of the equation are identical, then we know that Peter is receiving exactly his due whenever he wins, i.e. it is a mathematically *fair* game.

17

But what if Paul pays Peter only, say, 9/10ths of a unit every time the latter wins? Then we have . . .

$(1/)(9/10)=(1/2)(1)$, $9/20=1/2$, and 9/20 does *not* equal 10/20

As both sides of the equation are accordingly *not* identical, then we know the game is mathematically *unfair*, and we may state another rule:

Rule: In a mathematically *unfair* game the *negative* expectation *exceeds* the *positive* expectation, i.e. *qa exceeds pb*.

As in the above equation 10/20 (i.e. *qa*) exceeds 9/20 (i.e. *pb*), then by definition whenever he wins, Peter is not receiving as many units as he should from Paul.

If a game be mathematically unfair, to what degree is it unfair? In a casino game this degree is called the *Bank's percentage*, or colloquially, the *PC*, and shall be designated by the letter *y*. Its value is obtained by subtracting the positive expectation from the negative expectation, i.e. by substituting in *qa−pb*. Again let us state a rule:

Rule: The Bank's percentage *y* equals the positive expectation subtracted from the negative expectation.

Using the last equation as our example, we have $10/20-9/20=1/20$. What does this fraction signify? It means that every time Peter *bets a* units he *loses* on an average $(1/20)a$ units to Paul. This adverse effect will be elaborated anon.

For our second example let us use a dice-throwing game. Peter and Paul throw a pair of dice. At any given trial Peter's chance of throwing a pair of aces is $p=1/36$, that of not throwing a pair of aces is $q=35/36$. (It should be noted that $1-p$ always equals 1, signifying certainty.) Peter bets $a=1$ unit on each trial, and whenever he wins, Paul pays him $b=35$ units. Is this a mathematically unfair game to Peter?

$(1/36)(35)=(35/36)(1)$, $35/36=35/36$

Hence the game is mathematically fair to Peter, because *pb=qa*.

But what if Paul pays Peter only, say, 34 units every time the latter wins? Then we have . . .

$(1/36)(34)=(35/36)(1)$, and 34/36 does *not* equal 35/36

As both sides of the equation are *not* identical, then we know the game is mathematically unfair to Peter, and the degree to which it is unfair is $qa-pb=35/36-34/36=1/36$. This fraction signifies

18

that every time Peter *bets* $a$ units he *loses* on an average $(1/36)a$ units to Paul. Again this adverse effect will be elaborated shortly.

Rule and formula: if $p$ and $q$ signify respectively the favorable and unfavorable probabilities of an event at any given trial, $a$ the average amount of the gambler's=bet, and $b$ the Bank's pay-off odds to 1, then the following formula yields the *Bank's percentage*, signified by the letter $y$:

$$(qa - bp) = y$$

*The value of* $y$ is always in the form of a common or decimal fraction, but if one wishes it in terms of actual *percentage*, then, of course, one merely multiplies $y$ by 100. As the value of $y$ may be arduous to calculate, I have listed it (along with the values of $p$ and $q$) for each bet in all the games that we shall consider anon.

The value of $b$, the Bank's pay-off odds to 1, is never calculated by a player. It is always declared by the casino in the rules of its games.

Rule and formula: assuming the foregoing definitions of $a, b, p, q$, and $y$, and defining $n$ as the number of trials, then the following formula yields the gambler's *average rate of loss* at the end of $n$ owing to the Bank's percentage:

$$an(qa - bp) = any$$

Rule: To calculate the *average gain* in units at the end of $n$ trials in an *unfair game* one *subtracts any* from the average gain in units at the end of $n$ trials of the equivalent fair game.

To calculate the *average loss* in units at the end of $n$ trials in an *unfair game* one *adds any* to the average loss in units at the end of $n$ trials of the equivalent fair game.

Let us examine Table 11 below. The second or $z$ column repeats the $z$ column of Table 1 (p. 2), i.e. $z$ signifies the average gain or loss in units at the end of a fair coin-tossing game. To obtain the average gain of the equivalent unfair game one subtracts *any* from $z$ to get the figures of the *ufcw* column (cumulative net win at the end of the unfair game). And to obtain the average loss of the equivalent unfair game one adds *any* to $z$ to get the figures of the *ufcl* column (cumulative net loss at the end of the unfair game).

Let us assume that the Bank's percentage in this imaginary game is arbitrarily $y = 136 = 0.0277$, i.e. 2.77 per cent, a conservatively 'typical' PC.

19

TABLE 11

| n | z | ufcw | ufcl | any |
|---|---|---|---|---|
| 2 | 2.00 | 1.95 | −2.05 | −0.055 |
| 6 | 2.73 | 2.56 | −2.90 | −0.166 |
| 10 | 3.26 | 2.98 | −3.54 | −0.277 |
| 18 | 4.12 | 3.62 | −4.62 | −0.499 |
| 36 | 4.80 | 3.80 | −5.80 | −1.000 |
| 100 | 8.00 | 5.23 | −10.77 | −2.000 |
| 1000 | 25.28 | −2.42 | −52.98 | −27.700 |
| 10000 | 80.00 | −197.00 | −357.00 | −277.000 |
| 50000 | 178.44 | −1206.56 | −1563.44 | −1385.000 |
| 100000 | 252.80 | −2517.20 | −3022.80 | −2770.000 |

Table 11 illustrates all too clearly the adverse effect of a PC of 'only' 1/36 on a player's average gains and losses. As the number of trials increases from 1 to 100,000 or whatever. *the PC reduces every wager Peter makes, whether winning or losing*, by exactly 1/36=0.0277, i.e. 2.77 per cent. One might think of the PC as a sort of constant interest that favors the Bank rather than the investor or gambler.

Thus at the end of a fair game of 36 trials on an average one will win or lose 4.80 units. At the end of an unfair game of 36 trials, however, on an average one will win only 3.80 units and lose 5.80. At the end of a fair game of 100 trials on an average one will win or lose 8.00 units; if the game be unfair, however, one will win only 5.23 units and lose 10.77 – the average loss having now become *more than double* the gain. And as we observe, somewhere between 100 and 1,000 trials in the unfair game the average gain not only decreases to zero but becomes *a minus quantity, continuing so to infinity*. Thus at the end of an unfair game of 1,000 trials the average result is either at best a loss of 2.42 units or at worst a loss of 52.98 units. At the end of an unfair game of 10,000 trials our choice has become even more disheartening – between an average loss of 197 units and one of 357. And at the end of an unfair game of 100,000 trials we have only two enormous losses from which to choose – an average loss of 2,517.20 units and another of 3,022.80.

From the *any* column of Table 11 (p. 20) one may deduce the following rule: In order to break even at the end of an unfair game, one must win at least *any* units.

Thus to break even at the end of 36 trials one must win at least 1 unit, at the end of 100 trials at least 2.77 units, at the end of 1,000 trials at least 27, at the end of 10,000 at least 277, and so forth. And as *any* increases in constant ratio with the number of trials, it is obvious that to break even becomes more and more improbable – and *far more rapidly so* than in a fair game.

Whatever may be the intellectual approach of comprehending the Bank's percentage, however, in the end the latter's adverse effect will always be found to be the same: if the PC be represented by $y$ (a common or decimal fraction), then whether one win or lose any given bet, on an average one will lose $y$th of that bet to the casino.

In Table 12 below I have listed the eight most popular games played in casinos round the world.[1] Although five of the eight games offer in addition bets whose probability at any given trial is relatively small, we are considering here only their *even-money* bets, for which the values of $p$ and $q$ are close to $p = q = 1/2$, and for which the Bank's pay-off odds are 1 to 1. For each game I have listed the value of the Bank's percentage – in the lefthand column as a decimal fraction, in the middle column as a common fraction.

TABLE 12

*Even-money Bets*

| Game | PC | PC | $0.04/y^2$ |
|---|---|---|---|
| 1  baccara-en-banque | 0.00917... | 1/109 | 475 |
| 2  trente-et-quarante (*insured*) | 0.01000... | 1/100 | 400 |
| 3  baccara chemin-de-fer | 0.0115 .... | 1/87 | 304 |
| 4  trente-et-quarante (*uninsured*) | 0.0125 .... | 1/80 | 256 |
| 5  Nevada baccarat | 0.0127 .... | 1/79 | 248 |
| 6  European roulette (red or black) | 0.0141 .... | 1/71 | 201 |
| 7  craps (line) | 0.0141 .... | 1/71 | 201 |
| 8  American roulette | 0.0526 .... | 1/19 | 15 |
| 9  boule | 0.1111 .... | 1/9 | 3 |

For our present purpose we need know nothing more about each of these games than that from the standpoint of the Bank's percentage the most favorable one is that at the top of the list, baccara-en-banque, and the most unfavorable one is that at the bottom, boule. Thus from *purely* this standpoint it behooves a

[1] Because its PC may fluctuate from less than 0 per cent to almost 100 per cent, blackjack constitutes a special case and has therefore been excluded from this list. See Chapter XIV.

player, should the choice be upon him, always to pick the game closest to the top of the list.

Now to another though directly relevant question. At what trial in a given casino game does the Bank's percentage or PC, an unfavorable trend, absorb all the gain from the average plus digression, a favorable trend? In other words at what value of $n$ does the decreasing trend of the Bank's percentage bisect the increasing trend of the average plus digression? The answer, listed in the righthand column under $0.04/y^2$, is worth knowing, for at this unfortunate point all the player's average gain will have decreased to zero, and beyond this point his average gain becomes, like his average loss, a purely minus quantity, and continues so to infinity.

Let us read the righthand column from the bottom up. If we play boule, our average gain is completely absorbed as early as the 3rd trial, whereas if we play baccara-en-banque, this unfavorable point is postponed until the 475th trial. Similarly the average gain of an even-money bet at American roulette is absorbed as early as the 15th trial, whereas at craps or European roulette the absorption does not take place until the 201st trial.

Thus we come again to the same conclusion: all else being equal, a gambler should always pick the game offering the smallest PC.

# CHAPTER IV

# A Typical Game: European Roulette

In the United States the three most popular games in gambling casinos are blackjack, craps, and roulette in that order. Of these I have selected roulette as the most appropriate game to examine first. It is the most traditional game. It is the only one common to casinos in the United States, Europe, Central Europe, the Near East, the Far East, Africa, Central and South America, and the Caribbean. It is the only one for which authentic statistical data, like the Hartman sample (Chapter V anon), have been published.[1] And perhaps most important, as its mathematical structure is so simple to understand, roulette serves very well to illustrate the problems a gambler has to face no matter which he chooses.

When I speak of *European* roulette, I refer to the game on whose wheel are painted 36 numbers plus a *single* zero. As illustrated in Table 13 (p. 24) the roulette wheel is composed of a stationary wooden bowl (about two feet in diameter), in the center of which, revolving on a pivot, is the conical metal wheel head (about 20 inches in diameter), on the circumference of which, each marking the entrance to a slot (about an inch wide), are the 36 numbers plus the zero. As we observe, there is an alternation on the wheel of numbers which are red and black. After spinning the wheel with moderate velocity in one direction, the croupier spins the small white ball around the backtrack (circumference) of the bowl in the other. When gravity exceeds the momentum of the ball, it falls from the rim of the bowl into one of the spinning slots (perhaps deflected in its descent by one of the small rhomboid obstacles), whose number the croupier announces to the assembled players. Whether the number is red or black, odd or even, high or low is also

[1] An exception is for craps: see *Craps*, by Lena M. Stear, Las Vegas, 1961.

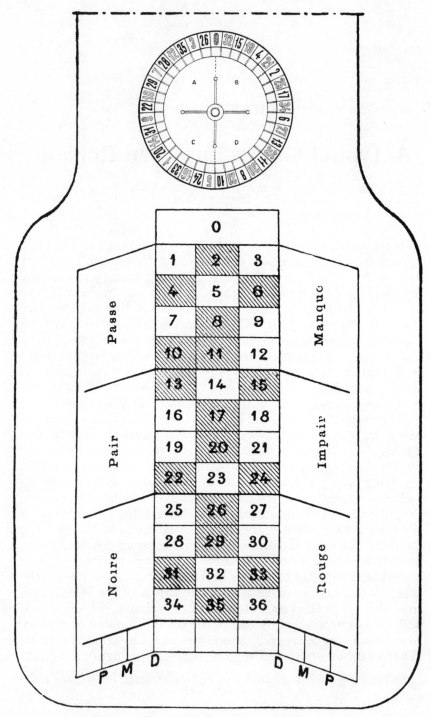

TABLE 13 *European Roulette*

announced. Given a mechanically accurate wheel, chance alone determines into which of the 37 pockets the white ball will fall.

As illustrated below the wheel in Table 13 (p. 24), the European roulette layout (about five feet long), headed by a space for zero, contains 36 squares, one for each number. These squares are flanked on the right by spaces for *rouge* (red), *impair* (odd), and *manque* (numbers 1 through 18); and on the left by spaces for *noir* (black), *pair* (even), and *passe* (numbers 19 through 36). The three unmarked squares at the foot of the layout are for wagers on the first, second, and third columns. And the three squares on either side of these, marked $12^p$, $12^m$, and $12^d$, are for wagers on the first, second, and third dozens.

# CHAPTER V

# The Result of One Week: 3,862 Spins

As each type of wager on the roulette layout deserves individual analysis, let us discuss them one by one, stipulating the values of $p$, $q$, $y$, and $b$ for each bet. Let us remember: $p$ signifies the probability of a favorable event in one trial; $q$ signifies the probability of an unfavorable event in one trial; $y$ signifies the Bank's percentage expressed as a decimal fraction; and $b$ signifies the actual pay-off odds to 1 in one trial.

To illustrate all the bets at roulette I have listed the results of an entire week's play at Table Number Two at the Monte Carlo Casino – a sample of 3,862 spins. The results comprise Table 14 (pp. 28–29).

*One Number*

$p=1/37$, $q=36/37$, $b=35$, $y=1/37$ or 0.027027 ...

Counting the plus and minus signs in the *units-won-or-lost* column, we observe that at the end of the 3,862 spins, of 37 numbers 12 end as winners and 25 as losers. Hence at pay-off odds of 35 to 1 the total won from all the winners is 3,228 units, the total lost from all the losers is 7,370 units, and the difference is a loss of 4,142 units.

As no individual gambler would bet simultaneously on all 37 numbers, however, let us examine just one number – say number 3.

At the end of 3,862 spins there should occur on an average $np=(3862)(1/37)=104$ number 3s (or any designated number for that matter). From the total of week (next to righthand column) column we note that number 3 occurred 109 times – 5 times more than theory prescribes.

At this point let us pause and remember the difference between two averages. The *theoretical average number* of occurrences of a favorable event is simply $p$ multiplied by $n$ trials, i.e. $pn$. The fluctuation, either in the plus or minus direction, *away* from this average number $pn$ we call the *average* (plus or minus) *digression* at the end of $n$ trials as we saw in Table 1 (p. 2). There are other *individual* digressions, of course, of exactly 1 or 2 or 3 or ... $z$ units, each with its own probability as we learned from Table 9 (p. 13).

If we wager constantly 1 unit on every spin, at the end of the week what is our total actual net gain or loss from number 3 (or from any designated number)? If $n$ signify the total number of spins, $w$ the total number of times our number occurred, $b$ the Bank's pay-off odds to 1, then $wb$ is our gross gain, $n-w$ is our gross loss, and the difference between these two is our total net gain or loss. In the case of number 3, therefore, we have $wb = (109)$ $(35) = 3815$ units won, $n-w = 3862 - 109 = 3753$ units lost, and the difference between these two is a net gain of 62 units, the amount noted in the *units-won-or-lost* column.

It is not the least surprising, of course, that 25 numbers ended as losers and only 12 as winners. With a Bank's percentage of 2.70 per cent on the numbers and 1.41 per cent on the even-money chances against a player at every spin, a whole week ending with more winning than losing numbers would be excessively rare indeed.[1] In other words at the end of this mathematically unfair game of 3,862 spins we should expect *considerable digressions* from the theoretical average rate of loss given by *any*.[2] Thus we have here any= (1) (3862) (1/37) = 104 = units. From the *units-won-or-lost* column we observe that the largest gain was 638 units (from number 16, which occurred 125 times) and the largest loss 802 units (from number 23, which occurred only 85 times). Neither of these digressions is especially improbable. At the end of every week there will be almost always a considerable excess of many numbers and a considerable deficiency of a few others.

Let us look at the gains and losses from the single numbers from another standpoint. If we divide the empirical results of the *units-*

---

[1] When calculating the number of spins at European roulette for an even-money chance, like red, black, high, low, odd, or even, the value of $n$ becomes $n-(3n/74)$, $p$ is 35/71, $q$ is 36/71, and $y$ is 1/71 or 0.014085; thus instead of 3862 spins we have 3705 spins on the even-money chances. See Appendix, 'In-Prison' rule.

[2] See Table 11 (p. 20).

27

## TABLE 14

One week's results at roulette Table Number Two at Monte Carlo

| Number | Monday | Tuesday | Wednesday | Thursday | Friday | Saturday | Sunday | Total of week | Units won or lost |
|---|---|---|---|---|---|---|---|---|---|
| 0 | 16 | 18 | 19 | 12 | 15 | 18 | 19 | 117 | +350 |
| 1 | 17 | 11 | 12 | 14 | 17 | 12 | 15 | 98 | −334 |
| 2 | 4 | 13 | 13 | 12 | 16 | 14 | 14 | 86 | −766 |
| 3 | 19 | 14 | 13 | 14 | 18 | 15 | 16 | 109 | + 62 |
| 4 | 9 | 14 | 18 | 21 | 13 | 15 | 10 | 100 | −262 |
| 5 | 16 | 14 | 13 | 9 | 22 | 18 | 15 | 107 | − 80 |
| 6 | 19 | 12 | 15 | 19 | 17 | 14 | 8 | 102 | −190 |
| 7 | 19 | 10 | 11 | 7 | 20 | 14 | 18 | 99 | −298 |
| 8 | 12 | 16 | 8 | 19 | 16 | 13 | 14 | 98 | −334 |
| 9 | 14 | 12 | 15 | 14 | 14 | 19 | 17 | 105 | − 82 |
| 10 | 14 | 16 | 17 | 20 | 8 | 23 | 13 | 111 | +134 |
| 11 | 18 | 13 | 15 | 20 | 7 | 19 | 10 | 102 | −190 |
| 12 | 20 | 16 | 28 | 13 | 16 | 13 | 14 | 120 | +458 |
| 13 | 20 | 7 | 15 | 24 | 15 | 12 | 13 | 106 | − 46 |
| 14 | 12 | 13 | 13 | 25 | 12 | 13 | 11 | 99 | −298 |
| 15 | 17 | 15 | 15 | 12 | 15 | 17 | 19 | 110 | + 98 |
| 16 | 21 | 16 | 11 | 20 | 19 | 22 | 16 | 125 | −638 |

Table 14 (continued)

| | | | | | | | | | |
|---|---|---|---|---|---|---|---|---|---|
| 17 | 5 | 14 | 16 | 23 | 18 | 11 | 19 | 106 | − 46 |
| 18 | 10 | 11 | 15 | 20 | 17 | 17 | 17 | 107 | − 80 |
| 19 | 15 | 11 | 12 | 14 | 14 | 14 | 16 | 96 | −406 |
| 20 | 16 | 11 | 21 | 14 | 13 | 14 | 21 | 110 | + 98 |
| 21 | 10 | 17 | 14 | 16 | 15 | 17 | 16 | 105 | − 82 |
| 22 | 17 | 11 | 12 | 16 | 9 | 11 | 12 | 88 | −694 |
| 23 | 14 | 12 | 10 | 15 | 12 | 10 | 12 | 85 | −802 |
| 24 | 14 | 15 | 12 | 16 | 24 | 14 | 8 | 103 | −154 |
| 25 | 16 | 18 | 17 | 16 | 12 | 18 | 12 | 107 | − 80 |
| 26 | 12 | 12 | 11 | 12 | 11 | 14 | 13 | 89 | −658 |
| 27 | 12 | 15 | 20 | 17 | 20 | 19 | 16 | 119 | +422 |
| 28 | 12 | 10 | 11 | 15 | 17 | 19 | 14 | 98 | −334 |
| 29 | 7 | 9 | 23 | 14 | 15 | 23 | 13 | 104 | −118 |
| 30 | 14 | 14 | 18 | 20 | 14 | 16 | 20 | 116 | +314 |
| 31 | 12 | 18 | 11 | 10 | 18 | 15 | 7 | 91 | −586 |
| 32 | 15 | 16 | 13 | 16 | 16 | 12 | 19 | 107 | − 80 |
| 33 | 15 | 23 | 16 | 14 | 18 | 17 | 10 | 113 | +206 |
| 34 | 20 | 8 | 21 | 13 | 19 | 18 | 20 | 119 | +422 |
| 35 | 12 | 13 | 13 | 15 | 14 | 16 | 14 | 97 | −370 |
| 36 | 7 | 18 | 12 | 20 | 15 | 20 | 16 | 108 | + 26 |
| | | | | | | | | 3862 | |

TABLE 14 (continued)

| Numbers | Monday | Tuesday | Wednesday | Thursday | Friday | Saturday | Sunday | Total of week | Units won or lost |
|---|---|---|---|---|---|---|---|---|---|
| 1–3 | 40 | 38 | 38 | 40 | 51 | 41 | 45 | 293 | −346 |
| 4–6 | 42 | 40 | 46 | 49 | 52 | 47 | 33 | 309 | −154 |
| 7–9 | 45 | 38 | 34 | 40 | 50 | 46 | 49 | 302 | −238 |
| 10–12 | 52 | 45 | 60 | 53 | 31 | 55 | 37 | 333 | +134 |
| 13–15 | 49 | 35 | 43 | 61 | 42 | 42 | 43 | 315 | − 82 |
| 16–18 | 36 | 41 | 42 | 63 | 54 | 50 | 52 | 338 | +194 |
| 19–21 | 41 | 39 | 47 | 44 | 42 | 45 | 53 | 311 | −130 |
| 22–24 | 45 | 38 | 34 | 47 | 45 | 35 | 32 | 276 | −550 |
| 25–27 | 42 | 45 | 48 | 45 | 43 | 51 | 41 | 315 | − 82 |
| 28–30 | 33 | 33 | 52 | 49 | 46 | 58 | 47 | 318 | − 46 |
| 31–33 | 42 | 57 | 40 | 40 | 52 | 44 | 36 | 311 | −130 |
| 34–36 | 39 | 39 | 46 | 48 | 48 | 54 | 50 | 324 | + 26 |
| 1–6 | 82 | 78 | 84 | 89 | 103 | 88 | 78 | 602 | −250 |
| 7–12 | 97 | 83 | 94 | 93 | 81 | 101 | 86 | 635 | − 52 |
| 13–18 | 85 | 76 | 85 | 124 | 96 | 92 | 95 | 653 | + 56 |
| 19–24 | 86 | 77 | 81 | 91 | 87 | 80 | 85 | 587 | −340 |
| 25–30 | 75 | 78 | 100 | 94 | 89 | 109 | 88 | 633 | − 64 |
| 31–36 | 81 | 96 | 86 | 88 | 100 | 98 | 86 | 635 | − 52 |

$$\text{T{\small ABLE} 14 (continued)}$$

| | | | | | | | | | | |
|---|---|---:|---:|---:|---:|---:|---:|---:|---:|---:|
| DOZENS | 1st. | 179 | 161 | 178 | 182 | 184 | 189 | 164 | 1237 | −151 |
| | 2nd. | 171 | 153 | 166 | 215 | 183 | 172 | 180 | 1240 | −142 |
| | 3rd. | 156 | 174 | 186 | 182 | 189 | 207 | 174 | 1268 | − 58 |
| COLUMNS | 1st. | 190 | 150 | 168 | 190 | 181 | 193 | 166 | 1238 | −148 |
| | 2nd. | 147 | 156 | 169 | 194 | 172 | 177 | 175 | 1190 | −292 |
| | 3rd. | 169 | 182 | 193 | 195 | 203 | 198 | 177 | 1317 | + 89 |
| RED: | | 269 | 246 | 268 | 283 | 292 | 287 | 286 | 1931 | + 58 |
| BLACK: | | 237 | 242 | 262 | 296 | 264 | 281 | 232 | 1814 | −176 |
| EVEN: | | 250 | 242 | 269 | 311 | 272 | 282 | 260 | 1886 | − 32 |
| ODD: | | 256 | 246 | 261 | 268 | 284 | 286 | 258 | 1859 | − 86 |
| HIGH: | | 242 | 251 | 267 | 273 | 276 | 287 | 259 | 1855 | − 94 |
| LOW: | | 264 | 237 | 263 | 306 | 280 | 281 | 259 | 1890 | − 24 |
| TOTAL SPINS:* | | 522 | 506 | 549 | 591 | 571 | 586 | 537 | 3862 | |

* Includes zeros.

*won-or-lost* column into quarters, we should find that at the end of 3,862 spins (or any number of spins for that matter) on an average 25 per cent of the 37 numbers, or (37) (0.25)=9.25 of them, will fall into each of the above four categories. In actual fact 8 are larger than plus 127 units, 12 fall between plus 127 units and minus 104 units, 10 fall between minus 104 units and minus 335 units, and lastly 7 are larger than minus 335 units. If we average 8+12+10+7=37, we have 37/4=9.25. In other words the empirical results for one number conform completely to theory.

### *1, 2, 3, 4, 6, 12, 18 (red or black, etc.), or 24 Numbers*

Let us assume that we shall sit down and play European roulette for 3,862 spins. As we know from Table 14 (pp. 28–31), at the Monte Carlo Casino such a period constitutes one week. Yet this period represents playing a daily session of 552 spins, from the moment the casino doors open (10:00 a.m.) to the moment they close (2:00 a.m.). If we assume 4 hours a day to be a more normal session of play, and 40 spins an hour to be the average number of trials, then 3,862 spins represent actually 24 days or about 3.5 weeks of play.

At European roulette there are 8 different ways of placing a wager on the layout, from a bet on a single number to one on 24 numbers. If we sit down at a Monte-Carlo roulette wheel and play a game of 1 unit per spin (*flat stakes*) for 3,862 spins, which of these 8 different ways should we select?

In Table 15 (p. 33) I have listed the theoretical results for all 8 different ways of betting. As observe, the figures under the four probabilities of 0.25 represent the median digressions divided into quarters. Naturally the figures are based on a session 3,862 long, except for the even-money chance (18/37), which is 3,705 spins long.[1]

It should be pointed out that when the Bank's percentage or PC reduces a figure in the righthand column to a minus quantity it should be interpreted, strictly speaking, in conjunction with 0. Thus, for example, when $p=6/37$, the figure in the righthand column is $-12$, signifying that we have a probability of 0.25 for a loss between $-12$ and 0, *and* a gain of more than 0 (i.e. of some indefinite amount). One interprets similarly $-45$, $-15$, and $-74$. I mention this, because it would be erroneous to conclude that there is no probability *at all* for a gain. What probability theory *does* tell

[1] See note 1 (p. 27).

us is that as the number of trials ($n$) *increases* in a mathematically unfair game (like roulette with its zero), the probability of winning anything at all becomes so small that it eventually becomes infinitesimal. This was illustrated not only in the *ufcw* and *ufcl* columns of Table 11 (p. 20) but also in the $0.04/y^2$ column of Table 12 (p. 21).

TABLE 15

$n=3862$

| $p$ | 0.25 more than | 0.25 between | | 0.25 between | | 0.25 more than |
|---|---|---|---|---|---|---|
| 1/37 | −335 | −335 | −104 | −104 | 127 | 127 |
| 2/37 | −268 | −268 | −104 | −104 | 60 | 60 |
| 3/37 | −239 | −239 | −104 | −104 | 31 | 31 |
| 4/37 | −219 | −219 | −104 | −104 | 11 | 11 |
| 6/37 | −196 | −196 | −104 | −104 | −12 | −12 |
| 12/37 | −163 | −163 | −104 | −104 | −45 | −45 |
| 18/37 | − 89 | − 89 | − 52 | − 52 | −15 | −15 |
| 24/37 | −134 | −134 | −104 | −104 | −74 | −74 |

Glancing down the second column from the left, we observe that the *largest loss* (335 units, and PC is 2.70 per cent) results from betting on a single number ($p=1/37$), and that the *smallest loss* (89 units, and PC is 1.41 per cent) results from betting on' an even-money chance (where $p=18/37$, or more precisely, 35/71 i.e. roughly 1/2). Table 15 (p. 33) shows how adversely the Bank's percentage has altered the symmetry of a mathematically fair game. If we bet on a single number at roulette, where $p$ is as small as 1/37, although our loss remains large (335 units), *our gain is only moderate* (127 units). Even worse, if we bet on an even-money

TABLE 16

$n=3862$

| $p$ | wins | losses | units won | units lost | final loss |
|---|---|---|---|---|---|
| 1/37 | 12 | 25 | 3,228 | 7,370 | 4,142 |
| 3/37 | 3 | 9 | 354 | 1,758 | 1,404 |
| 6/37 | 1 | 5 | 56 | 758 | 702 |
| 12/37 | 0 | 3 | 0 | 351 | 351 |
| 12/37 | 1 | 2 | 89 | 440 | 351 |
| 18/37 | 1 | 1 | 58 | 176 | 118 |

chance, like the red or black, although our loss is relatively small (89 units), *our gain has become a loss* (15 units).

So much for a theoretical table about Monte-Carlo roulette. Using the theoretical table as background, let us examine more thoroughly the results of Table 14 (pp. 28–31) and see what actually happened at the end of 3,862 spins.

Thus if we had bet on all 37 single numbers, we should have had a gross gain of 3,228 units, a gross loss of 7,370 units, and (the difference between these last two numbers) a final net loss of 4,142 units. And if we had bet on all 18 red numbers we should have had a gross gain of 58 units, a gross loss of 176 units, and a final net loss of 118 units.

# CHAPTER VI

# The Result of Three Months: 46,080 Spins: Betting on Just One Number

Attention ladies and gentlemen! Now that the pages of theory concluding with an *actual week* of Monte Carlo roulette have been examined, we come now to an examination of an *actual three months* of 46,080 spins. For our study we need the constant companionship of that perpetual gambler and charming adventurer, Mr Optimist!

'I've been with you since page one,' sighs Mr Optimist. 'A suffering, silent partner.'

'Did you understand the simple mathematics and graph of returns to equilibrium? Of plus and minus digressions both *at the end* of and *during* a game of *n* trials? And the adverse effect of the Bank's percentage?' I ask.

'Oh, as far as it went I understood. But theory isn't the same as this actual sample of 46,080 spins you've just spoken of,' replies Mr Optimist.

'That's why I wanted you to be right here with the reader to witness how well theory accords with fact,' I add.

'Well, let's get going. Where did you get the sample?'

'It comprises the entirety of a book, *Roulette Expert*, by Dr Hans Hartman, published in Berlin in 1934. The sample consists of all 46,080 numbers – about 600 spins a day – produced by the roulette wheel at Table #2 at Monte Carlo from January 1st, 1933, through March 25th of the same year, a period of almost three months. Now I want you, Mr Optimist, to pick any number from zero through 36 for our discussion.'

'Don't tell me you're going to ignore the red and black – and after all that gambling at heads and tails by Peter and Paul?

35

Thank God I've never gone to a game with those two. They never stop for a drink or a bite to eat. They don't even go to the men's room! Haven't they any kidneys?'

'Don't worry about the red and black – they'll be examined in the very next chapter. So pick a single number for our present discussion.'

'All right, let's take zero itself – it's as good as any other number. Besides I've always suspected that the croupier tries to shoot the ball into the general area of zero, "the House's Number", to make it come up more often than theory prescribes,' says Mr Optimist speaking, admittedly, with some pessimism.

'Tables 19 (p. 38) and 20 (p. 39) indicate that the total number of winning runs at the end of 46,080 spins is 1225.'

'How many times does theory prescribe?' asks Mr Optimist.

'At any specified spin the probability of a chosen number's occurrence is $p = 1/37$. At the end of 46,080 spins the number of runs of 1 (or more) zeros is 1212. Remember a *run*, signified by *r*, whether *winning* or *losing*, consists of the number of trials an event – here zero – occurs *repetitively*, that is, *in a row*.'

'So the number of actual runs of zero is $1225 - 1212 = 13$ in excess of the average!' crows Mr Optimist triumphantly.

'But, Mr Optimist, that's a small fluctuation of runs in such a large sample. In the very first chapter of this book didn't we learn that, if anything, just breaking even – a return to equilibrium – is highly unlikely? That a chance event will almost always fluctuate in the plus or minus direction? Remember we called such a fluctuation a plus or minus digression from the theoretical average. Look at the fluctuations, for example, of Professor Feller's sample of 10,000 coin tosses – Table 7, page 7!'

'But all those digressions concerned just *theoretical* heads and tails,' objects Mr Optimist.

'Not in Table 14, pp. 28–31 in the last chapter,' I repost. 'Note that except 29 every *actual* number *digresses* from the theoretical mean of 104 occurrences. You'll recall that in units *12* numbers are *ahead* and *25* are behind the average.'

'All right, you've got me convinced of the inevitability of digressions above and below the theoretical average. But what is the extent of these two digressions in the Hartman sample?'

'Let's examine first the *theory* of runs – then we'll be able to understand better the occurrence of *actual* runs in the Hartman sample.'

36

TABLE 17

Theoretical number of *winning* and *losing* runs exactly *r* spins
long at the end of 46,080 spins.

| Exactly r | winning runs (zeros) | r | losing runs (other numbers) |
|---|---|---|---|
| 1 | 1178.99 | 1 | 32.748 |
| 2 | 31.864 | 2 | 31.864 |
| 3 | 0.8612069 | 3 | 31.003 |
| 4+ | 0.0239223 | 4+ | 1116.126 |
| | 1211.7391292 | | 1211.741 |

'Notice,' I continue, 'that the theoretical total *number* of runs
exactly *r* spins in length, whether *winning* or *losing*, is identical – in
this particular case, 1212 – and this is true regardless of whether
we're betting on one number, the red or black, or any combination
or total of numbers. At the end of any sample of *n* spins the
theoretical number of *winning* runs always *equals* the number of
*losing* runs.'

'How about for the game of craps?' asks Mr Optimist.

'Exactly the same theory of runs applies to throws at craps.
Remember – we're examining roulette not just for itself but
because the conclusions we're gathering apply to other main casino
games. We're using roulette to illustrate matters in general.'

'Is the *sum* of all the winning runs always 1212 for 46,080 spins?'

'Even to infinity. But let's extend the winning-run portion of
Table 17 (p. 37) to include, say, runs of exactly 4, 5, 6, and 7 zeros
long.'

TABLE 18

Theoretical number of *winning* runs exactly *r* zeros long at
the end of 46,080 spins.

| Exactly r | winning runs (zeros) |
|---|---|
| 1 | 1178.99 |
| 2 | 31.864 |
| 3 | 0.8612067 |
| 4 | 0.0232758 |
| 5 | 0.0006290 |
| 6 | 0.0000169 |
| 7 | 0.0000004 |
| | 1211.7391288 |

37

'I see that at the end of 46,080 spins the number of winning runs of exactly 3 zeros is only 0.8612067th of a run,' comments Mr Optimist sadly. 'There isn't even theoretically a single whole one.'

'True – to get a whole run of exactly 3 zeros we should have to play longer – that is, get a theoretical sample larger than 46,080 spins. Now let's examine Table 19 (p. 38) below, the *actual* number of *winning* runs exactly *r* zeros long at the end of the 46,080 spins composing the Hartman sample.'

TABLE 19

Actual number of *winning* runs exactly *r* zeros long at the end of 46,080 spins.

| Exactly r | Actual | Theory | Difference |
|---|---|---|---|
| 1 | 1190 | 1179 | +11 |
| 2 | 34 | 32 | + 2 |
| 3 | 1 | 1 | 0 |
| | 1225 | 1212 | +13 |

'As we see, Mr Optimist, there are *actually* 1190 winning runs of exactly 1 zero, 34 winning runs of exactly 2 zeros, and 1 winning run of exactly 3 zeros. The second column shows that *theory* accords quite well with *actuality*.'

'There occur no runs of 4 (or more) zeros?'

'No, the winning run or 3 zeros is the longest winning run in the whole 46,080 spins. At any rate so much for *actual winning* runs.

'Table 20 (p. 39) lists all the *actual losing* runs *exactly r* spins long in the whole Hartman sample.'

'Across the top of the table are figures signifying the increasing lengths of the *actual losing* runs exactly *r* spins long, and across the bottom are figures signifying their *actual* declining frequency.

'Thus there occur *actually* 35 losing runs exactly 0 spins long, 29 losing runs *exactly* 1 spin long, 32 losing runs *exactly* 2 spins long, 26 losing runs *exactly* 3 spins long ... and finally 3 losing runs of anywhere from *exactly* 248 to 330 spins long. If we add up 29+32+26 ... and 3, we get naturally the previously stated total of 1225 *actual* losing runs for the whole 46,080 spins, and these bottom figures – 29,32,26,35,32 etc. – accord, of course, with the righthand column of *theoretical* figures of Table 17 (p. 37). Owing to the latter column's being theoretically longer than even 100

# TABLE 20

## Actual number of *losing* runs exactly *r* spins long at the end of 46,080 spins.

| Exactly *R*: | 0 | 1 | 2 | 3 | 4 | 5 | 6 | 7 | 8 | 9 | 10 | 11 | 12 | 13 | 14 | 15 | 16 | 17 | 18 | 19 | 20 | 21 | 22 | 23 | 24 | 25 | 26 | 27 | 28 | 29 | 30 | 31 | 32 |
|---|---|---|---|---|---|---|---|---|---|---|---|---|---|---|---|---|---|---|---|---|---|---|---|---|---|---|---|---|---|---|---|---|---|
| Group 1 | 3 | 3 | 4 | 1 | 5 | 2 | 3 | 2 | 3 | 1 | 4 | 3 | 1 | 6 | 1 | 3 | 6 | 0 | 1 | 5 | 2 | 2 | 1 | 1 | 2 | 4 | 1 | 0 | 0 | 3 | 1 | 4 | — |
| 2 | 8 | 6 | 2 | 2 | 4 | 3 | 5 | 1 | 4 | 3 | 3 | 4 | 2 | 6 | 2 | 1 | 6 | 2 | 3 | 3 | 1 | 3 | 2 | 3 | 2 | 3 | 4 | 2 | 3 | 2 | 1 | 2 | 1 |
| 3 | 4 | 4 | 2 | 3 | 3 | 2 | 7 | 4 | 2 | 5 | 4 | 1 | 4 | 3 | 3 | 2 | 2 | 1 | 3 | 3 | 3 | 3 | 3 | 2 | 2 | 2 | 2 | 2 | 2 | 3 | 2 | 2 | 0 |
| 4 | 3 | 2 | 3 | 4 | 6 | 6 | 4 | 2 | 6 | 4 | 4 | 1 | 1 | 7 | 1 | 4 | 2 | 3 | 3 | 0 | 6 | 6 | 4 | 3 | 0 | 3 | 0 | 2 | 3 | 0 | 2 | 0 | 3 |
| 5 | 1 | 3 | 5 | 3 | 3 | 2 | 2 | 2 | 1 | 4 | 4 | 5 | 1 | 4 | 5 | 3 | 8 | 1 | 5 | 5 | 1 | 2 | 0 | 2 | 1 | 1 | 0 | 2 | 3 | 0 | 1 | 2 | 1 |
| 6 | 5 | 3 | 5 | 3 | 1 | 4 | 4 | 5 | 5 | 2 | 1 | 2 | 2 | 1 | 3 | 0 | 0 | 1 | 5 | 2 | 5 | 3 | 3 | 0 | 1 | 2 | 1 | 0 | 2 | 2 | 3 | 1 | 1 |
| 7 | 4 | 2 | 3 | 1 | 3 | 4 | 1 | 4 | 2 | 2 | 2 | 5 | 2 | 1 | 2 | 2 | 1 | 1 | 2 | 2 | 2 | 1 | 4 | 1 | 1 | 1 | 1 | 2 | 0 | 0 | 1 | 3 | 2 |
| 8 | 5 | 3 | 1 | 1 | 6 | 4 | 4 | 3 | 5 | 2 | 5 | 3 | 2 | 1 | 2 | 2 | 3 | 3 | 6 | 0 | 4 | 2 | 3 | 3 | 5 | 1 | 5 | 3 | 0 | 0 | 3 | 0 | 3 |
| 9 | 2 | 1 | 3 | 7 | 4 | 1 | 4 | 4 | 1 | 4 | 1 | 1 | 3 | 2 | 2 | 1 | 0 | 2 | 3 | 0 | 2 | 0 | 4 | 0 | 0 | 2 | 0 | 2 | 0 | 2 | 2 | 2 | 0 |
| | 35 | 29 | 32 | 26 | 35 | 32 | 30 | 33 | 30 | 24 | 27 | 28 | 22 | 23 | 24 | 18 | 26 | 24 | 19 | 29 | 18 | 21 | 18 | 22 | 12 | 17 | 13 | 14 | 13 | 6 | 19 | 15 | 15 |

| | 33 | 34 | 35 | 36 | 37 | 38 | 39 | 40 | 41 | 42 | 43 | 44 | 45 | 46 | 47 | 48 | 49 | 50 | 51 | 52 | 53 | 54 | 55 | 56 | 57 | 58 | 59 | 60 | 61 | 62 | 63 | 64 | 65 |
|---|---|---|---|---|---|---|---|---|---|---|---|---|---|---|---|---|---|---|---|---|---|---|---|---|---|---|---|---|---|---|---|---|---|
| 1 | 3 | 0 | 1 | 2 | 1 | 5 | 3 | 2 | 0 | 2 | 1 | 2 | 1 | 5 | 0 | 1 | 2 | 0 | 2 | 0 | 0 | 1 | 1 | 1 | 1 | 3 | 0 | 0 | 1 | 3 | 0 | 0 | 0 |
| 2 | 4 | 1 | 4 | 4 | 1 | 3 | 1 | 0 | 0 | 0 | 2 | 5 | 3 | 0 | 1 | 4 | 0 | 0 | 1 | 2 | 1 | 0 | 1 | 1 | 1 | 1 | 4 | 0 | 1 | 0 | 1 | 0 | 2 |
| 3 | 2 | 1 | 2 | 0 | 2 | 2 | 0 | 2 | 0 | 2 | 2 | 2 | 0 | 1 | 1 | 2 | 0 | 0 | 0 | 1 | 1 | 0 | 0 | 2 | 0 | 0 | 0 | 0 | 0 | 2 | 0 | 0 | 0 |
| 4 | 1 | 2 | 1 | 0 | 3 | 0 | 2 | 2 | 0 | 1 | 0 | 1 | 1 | 0 | 1 | 1 | 1 | 0 | 1 | 0 | 0 | 1 | 0 | 0 | 2 | 0 | 0 | 1 | 0 | 0 | 1 | 0 | 1 |
| 5 | 1 | 2 | 2 | 1 | 0 | 1 | 1 | 0 | 0 | 1 | 2 | 0 | 0 | 0 | 0 | 0 | 3 | 2 | 1 | 0 | 1 | 0 | 0 | 1 | 0 | 2 | 0 | 0 | 0 | 0 | 0 | 0 | 0 |
| 6 | 2 | 3 | 1 | 1 | 1 | 0 | 0 | 0 | 1 | 2 | 0 | 1 | 0 | 1 | 0 | 0 | 0 | 1 | 0 | 1 | 1 | 1 | 0 | 0 | 1 | 0 | 0 | 0 | 1 | 0 | 0 | 0 | 1 |
| 7 | 1 | 1 | 1 | 1 | 2 | 1 | 1 | 0 | 1 | 1 | 3 | 0 | 1 | 1 | 0 | 0 | 2 | 2 | 1 | 2 | 1 | 1 | 1 | 1 | 1 | 0 | 0 | 0 | 0 | 1 | 0 | 0 | 0 |
| 8 | 3 | 1 | 0 | 1 | 0 | 0 | 2 | 1 | 2 | 0 | 0 | 3 | 2 | 0 | 1 | 0 | 0 | 1 | 2 | 1 | 2 | 0 | 1 | 0 | 1 | 1 | 1 | 1 | 1 | 2 | 0 | 0 | 0 |
| 9 | 2 | 1 | 2 | 2 | 1 | 2 | 1 | 3 | 0 | 0 | 1 | 2 | 1 | 3 | 3 | 1 | 1 | 1 | 2 | 1 | 0 | 1 | 0 | 4 | 4 | 0 | 1 | 1 | 0 | 0 | 0 | 0 | 0 |
| | 19 | 8 | 18 | 13 | 11 | 17 | 11 | 12 | 4 | 9 | 10 | 14 | 10 | 14 | 8 | 5 | 12 | 8 | 4 | 9 | 6 | 11 | 6 | 7 | 4 | 8 | 4 | 8 | 12 | 7 | 3 | 8 | 6 | 9 | 2 | 4 |

TABLE 20 (continued)

Actual number of *losing* runs exactly *r* spins long at the end of 46,080 spins

| Exactly | 66 | 67 | 68 | 69 | 70 | 71 | 72 | 73 | 74 | 75 | 76 | 77 | 78 | 79 | 80 | 81 | 82 | 83 | 84 | 85 | 86 | 87 | 88 | 89 | 90 | 91 | 92 | 93 | 94 | 95 | 96 | 97 | 98 |
|---|---|---|---|---|---|---|---|---|---|---|---|---|---|---|---|---|---|---|---|---|---|---|---|---|---|---|---|---|---|---|---|---|---|
| Group 1 | 0 | 0 | 0 | 0 | 1 | 1 | 1 | 0 | 0 | 0 | 0 | 2 | 2 | 0 | 0 | 0 | 1 | 0 | 2 | 2 | 0 | 0 | 0 | 0 | 0 | 0 | 1 | 1 | 0 | 0 | 0 | 0 | 0 |
| 2 | 1 | 1 | 1 | 1 | 0 | 0 | 1 | 0 | 0 | 0 | 0 | 0 | 0 | 0 | 1 | 0 | 0 | 2 | 0 | 0 | 0 | 1 | 0 | 1 | 0 | 0 | 0 | 0 | 0 | 1 | 0 | 0 | 0 |
| 3 | 0 | 0 | 1 | 0 | 0 | 0 | 0 | 1 | 1 | 1 | 0 | 0 | 0 | 1 | 1 | 0 | 1 | 0 | 1 | 1 | 0 | 0 | 1 | 1 | 1 | 0 | 0 | 0 | 0 | 0 | 0 | 0 | 0 |
| 4 | 0 | 0 | 0 | 0 | 0 | 0 | 1 | 0 | 1 | 1 | 1 | 1 | 1 | 1 | 1 | 1 | 0 | 1 | 0 | 2 | 0 | 0 | 0 | 0 | 1 | 1 | 0 | 0 | 1 | 0 | 0 | 0 | 0 |
| 5 | 0 | 0 | 0 | 0 | 0 | 0 | 0 | 0 | 2 | 2 | 0 | 0 | 1 | 1 | 1 | 1 | 1 | 1 | 1 | 1 | 1 | 1 | 0 | 0 | 0 | 1 | 0 | 1 | 0 | 1 | 0 | 0 | 1 |
| 6 | 0 | 0 | 0 | 0 | 0 | 1 | 0 | 0 | 0 | 0 | 1 | 0 | 0 | 0 | 2 | 0 | 3 | 0 | 0 | 0 | 0 | 0 | 1 | 1 | 1 | 2 | 1 | 1 | 1 | 1 | 1 | 0 | 1 |
| 7 | 0 | 0 | 0 | 0 | 0 | 0 | 1 | 0 | 1 | 0 | 0 | 0 | 1 | 2 | 1 | 1 | 0 | 0 | 0 | 0 | 0 | 0 | 0 | 0 | 2 | 2 | 0 | 0 | 0 | 0 | 1 | 0 | 2 |
| 8 | 2 | 1 | 1 | 2 | 0 | 0 | 0 | 0 | 0 | 0 | 0 | 0 | 0 | 0 | 1 | 1 | 0 | 0 | 0 | 1 | 0 | 0 | 0 | 0 | 0 | 0 | 0 | 1 | 0 | 1 | 2 | 0 | 2 |
| 9 | 2 | 0 | 0 | 2 | 1 | 2 | 0 | 0 | 0 | 0 | 3 | 0 | 1 | 1 | 0 | 0 | 0 | 0 | 1 | 0 | 1 | 0 | 0 | 2 | 1 | 0 | 1 | 0 | 0 | 0 | 0 | 0 | 0 |
| | 9 | 4 | 6 | 3 | 2 | 6 | 3 | 2 | 5 | 2 | 5 | 3 | 4 | 7 | 5 | 1 | 8 | 2 | 5 | 5 | 1 | 3 | 1 | 7 | 4 | 4 | 3 | 5 | 3 | 3 | 2 | 1 | 1 | 6 |

| | 99–106 | 107–114 | 115–125 | 126–139 | 140–164 | 165–247 | 248–330 | 331 or more |
|---|---|---|---|---|---|---|---|---|
| 1 | 2 | 1 | 1 | 1 | 2 | 1 | 0 | 0 |
| 2 | 0 | 1 | 0 | 2 | 0 | 2 | 0 | 0 |
| 3 | 2 | 0 | 2 | 2 | 1 | 1 | 1 | 0 |
| 4 | 0 | 1 | 2 | 3 | 1 | 1 | 1 | 0 |
| 5 | 1 | 1 | 3 | 0 | 0 | 3 | 0 | 0 |
| 6 | 2 | 5 | 2 | 1 | 1 | 2 | 0 | 0 |
| 7 | 4 | 1 | 1 | 0 | 2 | 0 | 1 | 0 |
| 8 | 6 | 0 | 3 | 1 | 1 | 0 | 0 | 0 |
| 9 | 3 | 0 | 2 | 1 | 2 | 3 | 0 | 0 |
| | 20 | 10 | 16 | 11 | 10 | 13 | 3 | 0  Total: 1225 |

significant figures, which we may infer from the top row of Table 20 (p. 39) that increases to losing runs as long as 330 spins, in the righthand column of *theoretical* figures of Table 17 (p 37) I have space for listing the figures for only the first three *losing* runs *exactly r* spins long. On the other hand in the lefthand column of Table 17 (p. 37), containing the *theoretical* figures for the *winning* runs of zero, I have also listed only the first three figures, because obviously fractional winning runs, which we extended in Table 18 (p. 37), don't exist in reality and consequently have no practical meaning for gamblers.'

'In Table 20 (p. 39) adding up the bottom figures signifying the decreasing frequency of the lengths of the *actual losing* runs, we find that approximately *50 per cent* of them occur before the *25*th losing spin, the remaining *50 per cent* occurring afterwards. Thus if we add $29+32+26+35\ldots+21+18+22+12$, we get 602 losing runs, and $1225-602=623$, and $(602/1225)=0.4914$, while $(623/1225)=0.5085$. Again adding the bottom figures, we find that approximately *75 per cent* of the losing runs occur before the *50*th losing spin, the remaining *25 per cent* occurring afterwards. Thus if we add $29+32+26+35\ldots+8+5+12+7$, we get 916 losing runs, and $1225-91\,6=309$, and $(916/1225)=0.7478$, while $(309/1225)=0.2552$.'

'But what do *losing* runs mean to a gambler?' asks Mr Optimist moving to his favorite point. 'I'll admit the term sounds bad.'

'Table 20 (p. 39) lists all the *actual* losing runs *exactly r* spins long of the Hartman sample in their ascending order of length *r*. Table 21 (p. 42) lists these very same losing runs *but in their actual order of occurrence*. It is against such a random order of losing runs that any gambler must play. Let's remember, Mr Optimist: winning runs take care of themselves, so to speak. It's the losing runs – and their order of occurrence – that we have to worry about.'

'All right,' says Mr Optimist, 'now tell me what the columns of numbers mean in Table 21 (p. 42).'

'The whole three months of 46,080 spins have been divided into 45 *sessions* each 1,024 spins long. In Table 21 (p. 42) the columns of numbers signify the *actual* losing runs precisely in their order of occurrence throughout the Hartman sample. Thus during the first session of 1,024 spins there occur 26 losing runs, beginning with those of length 1, 39, 21, 4 … spins and ending with those of length … 51, 93, 51, and 32 spins. The last losing run of each session – in the 1st its 32 spins – overlaps into the next session.'

41

## TABLE 21

Actual number of *losing* runs exactly *r* spins long at the end of
46,080 spins in the actual order of the runs' occurrences. The
Hartman sample divided into 45 sessions each 1,024 spins long.

| | | | | | | | |
|---|---|---|---|---|---|---|---|
| 1 | 3 | 36 | 38 | 19 | 23 | 45 | 25 |
| 39 | 113 | 38 | 30 | 28 | 184 | 57 | 38 |
| 21 | 20 | 84 | 2 | 82 | 7 <u>16</u> | 0 | 12 |
| 4 | 3 | 46 | 59 | 32 | 58 | 33 | 48 |
| 49 | 77 | 3 <u>16</u> | 12 | 22 | 35 | 52 | 8 |
| 159 | 21 | 25 | 2 | 35 | 1 | 1 | 36 |
| 8 | 58 | 9 | 30 | 45 | 30 | 44 | 14 |
| 44 | 13 | 33 | 1 | 0 | 0 | 24 | 29 |
| 3 | 30 | 22 | 17 | 65 | 64 | 38 | 4 |
| 66 | 5 | 131 | 84 | 0 | 134 | 36 | 28 |
| 14 | 26 | 0 | 82 | 73 | 26 | 69 | 5 |
| 62 | 36 | 49 | 10 | 56 | 19 | 68 | 35 |
| 25 | 38 | 32 | 43 | 6 <u>21</u> | 20 | 24 | 17 |
| 57 | 44 | 37 | 63 | 25 | 6 | 134 | 23 |
| 5 | 0 | 20 | 22 | 6 | 97 | 94 | 31 |
| 2 | 32 | 20 | 59 | 4 | 14 | 33 | 33 |
| 91 | 2 <u>42</u> | 12 | 100 | 15 | 35 | 28 | 44 |
| 32 | 19 | 55 | 11 | 10 | 31 | 10 | 0 |
| 7 | 15 | 24 | 33 | 14 | 12 | 9 <u>65</u> | 17 |
| 46 | 17 | 31 | 3 | 11 | 26 | 34 | 61 |
| 46 | 59 | 40 | 5 <u>17</u> | 44 | 14 | 0 | 27 |
| 5 | 35 | 70 | 43 | 14 | 6 | 4 | 44 |
| 51 | 39 | 6 | 59 | 4 | 61 | 2 | 10 <u>26</u> |
| 93 | 11 | 119 | 17 | 27 | 82 | 29 | 8 |
| 51 | 92 | 15 | 18 | 1 | 3 | 20 | 6 |
| 1 <u>32</u> | 5 | 71 | 53 | 232 | 16 | 43 | 61 |
| 17 | 6 | 27 | 6 | 17 | 36 | 2 | 60 |
| 69 | 11 | 77 | 13 | 36 | 7 | 45 | 1 |
| 16 | 100 | 56 | 85 | 62 | 38 | 0 | 31 |
| 8 | 7 | 4 <u>48</u> | 30 | 17 | 13 | 22 | 88 |
| 5 | 38 | 40 | 60 | 9 | 8 | 1 | 49 |
| 39 | 7 | 33 | 5 | 1 | 6 | 52 | 20 |
| 63 | 17 | 0 | 54 | 3 | 14 | 71 | 7 |
| 153 | 12 | 38 | 1 | 87 | 8 <u>108</u> | 44 | 20 |
| 45 | 185 | 46 | 66 | 39 | 80 | 12 | 9 |
| 1 | 9 | 9 | 11 | 33 | 12 | 9 | 149 |
| 16 | 46 | 20 | 26 | 0 | 61 | 17 | 23 |
| 17 | 42 | 11 | 5 | 61 | 9 | 8 | 3 |
| 23 | 20 | 63 | 20 | 18 | 37 | 8 | 52 |

| | | | | | | | |
|---|---|---|---|---|---|---|---|
| 10 | 192 | 23 | 17 | 11 | 4 | 30 | 16 |
| 5 | 22 | 17 | 7 | 9 | 18 63 | 15 | 3 |
| 49 | 27 | 19 | 37 | 7 | 79 | 27 | 202 |
| 19 | 28 | 85 | 18 | 10 | 19 | 7 | 5 |
| 30 | 0 | 39 | 6 | 3 | 6 | 37 | 20 |
| 49 | 16 | 83 | 10 | 21 | 66 | 132 | 19 |
| 61 | 11 | 120 | 24 | 33 | 18 | 12 | 10 |
| 85 | 74 | 9 | 10 | 74 | 135 | 43 | 1 |
| 99 | 8 | 11 | 48 | 62 | 1 | 25 | 31 |
| 11 4 | 5 | 10 | 13 | 268 | 19 | 13 | 22 |
| 22 | 84 | 6 | 72 | 1 | 13 | 22 | 82 |
| 16 | 100 | 6 | 23 | 17 49 | 9 | 33 | 35 |
| 18 | 10 | 66 | 35 | 38 | 121 | 9 | 64 |
| 36 | 57 | 15 | 24 | 9 | 2 | 73 | 35 |
| 39 | 27 | 14 35 | 14 | 23 | 5 | 19 | 92 |
| 59 | 13 | 25 | 21 | 6 | 16 | 30 | 68 |
| 58 | 21 | 15 | 94 | 8 | 16 | 20 114 | 26 |
| 2 | 58 | 44 | 34 | 31 | 57 | 120 | 71 |
| 12 | 4 | 52 | 15 | 13 | 89 | 19 | 22 98 |
| 11 | 2 | 22 | 5 | 13 | 31 | 15 | 7 |
| 14 | 45 | 6 | 11 | 27 | 90 | 16 | 33 |
| 1 | 30 | 37 | 0 | 18 | 55 | 80 | 20 |
| 26 | 25 | 6 | 3 | 3 | 0 | 84 | 6 |
| 75 | 78 | 37 | 23 | 8 | 21 | 20 | 65 |
| 7 | 79 | 9 | 4 | 66 | 8 | 112 | 54 |
| 24 | 17 | 260 | 42 | 38 | 35 | 13 | 49 |
| 24 | 0 | 26 | 13 | 15 | 21 | 3 | 28 |
| 3 | 10 | 28 | 46 | 21 | 63 | 28 | 85 |
| 0 | 13 | 35 | 22 | 121 | 9 | 43 | 46 |
| 11 | 9 | 123 | 45 | 136 | 19 31 | 40 | 49 |
| 20 | 13 43 | 15 | 6 | 32 | 160 | 9 | 30 |
| 40 | 72 | 0 | 11 | 7 | 28 | 10 | 22 |
| 7 | 41 | 137 | 15 | 52 | 5 | 24 | 12 |
| 9 | 89 | 38 | 32 | 5 | 57 | 36 | 34 |
| 23 | 6 | 35 | 28 | 4 | 16 | 22 | 42 |
| 55 | 68 | 7 | 16 5 | 40 | 22 | 168 | 56 |
| 14 | 19 | 35 | 78 | 13 | 4 | 79 | 32 |
| 21 | 14 | 15 3 | 43 | 45 | 9 | 74 | 5 |
| 82 | 1 | 40 | 9 | 8 | 3 | 21 20 | 16 |
| 47 | 66 | 28 | 16 | 23 | 21 | 24 | 42 |
| 128 | 55 | 77 | 205 | 10 | 7 | 55 | 16 |
| 4 | 1 | 2 | 46 | 76 | 47 | 18 | 0 |
| 6 | 25 | 32 | 87 | 4 | 7 | 15 | 11 |
| 12 30 | 31 | 4 | 19 | 0 | 24 | 25 | 8 |

| | | | | | | | |
|---|---|---|---|---|---|---|---|
| 49 | 12 | 20 | 31 | 33 | <u>31</u> 0 | 11 | 7 |
| 17 | 39 | 82 | 16 | 18 | 91 | 41 | 30 |
| 10 | 83 | 16 | 2 | 14 | 12 | 9 | 4 |
| 52 | 14 | 2 | 1 | 98 | 37 | 9 | 1 |
| 13 | 12 | 63 | 28 | 65 | 43 | 51 | 14 |
| 3 | 14 | 3 | 39 | 35 | 80 | 10 | 90 |
| 58 | 2 | 50 | 2 | 79 | 101 | 32 | 5 |
| 2 | 19 | 6 | 20 | 42 | 47 | 36 | 42 |
| 2 | 27 | 66 | 12 | 12 | 3 | 46 | 11 |
| 28 | 16 | 13 | 9 | 37 | 21 | 23 | 13 |
| <u>23</u> 11 | 50 | 24 | 51 | 30 | 15 | 2 | <u>34</u> 18 |
| 123 | 16 | 128 | 8 | 95 | 50 | 7 | 140 |
| 13 | 7 | 14 | 11 | 11 | 16 | <u>33</u> 21 | 101 |
| 172 | 4 | 0 | 0 | 106 | 16 | 91 | 23 |
| 17 | 75 | <u>26</u> 9 | 19 | 34 | 98 | 31 | 1 |
| 57 | 47 | 223 | 17 | 28 | 89 | 98 | 19 |
| 31 | 1 | 4 | <u>28</u> 89 | 58 | 55 | 4 | 4 |
| 7 | 7 | 68 | 94 | <u>30</u> 62 | 25 | 21 | 40 |
| 11 | 20 | 78 | 82 | 259 | 26 | 37 | 57 |
| 91 | 4 | 105 | 108 | 55 | 11 | 22 | 2 |
| 10 | 116 | 71 | 53 | 67 | 33 | 18 | 74 |
| 2 | 30 | 116 | 29 | 15 | 7 | 0 | 103 |
| 15 | 50 | 63 | 32 | 60 | 66 | 3 | 4 |
| 21 | 103 | 112 | 26 | 79 | 52 | 2 | 38 |
| 26 | 74 | <u>27</u> 76 | 87 | 14 | 13 | 72 | 35 |
| 16 | 8 | 112 | 7 | 44 | 0 | 85 | 78 |
| 21 | 38 | 0 | 8 | 22 | <u>32</u> 10 | 34 | 150 |
| 93 | 2 | 31 | 33 | 1 | 23 | 19 | 53 |
| 33 | 14 | 82 | 6 | 64 | 8 | 43 | 52 |
| 11 | 14 | 0 | 108 | 75 | 32 | 11 | 4 |
| 13 | <u>25</u> 58 | 25 | 1 | 3 | 26 | 8 | 42 |
| 12 | 44 | 80 | 23 | 31 | 90 | 2 | <u>35</u> 24 |
| 16 | 14 | 6 | 19 | 30 | 6 | 2 | 18 |
| 1 | 49 | 10 | 59 | 47 | 125 | 5 | 10 |
| 38 | 35 | 25 | 31 | 21 | 79 | 2 | 30 |
| 12 | 3 | 99 | 2 | 18 | 105 | 2 | 5 |
| 38 | 7 | 43 | 149 | 60 | 2 | 5 | 19 |
| 14 | 93 | 22 | 5 | 11 | 5 | 17 | 8 |
| 15 | 6 | 7 | 8 | 50 | 19 | 21 | 120 |
| 7 | 194 | 61 | 7 | 6 | 50 | 23 | 11 |
| 39 | 35 | 0 | 1 | 110 | 4 | 68 | 100 |
| 27 | 5 | 8 | 2 | 1 | 93 | 0 | 46 |
| 6 | 49 | 117 | <u>29</u> 48 | 5 | 17 | 19 | 130 |
| <u>24</u> 4 | 22 | 5 | 21 | 90 | 11 | 0 | 4 |
| 19 | 8 | 29 | 3 | 12 | 54 | 3 | 36 |

| | | | | | | | |
|---|---|---|---|---|---|---|---|
| 18 | 10 | 4 | 67 | 15 | 5 | 56 | 26 |
| 22 | 13 | 0 | 12 | 11 | 30 | 186 | <u>16</u> |
| 18 | 34 | 115 | 37 | 81 | 3 | 49 | |
| 32 | 2 | 33 | 49 | 15 | 47 | 9 | |
| 68 | 106 | 16 | 12 | 42 <u>58</u> | 103 | 42 | |
| 54 | 25 | 39 <u>5</u> | 76 | 34 | 46 | 30 | |
| 33 | 53 | 104 | 18 | 4 | 3 | 50 | |
| 99 | 27 | 32 | 5 | 13 | 44 <u>7</u> | 59 | |
| 44 | 98 | 44 | 8 | 170 | 8 | 74 | |
| 26 | 18 | 59 | 44 | 9 | 78 | 41 | |
| 36 <u>25</u> | 41 | 12 | 23 | 35 | 1 | 36 | |
| 62 | 30 | 17 | 2 | 8 | 29 | 63 | |
| 25 | 8 | 10 | 89 | 12 | 115 | 15 | |
| 63 | 89 | 41 | 0 | 27 | 122 | 48 | |
| 22 | 7 | 0 | 7 | 52 | 48 | 5 | |
| 42 | 46 | 0 | 40 | 10 | 38 | 4 | |
| 6 | 6 | 45 | 50 | 84 | 31 | 71 | |
| 145 | 38 <u>4</u> | 6 | 4 | 92 | 18 | 0 | |
| 39 | 95 | 67 | 27 | 5 | 71 | 46 <u>3</u> | |
| 4 | 25 | 2 | 4 | 57 | 46 | 125 | |
| 115 | 8 | 19 | 69 | 99 | 47 | 47 | |
| 55 | 98 | 8 | 4 | 33 | 4 | 32 | |
| 96 | 67 | 51 | 10 | 51 | 5 | 31 | |
| 1 | 27 | 3 | 23 | 33 | 62 | 4 | |
| 2 | 18 | 8 | 1 | 10 | 38 | 66 | |
| 40 | 0 | 36 | 37 | 8 | 23 | 11 | |
| 36 | 7 | 10 | 40 | 21 | 23 | 10 | |
| 58 | 44 | 56 | 58 | 79 | 40 | 43 | |
| 66 | 17 | 10 | 52 | 14 | 6 | 20 | |
| 23 | 27 | 50 | 41 <u>55</u> | 43 <u>71</u> | 16 | 167 | |
| 101 | 18 | 9 | 102 | 31 | 3 | 179 | |
| 33 | 40 | 19 | 76 | 4 | 58 | 166 | |
| 19 | 11 | 12 | 7 | 44 | 21 | 18 | |
| 37 <u>23</u> | 45 | 0 | 4 | 76 | 45 <u>58</u> | 8 | |
| 63 | 19 | 13 | 45 | 182 | 31 | 42 | |
| 14 | 15 | 6 | 39 | 30 | 5 | 27 | |
| 30 | 19 | 53 | 171 | 29 | 4 | 47 <u>26</u> | |
| 11 | 14 | 17 | 7 | 147 | 22 | 35 | |
| 1 | 61 | 54 | 14 | 19 | 31 | 73 | |
| 99 | 25 | 7 | 67 | 89 | 24 | 40 | |
| 21 | 52 | 32 | 148 | 86 | 17 | 11 | |
| 34 | 5 | 18 | 53 | 10 | 19 | 7 | |
| 47 | 1 | 40 <u>80</u> | 47 | 19 | 8 | 40 | |
| 36 | 16 | 136 | 70 | 19 | 6 | 16 | |
| 46 | 23 | 1 | 13 | 0 | 8 | 231 | |

45

'But what separates each losing run from the next?' asks Mr Optimist.

'An *unlisted zero*, the number we're betting on, at the end of each losing run.'

'In other words, a win?' he inquires happily.

'Exactly.'

'So there are as many *zeros* or *wins* in each session as there are *losing* runs?' he continues.

'Right,' I reply. 'And each combination of a losing run, ending in a zero, we'll call a *game*. So there are as many *games* in each session as there are *losing* runs. There occur 26 games in the 1st session, 31 in the 2nd, 27 in the 3rd, 26 in the 4th, 31 in the 5th, and so on, if you want to count them, through the 45th session. The single o's in the sample signify winning runs of 2 zeros, and the two o's in a row in the 40th session the sole winning run in the sample of 3 consecutive zeros.'

'But betting, say, 1 unit per spin how much do I win from all this?' asks Mr Optimist again getting right to his favorite point.

'All right, let's begin playing the 1st session of the Hartman sample, and as the numbers of Table 21 (p. 42) were generated by an actual roulette wheel at the Monte Carlo Casino, for all practical purposes we're really gambling at Monte Carlo.'

'Let's begin betting,' asserts Mr Optimist.

'The 1st losing run is 1 spin long, but for the unlisted zero, which immediately follows, the Bank pays us 35 units. So after only 2 spins we're $35-1=34$ units ahead.'

'This is the kind of game I like,' chimes in our happily adventurous companion.

'The 2nd losing run is 39 spins long, and again for the unlisted zero which immediately follows, the Bank pays us another 35 units. So after $2+40=42$ spins we've won $35+35=70$ units and lost $1+39=40$ units so we're still ahead $70-40=30$ units. Remember the simple procedure, Mr Optimist: to calculate the gross loss from any session we merely *add* its column of figures, which signify only losing runs, and to calculate the gross gain from any session we merely *multiply* the number of these losing runs by the Bank's pay-off odds to 1 for a single number at roulette, which are 35 to 1. And remember that the number you chose from among the 37 is zero.'

'While you were talking,' interjects Mr Optimist gloomily, 'I've

46

been staring at the next 4 losing runs, which are 21, 4, 49, and ... 159.'

'From the losing runs 21, 4, and 49 spins long our gross loss is simply 21+4+49=74 units, and from these 3 games our gross gain is 3×35=105 units. Hence for these last 3 games our net gain is 105−74=31 units. Added to the win of 30 units from the last 2 games our net gain from the 1st 5 games is 30+31=61 units. But happy though it may be, I know 61 isn't the figure on your mind.'

'That's right – I'm still staring at the 6th run – 159 spins long. Are you sure Dr Hans Hartman didn't make a mistake? Can there be really a losing run as long as 159 spins before the reoccurrence of zero?'

'Of course – look back at Table 20 (p. 39): for losing runs as long as 140 to 164 spins there occur as many as 10 losing runs in the whole sample of 46,080 spins. It's just that this run of 159 losses without the reoccurrence of a single zero is the first long run we've struck.'

'Leaving us with a net loss of 159−61=98 units before our reaching the unlisted zero on the 160th spin,' laments Mr Optimist, 'whose happy occurrence still leaves us with a net loss of 98−35=63 units, and subtracting our previous net gain of 61 units, all told we're still 2 units out of pocket. And we were doing so well!'

'Which only underlines perhaps the most important point about Table 21 (p. 42),' I reply sympathetically. 'If roulette – or any other casino game for that matter – were only lacking in *long* losing runs, then perhaps the gambler could win.'

'Is there no way of avoiding them?' asks Mr Optimist, ever hopeful.

'What mathematically must occur does occur, and that includes those very long losing runs. As we may see from our final net loss of 2 units, it takes only *one* long losing run to wipe out all our net profit from the previous 6 games.'

'Well, a net loss of only 2 units isn't much,' says Mr Optimist ever looking at the brighter side, 'and glancing down the losing runs of the 1st 12 sessions I'm happy to see all of them begin with short losing runs allowing us to build up a good backlog of profit before the long losing run occurs which may wipe us out.'

'Unfortunately you're taking too small a sample. If you look at the whole Hartman sample, you'll find that the 13th, 20th, 21st, 24th, 27th, 28th, 31st, 35th, 40th, 41st, and 42nd sessions all *start* with long losing runs respectively 192, 160, 120, 123, 223, 112,

47

259, 104, 136, and 102 spins long. So 11 out of 45 sessions, or almost 1 out of 4, begin *immediately* with a long losing run.'

'What's the *actual average longest* losing run for all 45 sessions?' asks Mr Optimist.

'It's *147.87* spins long,' I reply.

'Golly, that's not very short. Well what's the *longest* losing run among all 45 sessions?' asks Mr Optimist.

'If you glance at the sessions,' I reply, 'you may easily find it.'

'The longest losing run in all the Hartman sample,' announces Mr Optimist after scanning all 45 sessions, 'occurs as the 18th run in the 17th session. This losing run is 268 spins long. No zero for 268 spins is incredible!'

'No it isn't. Look back again at Table 20 (p. 39) and remember what we found: 50 per cent of the losing runs occur before the 25th spin and 75 per cent before the 50th spin, which means that as many as *25 per cent* of the runs – and these the longest ones, of course – occur *after* the 50th spin. Run your eye over the longest runs of the sample: between 99 and 106 spins occur 20 losing runs, between 107 and 114 spins occur 10 losing runs, and between runs as long as from even 165 to 247 spins occur 13 losing runs, and so on. And at this point it would be edifying, in Table 22 (p. 48), to list the longest losing run that occurs in each of the 45 sessions.'

TABLE 22

The longest losing run of zero *during* each of the 45 sessions of the Hartman sample of 46,080 spins.

| | | | | | | | |
|---|---|---|---|---|---|---|---|
| 1 | 159 | 13 | 192 | 25 | 116 | 37 | 145 |
| 2 | 153 | 14 | 120 | 26 | 194 | 38 | 106 |
| 3 | 185 | 15 | 260 | 27 | 223 | 39 | 115 |
| 4 | 131 | 16 | 94 | 28 | 117 | 40 | 104 |
| 5 | 100 | 17 | 268 | 29 | 149 | 41 | 136 |
| 6 | 85 | 18 | 136 | 30 | 106 | 42 | 171 |
| 7 | 232 | 19 | 135 | 31 | 259 | 43 | 170 |
| 8 | 134 | 20 | 160 | 32 | 101 | 44 | 182 |
| 9 | 134 | 21 | 168 | 33 | 125 | 45 | 122 |
| 10 | 71 | 22 | 202 | 34 | 98 | | |
| 11 | 149 | 23 | 85 | 35 | 140 | | 147.87 |
| 12 | 128 | 24 | 172 | 36 | 130 | spins (average) | |

'We still haven't finished with the 1st session,' says Mr Optimist shifting hopefully to a possibly less depressing compilation. 'What is our gain or loss at the end of the 1st 1,024 spins?'

'First we add up all the losing runs: 1+39+21+4 ...

+51+93+51+52=1013 units, our gross loss. And as there are 26 losing runs, each ending in a zero, we multiply 26×35=910 units, our gross gain. Their difference is 1013−910=103 units, our final net loss. But we don't always have to lose at the end of every session, so take heart!'

'I'm trying to take heart!' cries out Mr Optimist.

'*If we begin anew at the beginning of each session*, at the end of the 1st, 3rd, and 4th sessions we lose respectively 103, 67, and 154 units ...'

'Boo!'

'But at the end of the 2nd and 5th we win respectively 17 and 72 units.'

'Hooray! Where does that leave us at the end of the 1st 5 sessions?'

'Well, 103+67+154=324 units lost, and 17+72=89 units won, so we get 324−89=*235* units as our final net loss *at the end* of 5×1024=5120 spins.'

'Boo! By the way what is the largest minus digression *during* the first 5,120 spins?' asks Mr Optimist.

'The largest minus digression *during* the first 5 session is *312* units, occurring at the beginning of the 5th and last session. Which means a favorable digression then sets in and reduces our net loss to *235* units. Remember the lesson of Table 10 (p. 15): the digression *during* a game or session is on average larger than the one *at the end* of it.'

'The net loss could have been worse,' comments Mr Optimist philosophically.

'True. The theoretical average loss at the end of 5,120 spins is 256 units.'

'Perhaps we'd do better playing longer!' exclaims Mr Optimist. 'What if we play the whole Hartman sample of 45 sessions of 46,080 spins betting 1 unit per spin on our chosen number zero?'

'Table 23 (p. 50) contains the succinct answer,' I reply.

'Well, an *actual net loss of 684 units* isn't too bad after our playing for almost 3 months or 46,080 spins!' asserts Mr Optimist.

'True, and because zero occurs actually 13 times more than it should theoretically, our actual net loss from the Bank's percentage or PC of $(1/37)(100)=2.70$ per cent on any chosen number – here zero – is much smaller than usual,' I reply. 'Thus in theory with a total of 46,080 spins we should get as many as $np=(46,080)(1/37)=1245$ *units as our theoretical net loss*.'

49

'That clinches it – I'll always bet on zero!' exclaims Mr Optimist.

'But the plus digression of 13 extra zeros is just because of luck, Mr Optimist!'

'That's what I mean – zero is a lucky number!'

'Well, have it your way,' I reply resignedly. 'At any rate let's see how well or ill we do if we adopt a progressive staking system on one number – and we might as well use zero again.'

'Wonderful – by systematically raising and lowering stakes at

TABLE 23

Actual final *net loss* in units at the end of the Hartman sample of 46,080 spins, betting 1 unit per spin on zero at pay-off odds of 35 to 1.

| Actual number of winning runs at the end of 46,080 spins | | Length of run (exactly) r | | Bank's pay-off odds to 1 | | gross win units |
|---|---|---|---|---|---|---|
| 1190 | × | 1 | × | 35 | = | 41,650 |
| 34 | × | 2 | × | 35 | = | 2,380 |
| 1 | × | 3 | × | 35 | = | 105 |
| 1225 | | | | | | 44,135 |

| Actual number of winning runs | | Length of run (exactly) r | | Actual winning spins |
|---|---|---|---|---|
| 1190 | × | 1 | = | 1190 |
| 34 | × | 2 | = | 68 |
| 1 | × | 3 | = | 3 |
| 1225 | | | | 1261 |

| | |
|---|---|
| 46,080 | Actual total spins of Hartman sample |
| 1,261 | Actual total *winning* spins |
| 44,819 | Actual total *losing* spins (and gross loss units betting 1 unit per spin) |
| 44,819 | Actual gross loss in units |
| 44,135 | Actual gross gain in units |
| 684 | Actual final *net loss* in units at the end of the Hartman sample of 46,080 spins, betting 1 unit per spin on zero. |

opportune moments I see no reason why I shouldn't beat not only the PC of 2.70 per cent but win something extra besides! After all the casino can't *make* me bet just 1 unit or flat stakes all the time. The question is, of course, when should I increase my bet?'

'If only because of the ever-gnawing effect of the PC, we should choose only that staking system whose *average* stake is always the lowest possible amount,' I recommend.

'In other words we should increase our stake as slowly as possible?' asks Mr Optimist.

'In the present case, yes. Let's put it this way: we won't increase our stake until that spin on which, *if we win*, we'll wipe out all our previous losses but, conservatively, win nothing more.'

'How shall we know when we reach that spin?' asks Mr Optimist.

'By using the following simple formula, which applies to any bet at any casino game where you may increase your stake. Remember: we'll bet only the minimal number of *a* units until our cumulative *gross loss* forces us to increase *a* to some larger stake which, on *our winning just once*, bring in immediately a gross gain roughly equaling our gross loss and thereby cancelling out all our prior debt, allowing us to reduce our stake again to the minimal *a* units. Here is the formula:

$$(b/a)=k$$

... where *b* signifies the Bank's pay-off odds to 1, *a* our stake in units, and *k* the last spin when we may bet *a before* having to increase our stake to recoup our gross loss.'

'Can you show me how this staking system would work out for our one number at roulette?' asks Mr Optimist.

'In Table 24 (p. 52) I've set out the whole progressive staking system.'

'Is this staking system simple?' asks Mr Optimist.

'Very. We begin betting a=1 unit and keep betting 1 unit for $(b/a)=k=(35/1)=35$ spins, the number heading the column under *k*. To be conservative we assume all along we haven't won before the 35th spin.'

'If we do win, how much is it?'

'It is the pay-off adds to 1 – here 35 – minus the number of losing bets we've already made.'

'So if zero comes up at, say, the 20th spin, we win $35-20=15$ units.'

'Right. After the 35th spin, however, to recoup our past losses

51

TABLE 24

Progressive staking system on one roulette number.

| ka | k | a | r | gl | gg | net gain or loss | cumulative net gain or loss |
|----|----|----|-----|-----|-----|------|------|
| 35 | 35 | 1 | 35 | 35 | 35 | 0 | 0 |
| 36 | 18 | 2 | 53 | 71 | 70 | −1 | −1 |
| 36 | 12 | 3 | 65 | 107 | 105 | −2 | −3 |
| 32 | 8 | 4 | 73 | 139 | 140 | +1 | −2 |
| 35 | 7 | 5 | 80 | 174 | 175 | +1 | −1 |
| 36 | 6 | 6 | 86 | 210 | 210 | 0 | −1 |
| 35 | 5 | 7 | 91 | 245 | 245 | 0 | −1 |
| 32 | 4 | 8 | 95 | 277 | 280 | +3 | +2 |
| 36 | 4 | 9 | 99 | 313 | 315 | +2 | +4 |
| 40 | 4 | 10 | 103 | 353 | 350 | −3 | −1 |
| 33 | 3 | 11 | 106 | 386 | 385 | −1 | −2 |
| 36 | 3 | 12 | 109 | 422 | 420 | −2 | −4 |
| 26 | 2 | 13 | 111 | 448 | 455 | +7 | +3 |
| 26 | 2 | 13 | 113 | 461 | 455 | −6 | −3 |
| 28 | 2 | 14 | 115 | 489 | 490 | +1 | −2 |
| 30 | 2 | 15 | 117 | 519 | 525 | +6 | +4 |

we have to begin increasing our bet. As shown under the column *a*, signifying the *amounts bet* as we go along, when we do increase our bet it's always by 1 unit except on the 13th hike, when there is momentarily no increase.'

'What is *r*?'

'The letter *r* continues to signify the *length* of the *uninterrupted losing run*. Continuing to assume we don't win *even once*, we must bet 1 unit for the 1st 35 spins, 2 units from the 36th to the 53rd spin, 3 units from the 54th to the 65th spin, 4 units from the 66th to the 73rd spin, and so on until the 117th spin.'

'What happens if we win any time between the 36th and the 117th spin?' asks Mr Optimist.

'It all depends on how long we've been betting. The letters *gl* and *gg* signify our *gross loss* and *gross gain* if we don't or do win at any designated spin. The very righthand column gives the *cumulative net gain or loss if we win*.'

'And *if we don't*?'

'Then our *cumulative net loss* equals the last number in the *gl* or *gross loss* column. So if we've been betting for *r*=53 spins without a single win, our final net loss is $gl=71$ units. If we keep betting for $r=65$ spins without a win, our final net loss is 107 units, and so on until the 117th spin where, betting $a=15$ units, our final net loss is as much as 519 units.'

'But *if we ever do win?*' asks Mr Optimist eagerly.

'Our *final net gain* or *loss* is listed in the righthand column. Notice that, *if we win*, our final net gain or loss doesn't go above or below 4 units, for as progressive staking systems go, this one is as tight as I could make it.'

'Why does the progression stop at the 117th spin?'

'Because after that everything gets out of hand: our bet must increase $a=1$ unit per spin, and only 10 spins later our *gl* or *gross loss* becomes as much as 724 units – unacceptedly large, I hope you agree.'

'I'm afraid so,' replies Mr Optimist. 'How often do we reach that unfortunate 117th spin without every hitting a single zero?'

'We may get a rough idea by examining Table 22 (p. 48) and merely note how many of the longest losing runs, among the 45 sessions, are longer than $r=117$ *spins or more.*'

'Then we win on the 5th, 6th, 10th, 16th, 23rd, 25th, 30th, 32nd, 34th, 38th, and 40th,' counts Mr Optimist, 'or a total of 11 sessions out of 45.'

'And we lose regretfully in $45-11=34$ sessions,' I reply. 'Note that *we go bankrupt* in *every one of the first 4 sessions*. And this result after adopting the most *conservative* progressive staking system. In other words if we increase our bet at any rate faster than that of column $a$, Table 24 (p. 52) we'll go bankrupt much more often.'

'Again, how often do we reach the unfortunate 117th spin without every hitting a single zero?' asks Mr Optimist again.

'The answer is we go bankrupt on an average once every 919 spins,' I reply.

'And every session is 1,024 spins long,' muses Mr Optimist somewhat sadly.

'I'm afraid so, old man.'

'Well, I guess we'd better not adopt even this most conservative progression on a single number,' concludes Mr Optimist ruefully. 'It seems pretty dangerous.'

'I agree.'

'But we can look on the brighter side,' he adds perking up. 'We suffered only disastrous *paper* losses.'

'That's why a gambler should *never try out* a betting system at the gaming table itself,' I emphasize.

'The PC for a single-zero roulette wheel here is 2.70 per cent, isn't it?' asks Mr Optimist.

'Just as we've examined,' I reply.

'What is it for such a wheel on the red or black, or some other even-money chance?'

'Much less – only 1.41 per cent – by coincidence exactly the same PC as for the Pass or Don't Pass line bets at craps,' I conclude.

'Then on to 1.41 per cent!' cries Mr Optimist.

'As you wish, my friend. Let's just not forget what we've learned.'

# CHAPTER VII

# The Result of Three Months: 50,000 Spins: Betting on 18 Numbers (Red)

'I feel much more at home,' remarks Mr Optimist, 'betting on even-money chances such as the red or black at roulette, the Pass or Don't Pass line at craps, or the ordinary bet at blackjack – especially as the Bank's Percentage or PC, as you call it, is only 1.41 per cent of every bet for at least the first two games. How do we come out on the even-money chances in the Hartman sample?'

'I've divided his 50,000-spin sample into 1 game of 50,000 spins, 10 games of 5,000 spins each, and lastly 500 games of 100 spins each,' I reply.

'How do we do at the end of the large 1 game of 50,000 spins?' asks Mr Optimist.

'Table 25 (p. 55) shows the results for the single game of 50,000 spins. We assume we're betting on all the 18 red numbers, so when we win, we get paid off at even-money i.e., odds of 1 to 1.'

TABLE 25

$n = 50,000$

|  | Red | Black | Zero |
|---|---|---|---|
| Theory: | 24,325 | 24,325 | 1,351 |
| Actual: | 24,479 | 24,171 | 1,348 |
|  | +154 | −154 | −3 |

'So the 18 black numbers plus zero are against us?' asks Mr Optimist.

'Exactly.'

'Then we win! Look – there are 154 more reds than blacks.'

'We have to discuss these figures. Yes, there are 154 more reds

55

than blacks – but Table 25 (p. 55) doesn't show the loss from the 1,348 zeros on our final net gain or loss in *units*. If we count every zero as a black without further qualification, then at the end of 50,000 spins our *actual* final net loss is 1,040 units.'

'Why?'

'We win 24,479 spins, which signifies also reds and gross units. We lose 24171+1348=25519 spins, which signifies blacks plus zeros, and gross units. Thus at the end of 50,000 spins, without further qualification, our final *actual* net loss is 25519−24479=1040. Were the 1,348 zeros not there, we should *win* 24479−24171=308 units from betting on red. Or more simply, 154×2=308 units. But we can't pretend the zeros aren't there, so our *actual* final net loss is 1,040 units as I mentioned.'

'Tell me, if we play the 10 games of 5,000 spins each that you mentioned, would we fare any better?' asks Mr Optimist.

'In the last chapter, when betting on a single number, we tried beginning anew at the start of each session of 1,024 spins, but this strategy didn't alter the final result. In the present matter of betting on red against black and zero let's divide the 50,000 spins into 10 games of 5,000 spins each. The result at the end of every 5,000 spins is listed in Table 26 (p. 56).'

TABLE 26

Number of units won and lost at the end of 50,000 spins, the latter divided into 10 games 5,000 spins long. (Each game below sums cumulatively by 10 the 100 500-spin figures of column 8, Table 27, p. 59.)

| Game | Units Won | Units Lost | | |
|------|-----------|------------|--------|--------------------------|
| 1 | 34 | 110 | | |
| 2 | 16 | 154 | | |
| 3 | 46 | 138 | | |
| 4 | 102 | 74 | | |
| 5 | 36 | 110 | | |
| 6 | 24 | 266 | | |
| 7 | 28 | 238 | | |
| 8 | 62 | 112 | | |
| 9 | 22 | 144 | −1458 | |
| 10 | 48 | 112 | + 418 | |
| | 418 | 1458 | −1040 | final net loss (including zeros) |

'So at the end of the 1st game 5,000 spins long we win 34 units and lose 110. At the end of the 2nd game 5,000 spins long we win 16 units and lose 154, and so on for the whole 10 games,' I continue.

'I see we are ahead in only the 4th game, winning 102−74=28 units,' notes Mr Optimist with a sigh.

'Yes, and this is just another proof of what the PC of 2.70 per cent loses us in the long run. At the end of the 10 games each 5,000 spins long our *actual* final net loss is 1,040 units, so again we have proved that it makes no difference whether we play 1 game 50,000 spins long or 10 games 5,000 spins long: the result is identical.'

'In the last chapter you promised that on the even-money chances of roulette or craps the PC would be 1.41 per cent, so why have you used so far the figure 2.70 per cent?' asks Mr Optimist.

'You might note that heretofore in this chapter my use of the phrase "without further qualification". In other words zero occurs once every 37 spins – giving us a loss of 1/37th or (1/37) (100)=2.70 per cent of every bet we make. This is entirely true in the last chapter on a single number. And it holds true for several numbers. But on a Monte-Carlo roulette wheel, used in most European countries, they have a rule called "In Prison" for the even-money chances, whereby we lose only *about half* of 2.70 per cent, or in truth 1.41 per cent.'

'Thus at the end of 50,000 spins we should lose *theoretically* from the PC, any=(1) (50000) (0.027027027)=1351 units as shown in Table 25 (p. 55), that is to say, our loss in units is identical to the number of zeros. But with a PC of 1.41 per cent the true *theoretical* loss in units is only any=(1) (50000) (0.0141)=705 units. Now, at the end of 50,000 spins in a mathematically *fair* game i.e., one without any PC favoring the Bank, we should expect to *win* or *lose* on an *average* 183 units. With the true PC of 1.41 per cent, however, this gain or loss becomes an *average loss* of 183−705=*522* units or a *worse average loss* of 183+705=*888* units. So we should be thankful to the Monte-Carlo "In Prison" rule, which reduces by almost half the loss on the even chances, such as the red and black, as opposed to that on one or more numbers themselves.'

'That's the way to look at things – optimistically!' cries Mr Optimist. 'Our theoretical loss is *smaller* rather than *larger*. And you say that at craps on the Pass and Don't Pass line bets the PC is also only 1.41 per cent?'

'Absolutely. Now shall we move on to the third and last division of games – 500 games of 100 spins each?'

'Onward!' cries Mr Optimist.

'Just as Table 21 (p. 42) gave the system player the step-by-step results for an *actual* single number in 46,080 spins at roulette, so Table 27 (p. 59) gives the results for the *actual* red or 18 numbers in 50,000 spins. Table 27 (p. 59) has 8 columns. Let's discuss each column slowly and carefully.'

'I hope so,' says Mr Optimist.

'And remember – without our making the "In Prison" rule adjustment, every zero will continue to be counted simply as a black or 1 unit lost,' I add. 'We assume, of course, that we are always betting 1 unit on red to win. And now to Table 27 (p. 59). Although a long table, it is very easy to understand.'

'I'm delighted to hear that,' responds Mr Optimist.

'I have divided the 1 sample of 50,000 spins into 500 samples or *games* of 100 spins each, and you'll note that these games are numbered, on the lefthand side of the table, from 1 to 500.

'*At the end* of these 500 games 40 result in a return to equilibrium, 187 result in a plus digression, and 273 result in a minus digression, which we may easily deduce using the figures in column 6 of Table 27 (p. 59). Or expressed in percentages we break even at the end of (40/500) (100)=8 per cent of the 500 games, win something at the end of (187/500) (100)=37.4 per cent of the 500 games, and lose something at the end of (273/500) (100)=54.6 per cent of the games.

'I should emphasize that, taken as one game 50,000 spins long, the last return to equilibrium *during* the game occurs at the 136th spin. It is the 29th return, and after this occurrence, betting always 1 unit on red during the 50,000 spins, the player never again breaks even let alone wins anything. Such is the adverse effect of the PC, here the simple zero of 2.70 per cent.

'Column 1 of Table 27 (p. 59) lists the *number* of returns to equilibrium during each game of 100 spins. We observe that there occur 23 returns during the 3rd game, 6 returns during the 2nd game, 12 returns during the 3rd game, and so on for 500 games.

'Table 28 (p. 72) lists the distribution of these returns to equilibrium *during* the 500 games. Thus 30 of the 500 games contain no returns at all, 39 of them contain only 1 return, 49 contain 2 returns ... and 1 game contains as many as 30 returns. The sum of 39+49+30 ... 1 is 469 games containing a return to equilibrium

# THE RESULT OF THREE MONTHS: 50,000 SPINS

## TABLE 27

|  |  | 1 | 2 | 3 | During + 4 | − 5 | End ± 6 | 7 | 8 |
|---|---|---|---|---|---|---|---|---|---|
| Game: | 1 | 23 | 100 | 10 | 8 | 4 | 0 | 52 |  |
|  | 2 | 6 | 36 | 3 | 3 | 24 | −24 | 20 |  |
|  | 3 | 12 | 36 | 9 | 3 | 12 | −12 | 28 |  |
|  | 4 | 1 | 16 | 0 | 0 | 10 | − 2 | 0 |  |
|  | 5 | 4 | 52 | 1 | 10 | 4 | + 4 | 78 | −34 |
|  | 6 | 8 | 22 | 4 | 10 | 2 | + 4 | 84 |  |
|  | 7 | 2 | 12 | 1 | 2 | 17 | −12 | 6 |  |
|  | 8 | 11 | 94 | 4 | 7 | 7 | − 2 | 36 |  |
|  | 9 | 10 | 46 | 6 | 8 | 3 | + 6 | 86 |  |
|  | 10 | 13 | 76 | 7 | 8 | 7 | + 6 | 36 | +2 |
|  | 11 | 0 | — | 0 | 23 | 0 | +22 | 100 |  |
|  | 12 | 8 | 44 | 5 | 4 | 21 | −20 | 30 |  |
|  | 13 | 14 | 82 | 9 | 7 | 5 | − 2 | 66 |  |
|  | 14 | 5 | 34 | 4 | 20 | 3 | +12 | 88 |  |
|  | 15 | 4 | 8 | 2 | 1 | 16 | −16 | 6 | −4 |
|  | 16 | 2 | 8 | 1 | 3 | 19 | −18 | 6 |  |
|  | 17 | 6 | 74 | 2 | 6 | 10 | −10 | 26 |  |
|  | 18 | 5 | 94 | 3 | 6 | 12 | + 2 | 44 |  |
|  | 19 | 2 | 8 | 2 | 1 | 16 | −14 | 2 |  |
|  | 20 | 8 | 46 | 2 | 7 | 2 | + 6 | 96 | −34 |
|  | 21 | 0 | — | 0 | 11 | 0 | + 4 | 100 |  |
|  | 22 | 4 | 12 | 1 | 3 | 22 | −22 | 10 |  |
|  | 23 | 6 | 96 | 3 | 10 | 3 | − 2 | 86 |  |
|  | 24 | 19 | 86 | 10 | 5 | 3 | − 2 | 38 |  |
|  | 25 | 11 | 64 | 7 | 11 | 4 | + 8 | 70 | −14 |
|  | 26 | 5 | 100 | 2 | 3 | 6 | 0 | 10 |  |
|  | 27 | 4 | 8 | 1 | 19 | 1 | +18 | 98 |  |
|  | 28 | 8 | 94 | 6 | 7 | 7 | − 4 | 52 |  |
|  | 29 | 12 | 92 | 7 | 11 | 4 | −4 | 54 |  |
|  | 30 | 7 | 20 | 5 | 3 | 24 | −22 | 88 | −12 |
|  | 31 | 2 | 6 | 1 | 12 | 2 | +10 | 94 |  |
|  | 32 | 5 | 86 | 2 | 5 | 10 | −10 | 24 |  |
|  | 33 | 1 | 2 | 1 | 24 | 1 | +22 | 98 |  |
|  | 34 | 3 | 8 | 0 | 0 | 14 | −14 | 0 |  |
|  | 35 | 8 | 96 | 5 | 6 | 6 | − 2 | 50 | +6 |
|  | 36 | 2 | 20 | 1 | 3 | 15 | − 6 | 16 |  |
|  | 37 | 14 | 62 | 9 | 5 | 8 | − 2 | 34 |  |
|  | 38 | 1 | 2 | 1 | 18 | 1 | +14 | 98 |  |
|  | 39 | 7 | 48 | 2 | 12 | 3 | +12 | 80 |  |

TABLE 27 (continued)

| | 1 | 2 | 3 | During<br>+<br>4 | −<br>·5 | End<br>±<br>6 | 7 | 8 |
|---|---|---|---|---|---|---|---|---|
| 40 | 4 | 100 | 2 | 9 | 1 | 0 | 98 | +18 |
| 41 | 7 | 100 | 2 | 11 | 3 | 0 | 78 | |
| 42 | 20 | 78 | 11 | 3 | 8 | − 6 | 24 | |
| 43 | 11 | 78 | 9 | 7 | 14 | −12 | 66 | |
| 44 | 18 | 96 | 8 | 4 | 6 | + 4 | 28 | |
| 45 | 4 | 52 | 1 | 14 | 1 | + 2 | 98 | −12 |
| 46 | 3 | 10 | 2 | 12 | 2 | +10 | 94 | |
| 47 | 9 | 34 | 4 | 1 | 14 | −10 | 10 | |
| 48 | 18 | 74 | 9 | 9 | 5 | + 6 | 52 | |
| 49 | 16 | 90 | 10 | 2 | 8 | − 8 | 18 | |
| 50 | 2 | 4 | 2 | 12 | 1 | +10 | 98 | +8 |
| 51 | 13 | 100 | 8 | 3 | 14 | 0 | 26 | |
| 52 | 12 | 90 | 4 | 2 | 8 | − 2 | 14 | |
| 53 | 5 | 98 | 2 | 11 | 4 | + 2 | 80 | |
| 54 | 8 | 100 | 3 | 5 | 10 | 0 | 22 | |
| 55 | 8 | 56 | 0 | 0 | 12 | −12 | 0 | −12 |
| 56 | 10 | 92 | 7 | 5 | 7 | − 6 | 20 | |
| 57 | 4 | 20 | 3 | 16 | 2 | +16 | 94 | |
| 58 | 12 | 100 | 6 | 2 | 10 | 0 | 20 | |
| 59 | 8 | 86 | 5 | 11 | 9 | +10 | 20 | |
| 60 | 2 | 8 | 1 | 2 | 8 | − 4 | 6 | +16 |
| 61 | 1 | 4 | 0 | 0 | 15 | − 6 | 0 | |
| 62 | 8 | 26 | 2 | 1 | 20 | −12 | 8 | |
| 63 | 0 | — | 0 | 18 | −16 | 0 | | |
| 64 | 3 | 24 | 2 | 1 | 14 | −12 | 2 | |
| 65 | 15 | 90 | 7 | 5 | 6 | + 2 | 30 | −44 |
| 66 | 12 | 90 | 7 | 6 | 6 | − 4 | 58 | |
| 67 | 1 | 2 | 0 | 0 | 16 | −16 | 0 | |
| 68 | 2 | 12 | 0 | 0 | 17 | −14 | 0 | |
| 69 | 12 | 86 | 7 | 8 | 5 | + 6 | 58 | |
| 70 | 17 | 96 | 10 | 6 | 4 | − 2 | 62 | −30 |
| 71 | 11 | 32 | 7 | 15 | 2 | +10 | 84 | |
| 72 | 5 | 34 | 4 | 5 | 13 | −12 | 20 | |
| 73 | 0 | — | 0 | 0 | 9 | − 6 | 0 | |
| 74 | 4 | 42 | 4 | 12 | 3 | + 6 | 90 | |
| 75 | 4 | 12 | 1 | 1 | 12 | − 6 | 4 | −8 |
| 76 | 1 | 2 | 0 | 0 | 14 | −12 | 0 | |
| 77 | 3 | 6 | 2 | 1 | 15 | −14 | 2 | |
| 78 | 6 | 48 | 4 | 11 | 3 | + 6 | 88 | |

TABLE 27 (continued)

| | 1 | 2 | 3 | During + 4 | − 5 | End ± 6 | 7 | 8 |
|---|---|---|---|---|---|---|---|---|
| 79 | 11 | 66 | 7 | 11 | 6 | +10 | 50 | |
| 80 | 16 | 86 | 7 | 3 | 11 | − 6 | 24 | −16 |
| 81 | 3 | 14 | 1 | 4 | 8 | − 8 | 14 | |
| 82 | 6 | 96 | 3 | 14 | 3 | − 2 | 90 | |
| 83 | 20 | 94 | 8 | 6 | 3 | + 2 | 62 | |
| 84 | 7 | 98 | 4 | 5 | 9 | + 2 | 56 | |
| 85 | 8 | 82 | 3 | 6 | 2 | + 2 | 86 | −4 |
| 86 | 6 | 60 | 3 | 8 | 10 | − 8 | 56 | |
| 87 | 4 | 28 | 2 | 9 | 1 | + 4 | 96 | |
| 88 | 1 | 2 | 1 | 15 | 1 | + 2 | 98 | |
| 89 | 5 | 16 | 2 | 1 | 15 | − 6 | 6 | |
| 90 | 5 | 32 | 2 | 2 | 12 | − 4 | 6 | −12 |
| 91 | 8 | 48 | 5 | 7 | 10 | − 8 | 22 | |
| 92 | 12 | 90 | 4 | 8 | 8 | − 8 | 66 | |
| 93 | 7 | 36 | 2 | 1 | 16 | − 8 | 2 | |
| 94 | 20 | 96 | 10 | 4 | 4 | + 2 | 62 | |
| 95 | 6 | 86 | 3 | 1 | 7 | − 2 | 4 | −24 |
| 96 | 14 | 70 | 5 | 8 | 4 | + 4 | 66 | |
| 97 | 2 | 28 | 1 | 1 | 13 | −10 | 2 | |
| 98 | 8 | 36 | 5 | 13 | 3 | + 8 | 80 | |
| 99 | 13 | 58 | 6 | 4 | 7 | − 2 | 44 | |
| 100 | 14 | 76 | 9 | 8 | 7 | − 4 | 56 | −4 |
| 101 | 6 | 58 | 4 | 5 | 13 | −12 | 34 | |
| 102 | 10 | 98 | 7 | 5 | 10 | + 2 | 34 | |
| 103 | 7 | 26 | 3 | 2 | 7 | − 2 | 14 | |
| 104 | 9 | 36 | 5 | 5 | 11 | − 4 | 32 | |
| 105 | 4 | 10 | 3 | 21 | 2 | +20 | 94 | +4 |
| 106 | 3 | 8 | 2 | 15 | 1 | +12 | 98 | |
| 107 | 2 | 54 | 0 | 0 | 9 | − 4 | 0 | |
| 108 | 2 | 20 | 2 | 16 | 3 | +14 | 90 | |
| 109 | 0 | — | 0 | 0 | 15 | −12 | 0 | |
| 110 | 0 | — | 0 | 0 | 20 | −18 | 0 | −8 |
| 111 | 18 | 98 | 4 | 5 | 2 | + 2 | 78 | |
| 112 | 12 | 82 | 5 | 4 | 7 | − 4 | 24 | |
| 113 | 4 | 28 | 0 | 0 | 14 | −14 | 0 | |
| 114 | 2 | 4 | 1 | 11 | 1 | + 4 | 96 | |
| 115 | 2 | 30 | 2 | 7 | 8 | − 8 | 28 | −20 |
| 116 | 8 | 98 | 3 | 2 | 8 | +2 | 6 | |
| 117 | 6 | 36 | 1 | 4 | 13 | − 8 | 22 | |

61

TABLE 27 (continued)

| | 1 | 2 | 3 | During + 4 | – 5 | End ± 6 | 7 | 8 |
|---|---|---|---|---|---|---|---|---|
| 118 | 6 | 86 | 4 | 8 | 3 | + 4 | 90 | |
| 119 | 13 | 52 | 6 | 2 | 11 | −10 | 24 | |
| 120 | 1 | 6 | 0 | 17 | 0 | + 2 | 100 | −10 |
| 121 | 3 | 40 | 2 | 11 | 1 | +10 | 96 | |
| 122 | 4 | 14 | 2 | 1 | 17 | −12 | 2 | |
| 123 | 12 | 68 | 5 | 10 | 4 | +10 | 74 | |
| 124 | 0 | — | 0 | 15 | 0 | +14 | 100 | |
| 125 | 10 | 30 | 8 | 11 | 3 | + 4 | 86 | +26 |
| 126 | 1 | 8 | 1 | 4 | 27 | −26 | 8 | |
| 127 | 19 | 80 | 11 | 5 | 6 | − 4 | 56 | |
| 128 | 16 | 66 | 4 | 4 | 6 | − 4 | 52 | |
| 129 | 14 | 76 | 7 | 8 | 6 | − 6 | 56 | |
| 130 | 3 | 12 | 1 | 1 | 14 | − 6 | 2 | −46 |
| 131 | 0 | — | 0 | 12 | 0 | + 2 | 100 | |
| 132 | 4 | 62 | 1 | 13 | 3 | +12 | 88 | |
| 133 | 4 | 60 | 1 | 12 | 8 | − 2 | 56 | |
| 134 | 0 | — | 0 | 0 | 14 | −12 | 0 | |
| 135 | 9 | 26 | 4 | 2 | 12 | −10 | 10 | −10 |
| 136 | 4 | 32 | 3 | 12 | 6 | + 4 | 70 | |
| 137 | 4 | 66 | 2 | 8 | 1 | + 6 | 98 | |
| 138 | 12 | 80 | 4 | 8 | 6 | − 6 | 40 | |
| 139 | 15 | 98 | 8 | 3 | 5 | − 2 | 22 | |
| 140 | 0 | — | 0 | 0 | 31 | −26 | 0 | −24 |
| 141 | 2 | 38 | 1 | 1 | 20 | −18 | 2 | |
| 142 | 2 | 4 | 2 | 1 | 13 | − 8 | 2 | |
| 143 | 1 | 2 | 0 | 0 | 12 | − 4 | 0 | |
| 144 | 0 | — | 0 | 32 | 0 | +32 | 100 | |
| 145 | 3 | 24 | 1 | 20 | 7 | +14 | 76 | +16 |
| 146 | 4 | 8 | 2 | 1 | 10 | − 2 | 2 | |
| 147 | 1 | 20 | 1 | 1 | 17 | −14 | 2 | |
| 148 | 7 | 50 | 5 | 5 | 10 | − 8 | 24 | |
| 149 | 21 | 84 | 6 | 6 | 2 | + 4 | 70 | |
| 150 | 8 | 100 | 4 | 4 | 7 | 0 | 26 | −20 |
| 151 | 5 | 38 | 2 | 11 | 4 | + 8 | 64 | |
| 152 | 6 | 14 | 3 | 21 | 2 | +14 | 92 | |
| 153 | 16 | 100 | 9 | 8 | 6 | 0 | 52 | |
| 154 | 0 | — | 0 | 0 | 15 | − 2 | 0 | |
| 155 | 9 | 72 | 4 | 6 | 5 | − 4 | 52 | +16 |
| 156 | 11 | 98 | 7 | 4 | 9 | − 2 | 42 | |

TABLE 27 (continued)

| | 1 | 2 | 3 | During + 4 | – 5 | End ± 6 | 7 | 8 |
|---|---|---|---|---|---|---|---|---|
| 157 | 5 | 24 | 1 | 5 | 11 | − 4 | 22 | |
| 158 | 2 | 100 | 0 | 9 | 0 | 0 | 100 | |
| 159 | 4 | 30 | 2 | 6 | 12 | −10 | 28 | |
| 160 | 5 | 92 | 4 | 11 | 2 | + 4 | 92 | −12 |
| 161 | 12 | 100 | 6 | 7 | 2 | 0 | 80 | |
| 162 | 12 | 88 | 4 | 9 | 7 | − 6 | 40 | |
| 163 | 11 | 60 | 7 | 3 | 13 | −12 | 32 | |
| 164 | 8 | 80 | 4 | 8 | 2 | + 4 | 92 | |
| 165 | 11 | 54 | 9 | 3 | 11 | −10 | 16 | −24 |
| 166 | 4 | 16 | 0 | 0 | 14 | − 4 | 0 | |
| 167 | 5 | 14 | 3 | 2 | 23 | −16 | 8 | |
| 168 | 12 | 60 | 8 | 3 | 10 | −10 | 26 | |
| 169 | 4 | 86 | 2 | 5 | 9 | + 2 | 30 | |
| 170 | 9 | 48 | 4 | 2 | 7 | − 4 | 8 | −32 |
| 171 | 0 | — | 0 | 15 | 0 | + 6 | 100 | |
| 172 | 11 | 50 | 7 | 6 | 5 | + 4 | 64 | |
| 173 | 3 | 20 | 3 | 16 | 4 | +12 | 82 | |
| 174 | 0 | — | 0 | 0 | 37 | −36 | 0 | |
| 175 | 7 | 38 | 2 | 16 | 2 | +12 | 96 | −2 |
| 176 | 3 | 56 | 2 | 1 | 9 | − 6 | 2 | |
| 177 | 0 | — | 0 | 14 | 0 | +14 | 100 | |
| 178 | 18 | 96 | 9 | 4 | 6 | − 4 | 36 | |
| 179 | 2 | 20 | 1 | 15 | 5 | +14 | 80 | |
| 180 | 10 | 88 | 6 | 4 | 9 | + 4 | 28 | +22 |
| 181 | 1 | 2 | 1 | 1 | 9 | − 6 | 2 | |
| 182 | 18 | 88 | 9 | 6 | 6 | − 6 | 42 | |
| 183 | 0 | — | 0 | 22 | 0 | +18 | 100 | |
| 184 | 15 | 76 | 8 | 4 | 6 | − 4 | 34 | |
| 185 | 0 | — | 0 | 30 | 0 | +30 | 100 | +32 |
| 186 | 9 | 42 | 6 | 4 | 16 | −16 | 28 | |
| 187 | 15 | 48 | 6 | 12 | 4 | +12 | 76 | |
| 188 | 10 | 98 | 4 | 6 | 4 | − 2 | 58 | |
| 189 | 8 | 46 | 7 | 3 | 10 | − 8 | 20 | |
| 190 | 1 | 14 | 1 | 19 | 3 | +14 | 86 | 0 |
| 191 | 1 | 2 | 1 | 20 | 1 | +20 | 98 | |
| 192 | 2 | 6 | 0 | 0 | 12 | −12 | 0 | |
| 193 | 2 | 6 | 1 | 2 | 19 | −18 | 4 | |
| 194 | 1 | 4 | 0 | 17 | 0 | +10 | 100 | |
| 195 | 16 | 50 | 8 | 2 | 12 | − 4 | 24 | −4 |
| 196 | 4 | 30 | 4 | 22 | 3 | +22 | 78 | |

TABLE 27 (continued)

| | 1 | 2 | 3 | During + 4 | − 5 | End ± 6 | 7 | 8 |
|---|---|---|---|---|---|---|---|---|
| 197 | 6 | 100 | 2 | 1 | 8 | 0 | 4 | |
| 198 | 4 | 10 | 2 | 13 | 2 | + 4 | 92 | |
| 199 | 14 | 82 | 11 | 8 | 4 | + 2 | 76 | |
| 200 | 8 | 80 | 6 | 6 | 6 | + 4 | 52 | +32 |
| 201 | 5 | 42 | 4 | 7 | 14 | −12 | 28 | |
| 202 | 2 | 6 | 2 | 13 | 2 | + 4 | 96 | |
| 203 | 7 | 32 | 4 | 2 | 18 | −18 | 10 | |
| 204 | 1 | 2 | 1 | 1 | 33 | −32 | 2 | |
| 205 | 7 | 28 | 4 | 2 | 11 | − 2 | 14 | −60 |
| 206 | 6 | 42 | 5 | 5 | 12 | − 6 | 26 | |
| 207 | 11 | 98 | 7 | 8 | 5 | + 2 | 56 | |
| 208 | 3 | 20 | 1 | 2 | 12 | − 6 | 6 | |
| 209 | 7 | 98 | 2 | 1 | 8 | − 2 | 4 | |
| 210 | 6 | 100 | 3 | 4 | 10 | 0 | 20 | −12 |
| 211 | 0 | — | 0 | 17 | 0 | +10 | 100 | |
| 212 | 9 | 62 | 5 | 12 | 6 | + 4 | 46 | |
| 213 | 13 | 100 | 7 | 7 | 5 | 0 | 76 | |
| 214 | 15 | 76 | 9 | 4 | 9 | − 6 | 30 | |
| 215 | 7 | 40 | 5 | 2 | 17 | −16 | 10 | − 8 |
| 216 | 6 | 28 | 5 | 3 | 14 | −14 | 10 | |
| 217 | 11 | 70 | 4 | 7 | 2 | + 2 | 90 | |
| 218 | 1 | 4 | 1 | 1 | 11 | − 2 | 4 | |
| 219 | 2 | 94 | 0 | 12 | 0 | + 6 | 100 | |
| 220 | 4 | 12 | 2 | 17 | 2 | +12 | 92 | +4 |
| 221 | 0 | — | 0 | 20 | 0 | +10 | 100 | |
| 222 | 11 | 40 | 2 | 3 | 12 | −10 | 30 | |
| 223 | 3 | 14 | 1 | 3 | 28 | −26 | 14 | |
| 224 | 19 | 92 | 10 | 7 | 5 | − 4 | 74 | |
| 225 | 1 | 2 | 0 | 13 | 0 | +10 | 100 | −20 |
| 226 | 6 | 24 | 3 | 14 | 2 | + 4 | 78 | |
| 227 | 3 | 22 | 2 | 5 | 11 | −10 | 16 | |
| 228 | 15 | 56 | 7 | 8 | 3 | + 8 | 76 | |
| 229 | 14 | 88 | 8 | 8 | 7 | − 6 | 68 | |
| 230 | 4 | 30 | 0 | 12 | 0 | + 6 | 100 | +2 |
| 231 | 13 | 58 | 4 | 9 | 3 | + 2 | 90 | |
| 232 | 6 | 92 | 2 | 8 | 6 | − 6 | 80 | |
| 233 | 16 | 94 | 9 | 6 | 3 | + 4 | 78 | |
| 234 | 2 | 4 | 0 | 18 | 0 | + 8 | 100 | |
| 235 | 3 | 8 | 1 | 2 | 17 | − 8 | 6 | 0 |

| TABLE 27 (continued) | | | During | | End | | |
| | | | + | − | ± | | |
| 1 | 2 | 3 | 4 | 5 | 6 | 7 | 8 |
|---|---|---|---|---|---|---|---|
| 236 | 13 | 78 | 7 | 5 | 7 | − 4 | 46 | |
| 237 | 10 | 78 | 4 | 10 | 3 | + 4 | 84 | |
| 238 | 13 | 60 | 5 | 2 | 13 | −12 | 18 | |
| 239 | 7 | 68 | 5 | 15 | 7 | +12 | 40 | |
| 240 | 5 | 62 | 4 | 10 | 11 | − 8 | 50 | −8 |
| 241 | 10 | 70 | 3 | 10 | 3 | + 8 | 58 | |
| 242 | 5 | 44 | 2 | 8 | 7 | + 2 | 28 | |
| 243 | 13 | 98 | 9 | 7 | 3 | − 2 | 80 | |
| 244 | 6 | 54 | 1 | 1 | 13 | −10 | 2 | |
| 245 | 19 | 100 | 11 | 9 | 2 | 0 | 68 | −2 |
| 246 | 14 | 62 | 6 | 19 | 2 | +18 | 88 | |
| 247 | 2 | 12 | 1 | 16 | 1 | + 4 | 98 | |
| 248 | 2 | 8 | 1 | 11 | 1 | +10 | 98 | |
| 249 | 8 | 98 | 1 | 6 | 3 | + 2 | 90 | |
| 250 | 18 | 68 | 10 | 2 | 7 | − 4 | 18 | +30 |
| | | | | | | | | |
| 251 | 2 | 46 | 2 | 6 | 11 | −10 | 36 | |
| 252 | 4 | 20 | 4 | 13 | 1 | +12 | 96 | |
| 253 | 9 | 70 | 6 | 3 | 13 | −10 | 18 | |
| 254 | 0 | — | 0 | 0 | 21 | −18 | 0 | |
| 255 | 4 | 30 | 2 | 6 | 16 | −12 | 24 | −38 |
| 256 | 14 | 58 | 7 | 1 | 8 | − 6 | 14 | |
| 257 | 23 | 98 | 11 | 5 | 3 | + 2 | 48 | |
| 258 | 1 | 24 | 1 | 3 | 18 | −18 | 24 | |
| 259 | 8 | 22 | 3 | 2 | 20 | −16 | 14 | |
| 260 | 7 | 68 | 3 | 5 | 14 | −14 | 28 | −52 |
| 261 | 11 | 100 | 6 | 5 | 9 | 0 | 30 | |
| 262 | 5 | 94 | 2 | 10 | 2 | + 2 | 90 | |
| 263 | 7 | 34 | 3 | 3 | 15 | − 8 | 18 | |
| 264 | 5 | 30 | 0 | 12 | 0 | + 2 | 100 | |
| 265 | 4 | 26 | 2 | 12 | 3 | + 4 | 78 | 0 |
| 266 | 1 | 8 | 0 | 0 | 25 | −20 | 0 | |
| 267 | 11 | 98 | 8 | 4 | 9 | + 2 | 32 | |
| 268 | 1 | 44 | 1 | 6 | 11 | −10 | 44 | |
| 269 | 15 | 82 | 6 | 6 | 8 | − 6 | 36 | |
| 270 | 7 | 100 | 2 | 8 | 1 | 0 | 98 | −34 |
| 271 | 6 | 54 | 4 | 9 | 3 | + 6 | 88 | |
| 272 | 1 | 94 | 0 | 18 | 0 | + 2 | 100 | |
| 273 | 7 | 100 | 4 | 9 | 1 | 0 | 92 | |
| 274 | 12 | 100 | 6 | 4 | 9 | 0 | 48 | |

TABLE 27 (continued)

| | 1 | 2 | 3 | During + 4 | − ·5 | End ± 6 | 7 | 8 |
|---|---|---|---|---|---|---|---|---|
| 275 | 8 | 92 | 4 | 13 | 4 | + 6 | 84 | +14 |
| 276 | 19 | 98 | 6 | 1 | 6 | − 2 | 14 | |
| 277 | 7 | 100 | 4 | 2 | 9 | 0 | 8 | |
| 278 | 1 | 2 | 1 | 1 | 15 | − 4 | 2 | |
| 279 | 14 | 88 | 10 | 6 | 3 | + 4 | 64 | |
| 280 | 8 | 66 | 3 | 4 | 12 | − 8 | 48 | −10 |
| 281 | 6 | 96 | 2 | 2 | 10 | + 2 | 16 | |
| 282 | 4 | 50 | 3 | 8 | 16 | −16 | 48 | |
| 283 | 2 | 94 | 0 | 9 | 0 | + 2 | 100 | |
| 284 | 6 | 44 | 4 | 3 | 17 | −16 | 12 | |
| 285 | 5 | 12 | 2 | 2 | 16 | − 8 | 4 | −36 |
| 286 | 0 | — | 0 | 0 | 19 | −14 | 0 | |
| 287 | 7 | 26 | 2 | 4 | 16 | −14 | 14 | |
| 288 | 2 | 18 | 0 | 0 | 15 | −12 | 0 | |
| 289 | 0 | — | 0 | 0 | 16 | −12 | 0 | |
| 290 | 3 | 10 | 1 | 2 | 19 | −14 | 10 | −66 |
| 291 | 4 | 32 | 1 | 16 | 1 | +10 | 98 | |
| 292 | 0 | — | 0 | 0 | 18 | −12 | 0 | |
| 293 | 9 | 96 | 5 | 8 | 5 | − 4 | 84 | |
| 294 | 3 | 10 | 1 | 2 | 19 | −18 | 8 | |
| 295 | 8 | 62 | 1 | 8 | 11 | − 6 | 54 | −30 |
| 296 | 1 | 38 | 1 | 6 | 19 | −16 | 38 | |
| 297 | 1 | 2 | 0 | 23 | 0 | +14 | 100 | |
| 298 | 15 | 86 | 6 | 2 | 5 | − 2 | 10 | |
| 299 | 5 | 22 | 3 | 14 | 3 | +12 | 80 | |
| 300 | 17 | 94 | 13 | 6 | 7 | + 2 | 52 | +10 |
| 301 | 6 | 34 | 1 | 3 | 11 | − 4 | 6 | |
| 302 | 4 | 20 | 2 | 1 | 14 | − 8 | 4 | |
| 303 | 4 | 24 | 4 | 2 | 26 | −22 | 6 | |
| 304 | 8 | 98 | 4 | 2 | 7 | + 2 | 6 | |
| 305 | 1 | 6 | 1 | 2 | 15 | − 8 | 6 | −40 |
| 306 | 4 | 8 | 2 | 1 | 24 | −24 | 2 | |
| 307 | 5 | 16 | 1 | 17 | 1 | +16 | 94 | |
| 308 | 7 | 44 | 2 | 1 | 15 | −14 | 2 | |
| 309 | 3 | 10 | 2 | 12 | 2 | + 4 | 94 | |
| 310 | 6 | 14 | 2 | 1 | 13 | −10 | 2 | −28 |
| 311 | 5 | 42 | 1 | 12 | 4 | +10 | 58 | |
| 312 | 5 | 34 | 5 | 9 | 1 | + 6 | 94 | |
| 313 | 3 | 6 | 2 | 1 | 17 | − 8 | 4 | |

| TABLE 27 (continued) | | | During | | End | | |
| --- | --- | --- | --- | --- | --- | --- | --- |
| | | | + | − | ± | | |
| 1 | 2 | 3 | 4 | 5 | 6 | 7 | 8 |
| 314 | 6 | 14 | 3 | 17 | 1 | +16 | 96 | |
| 315 | 2 | 78 | 2 | 12 | 8 | − 8 | 76 | +16 |
| 316 | 9 | 98 | 5 | 3 | 8 | − 2 | 14 | |
| 317 | 8 | 92 | 5 | 11 | 3 | + 2 | 84 | |
| 318 | 10 | 46 | 8 | 4 | 6 | − 4 | 14 | |
| 319 | 14 | 74 | 5 | 13 | 2 | +12 | 90 | |
| 320 | 6 | 52 | 3 | 7 | 5 | + 4 | 50 | +12 |
| 321 | 2 | 30 | 2 | 2 | 9 | − 8 | 4 | |
| 322 | 12 | 62 | 8 | 4 | 22 | −22 | 34 | |
| 323 | 6 | 36 | 4 | 6 | 14 | −14 | 22 | |
| 324 | 11 | 100 | 7 | 6 | 4 | 0 | 60 | |
| 325 | 7 | 22 | 2 | 18 | 2 | +16 | 90 | −28 |
| 326 | 13 | 46 | 8 | 8 | 1 | + 2 | 90 | |
| 327 | 1 | 4 | 1 | 2 | 22 | −16 | 4 | |
| 328 | 5 | 20 | 3 | 2 | 13 | − 8 | 12 | |
| 329 | 2 | 4 | 0 | 11 | 0 | +10 | 100 | |
| 330 | 1 | 2 | 1 | 1 | 21 | −18 | 2 | −30 |
| 331 | 11 | 38 | 4 | 13 | 1 | + 8 | 94 | |
| 332 | 8 | 72 | 3 | 5 | 10 | − 8 | 58 | |
| 333 | 3 | 32 | 0 | 0 | 14 | −12 | 0 | |
| 334 | 2 | 4 | 2 | 1 | 22 | −16 | 2 | |
| 335 | 6 | 42 | 1 | 5 | 12 | − 8 | 26 | −36 |
| 336 | 2 | 16 | 1 | 10 | 5 | + 6 | 84 | |
| 337 | 16 | 88 | 12 | 8 | 5 | + 8 | 56 | |
| 338 | 4 | 52 | 3 | 9 | 10 | − 8 | 48 | |
| 339 | 7 | 86 | 2 | 1 | 6 | − 14 | 4 | |
| 340 | 2 | 18 | 1 | 5 | 15 | −14 | 14 | −12 |
| 341 | 0 | — | 0 | 0 | 16 | −16 | 0 | |
| 342 | 5 | 18 | 2 | 2 | 22 | −22 | 16 | |
| 343 | 7 | 56 | 3 | 4 | 13 | −12 | 24 | |
| 344 | 2 | 8 | 2 | 2 | 9 | − 4 | 4 | |
| 345 | 3 | 40 | 2 | 9 | 2 | + 6 | 96 | −48 |
| 346 | 8 | 80 | 2 | 3 | 9 | − 8 | 28 | |
| 347 | 13 | 44 | 6 | 4 | 8 | − 8 | 22 | |
| 348 | 11 | 90 | 7 | 6 | 4 | − 4 | 80 | |
| 349 | 11 | 94 | 7 | 6 | 10 | − 2 | 38 | |
| 350 | 2 | 12 | 2 | 17 | 1 | + 6 | 98 | −16 |
| 351 | 1 | 4 | 1 | 2 | 14 | −10 | 4 | |
| 352 | 12 | 96 | 8 | 9 | 3 | − 2 | 68 | |

Table 27 (continued)

| | 1 | 2 | 3 | During + 4 | − 5 | End ± 6 | 7 | 8 |
|---|---|---|---|---|---|---|---|---|
| 353 | 9 | 48 | 4 | 4 | 16 | −16 | 22 | |
| 354 | 0 | — | 0 | 12 | 0 | + 4 | 100 | |
| 355 | 10 | 100 | 8 | 6 | 3 | 0 | 76 | −24 |
| 356 | 3 | 10 | 1 | 1 | 11 | − 6 | 2 | |
| 357 | 0 | — | 0 | 0 | 15 | −14 | 0 | |
| 358 | 3 | 98 | 2 | 7 | 4 | + 2 | 86 | |
| 359 | 5 | 34 | 2 | 10 | 3 | +10 | 80 | |
| 360 | 10 | 52 | 6 | 6 | 11 | − 8 | 36 | −16 |
| 361 | 13 | 100 | 5 | 7 | 4 | 0 | 58 | |
| 362 | 16 | 86 | 9 | 4 | 9 | − 4 | 56 | |
| 363 | 13 | 64 | 5 | 5 | 3 | + 4 | 78 | |
| 364 | 7 | 98 | 1 | 1 | 9 | − 2 | 2 | |
| 365 | 1 | 6 | 0 | 27 | 0 | +24 | 100 | +22 |
| 366 | 14 | 100 | 9 | 3 | 6 | 0 | 20 | |
| 367 | 14 | 96 | 8 | 5 | 6 | − 4 | 40 | |
| 368 | 1 | 6 | 1 | 3 | 17 | −14 | 6 | |
| 369 | 11 | 100 | 6 | 2 | 10 | 0 | 12 | |
| 370 | 13 | 100 | 5 | 6 | 5 | 0 | 54 | −18 |
| 371 | 2 | 68 | 2 | 1 | 8 | − 8 | 2 | |
| 372 | 12 | 98 | 7 | 12 | 4 | − 2 | 66 | |
| 373 | 4 | 64 | 2 | 14 | 2 | + 6 | 92 | |
| 374 | 5 | 52 | 3 | 12 | 8 | + 6 | 76 | |
| 375 | 9 | 42 | 4 | 1 | 13 | −12 | 4 | −10 |
| 376 | 8 | 20 | 4 | 1 | 18 | −18 | 8 | |
| 377 | 12 | 58 | 7 | 10 | 4 | + 8 | 62 | |
| 378 | 11 | 60 | 5 | 12 | 7 | +12 | 60 | |
| 379 | 0 | — | 0 | 0 | 11 | −10 | 0 | |
| 380 | 6 | 20 | 2 | 28 | 1 | +24 | 94 | +16 |
| 381 | 6 | 40 | 3 | 17 | 7 | +16 | 62 | |
| 382 | 9 | 92 | 4 | 6 | 2 | + 2 | 98 | |
| 383 | 14 | 78 | 4 | 9 | 7 | + 6 | 54 | |
| 384 | 6 | 16 | 2 | 2 | 18 | −12 | 8 | |
| 385 | 9 | 52 | 7 | 7 | 8 | − 6 | 46 | +6 |
| 386 | 4 | 36 | 3 | 7 | 14 | − 2 | 32 | |
| 387 | 12 | 70 | 4 | 4 | 13 | −12 | 32 | |
| 388 | 8 | 72 | 3 | 6 | 9 | + 6 | 48 | |
| 389 | 5 | 18 | 3 | 1 | 11 | − 6 | 4 | |
| 390 | 15 | 80 | 7 | 5 | 8 | − 8 | 38 | −22 |
| 391 | 2 | 96 | 1 | 1 | 12 | − 4 | 2 | |
| 392 | 3 | 58 | 0 | 0 | 13 | −10 | 0 | |

| Table 27 (continued) | | | During | | End | | |
| | | | + | − | ± | | |
| 1 | 2 | 3 | 4 | 5 | 6 | 7 | 8 |
|---|---|---|---|---|---|---|---|
| 393 | 15 | 70 | 7 | 6 | 3 | + 4 | 62 | |
| 394 | 6 | 70 | 3 | 5 | 9 | + 2 | 32 | |
| 395 | 6 | 12 | 3 | 1 | 16 | −14 | 4 | −22 |
| 396 | 15 | 100 | 7 | 6 | 5 | 0 | 40 | |
| 397 | 8 | 80 | 5 | 6 | 5 | +6 | 62 | |
| 398 | 11 | 64 | 7 | 7 | 3 | + 4 | 72 | |
| 399 | 3 | 20 | 2 | 14 | 1 | + 8 | 98 | |
| 400 | 10 | 100 | 4 | 8 | 8 | 0 | 56 | +18 |
| 401 | 19 | 96 | 9 | 2 | 4 | − 2 | 24 | |
| 402 | 8 | 88 | 3 | 7 | 4 | + 2 | 72 | |
| 403 | 7 | 22 | 3 | 3 | 9 | − 4 | 20 | |
| 404 | 16 | 100 | 11 | 6 | 3 | 0 | 68 | |
| 405 | 9 | 92 | 7 | 4 | 7 | − 2 | 42 | −6 |
| 406 | 7 | 96 | 3 | 3 | 6 | − 2 | 22 | |
| 407 | 7 | 96 | 4 | 2 | 11 | + 2 | 14 | |
| 408 | 0 | — | 0 | 0 | 20 | −16 | 0 | |
| 409 | 12 | 62 | 6 | 7 | 5 | + 4 | 72 | |
| 410 | 6 | 84 | 4 | 11 | 9 | − 8 | 70 | −20 |
| 411 | 5 | 38 | 3 | 4 | 11 | − 6 | 34 | |
| 412 | 2 | 4 | 0 | 15 | 0 | + 8 | 100 | |
| 413 | 6 | 34 | 3 | 21 | 5 | +20 | 76 | |
| 414 | 13 | 74 | 6 | 5 | 6 | − 4 | 48 | |
| 415 | 9 | 48 | 2 | 7 | 12 | − 8 | 40 | +10 |
| 416 | 3 | 8 | 2 | 2 | 19 | −18 | 4 | |
| 417 | 13 | 90 | 6 | 2 | 8 | − 4 | 22 | |
| 418 | 2 | 18 | 0 | 0 | 13 | −12 | 0 | |
| 419 | 21 | 84 | 15 | 3 | 8 | − 6 | 24 | |
| 420 | 7 | 100 | 4 | 5 | 7 | 0 | 20 | −40 |
| 421 | 5 | 40 | 4 | 5 | 15 | −14 | 20 | |
| 422 | 1 | 2 | 0 | 15 | 0 | + 6 | 100 | |
| 423 | 14 | 100 | 9 | 4 | 10 | 0 | 26 | |
| 424 | 7 | 84 | 5 | 7 | 7 | − 6 | 60 | |
| 425 | 13 | 96 | 4 | 4 | 6 | − 2 | 30 | −16 |
| 426 | 4 | 20 | 0 | 19 | 0 | +16 | 100 | |
| 427 | 11 | 96 | 5 | 4 | 6 | − 2 | 36 | |
| 428 | 0 | — | 0 | 0 | 14 | − 8 | 0 | |
| 429 | 2 | 46 | 2 | 1 | 12 | − 4 | 2 | |
| 430 | 4 | 94 | 0 | 0 | 16 | − 2 | 0 | 0 |
| 431 | 6 | 74 | 5 | 8 | 8 | − 8 | 66 | |

TABLE 27 (continued)

| | 1 | 2 | 3 | During + 4 | − 5 | End ± 6 | 7 | 8 |
|---|---|---|---|---|---|---|---|---|
| 432 | 8 | 84 | 3 | 8 | 9 | − 8 | 80 | |
| 433 | 5 | 12 | 4 | 1 | 29 | −26 | 4 | |
| 434 | 1 | 2 | 1 | 1 | 19 | −18 | 2 | |
| 435 | 6 | 98 | 4 | 7 | 7 | − 2 | 66 | −62 |
| 436 | 11 | 100 | 5 | 10 | 3 | 0 | 78 | |
| 437 | 9 | 40 | 6 | 4 | 21 | −20 | 26 | |
| 438 | 8 | 74 | 5 | 8 | 2 | + 6 | 90 | |
| 439 | 6 | 50 | 4 | 4 | 14 | −12 | 32 | |
| 440 | 1 | 22 | 0 | 26 | 0 | +26 | 100 | 0 |
| 441 | 8 | 20 | 4 | 10 | 2 | + 4 | 94 | |
| 442 | 13 | 82 | 5 | 6 | 5 | + 6 | 42 | |
| 443 | 12 | 100 | 6 | 3 | 7 | 0 | 26 | |
| 444 | 30 | 94 | 18 | 3 | 4 | − 2 | 44 | |
| 445 | 3 | 62 | 2 | 7 | 5 | − 4 | 60 | +4 |
| 446 | 9 | 56 | 6 | 1 | 8 | − 6 | 8 | |
| 447 | 6 | 78 | 3 | 10 | 8 | − 4 | 62 | |
| 448 | 4 | 16 | 3 | 26 | 2 | +24 | 94 | |
| 449 | 6 | 20 | 3 | 2 | 11 | − 6 | 10 | |
| 450 | 16 | 100 | 11 | 8 | 6 | 0 | 58 | +8 |
| | | | | | | | | |
| 451 | 6 | 14 | 4 | 16 | 1 | +16 | 94 | |
| 452 | 8 | 78 | 3 | 4 | 9 | − 8 | 18 | |
| 453 | 7 | 64 | 4 | 9 | 2 | + 4 | 86 | |
| 454 | 8 | 100 | 3 | 13 | 1 | 0 | 92 | |
| 455 | 10 | 100 | 5 | 7 | 5 | 0 | 60 | +12 |
| 456 | 1 | 2 | 1 | 30 | 1 | +30 | 98 | |
| 457 | 8 | 66 | 2 | 5 | 8 | − 8 | 34 | |
| 458 | 10 | 30 | 4 | 14 | 3 | + 8 | 80 | |
| 459 | 14 | 62 | 6 | 2 | 24 | −24 | 20 | |
| 460 | 2 | 18 | 1 | 4 | 8 | − 2 | 18 | +4 |
| 461 | 2 | 8 | 1 | 23 | 1 | + 8 | 98 | |
| 462 | 2 | 8 | 1 | 2 | 17 | −16 | 6 | |
| 463 | 1 | 100 | 0 | 0 | 9 | 0 | 0 | |
| 464 | 2 | 98 | 0 | 0 | 9 | − 2 | 0 | |
| 465 | 13 | 46 | 8 | 3 | 9 | − 4 | 22 | −14 |
| 466 | 11 | 92 | 6 | 6 | 7 | − 2 | 68 | |
| 467 | 3 | 12 | 1 | 10 | 3 | + 8 | 88 | |
| 468 | 6 | 38 | 5 | 1 | 12 | −10 | 8 | |
| 469 | 10 | 98 | 4 | 11 | 3 | + 2 | 80 | |
| 470 | 1 | 10 | 0 | 23 | 0 | +16 | 100 | +14 |

TABLE 27 (continued)

| | | | During | | End | | |
| | | | + | − | ± | | |
| 1 | 2 | 3 | 4 | 5 | 6 | 7 | 8 |
|---|---|---|---|---|---|---|---|
| 471 | 12 | 66 | 10 | 2 | 8 | − 4 | 14 | |
| 472 | 0 | — | 0 | 16 | 0 | + 6 | 100 | |
| 473 | 1 | 2 | 1 | 1 | 16 | −16 | 2 | |
| 474 | 2 | 6 | 0 | 0 | 32 | −32 | 0 | |
| 475 | 3 | 12 | 2 | 2 | 12 | − 8 | 8 | −54 |
| 476 | 12 | 64 | 5 | 1 | 16 | −16 | 8 | |
| 477 | 2 | 4 | 0 | 0 | 18 | −16 | 0 | |
| 478 | 7 | 74 | 2 | 6 | 2 | + 4 | 92 | |
| 479 | 15 | 100 | 7 | 10 | 4 | 0 | 74 | |
| 480 | 7 | 96 | 3 | 12 | 3 | − 2 | 92 | −30 |
| 481 | 2 | 4 | 2 | 17 | 1 | +14 | 98 | |
| 482 | 17 | 100 | 8 | 4 | 7 | 0 | 26 | |
| 483 | 1 | 40 | 0 | 0 | 19 | −16 | 0 | |
| 484 | 5 | 30 | 2 | 3 | 13 | −12 | 8 | |
| 485 | 8 | 100 | 4 | 5 | 7 | 0 | 52 | −14 |
| 486 | 5 | 44 | 2 | 1 | 17 | −14 | 2 | |
| 487 | 7 | 70 | 4 | 12 | 2 | +12 | 90 | |
| 488 | 2 | 74 | 0 | 0 | 8 | − 6 | 0 | |
| 489 | 2 | 8 | 1 | 12 | 2 | +10 | 96 | |
| 490 | 8 | 72 | 3 | 11 | 6 | + 8 | 32 | +10 |
| 491 | 5 | 10 | 1 | 1 | 16 | −14 | 2 | |
| 492 | 5 | 30 | 3 | 12 | 6 | + 4 | 74 | |
| 493 | 9 | 64 | 5 | 5 | 6 | + 4 | 54 | |
| 494 | 12 | 40 | 5 | 15 | 3 | +12 | 84 | |
| 495 | 13 | 80 | 9 | 4 | 8 | − 6 | 52 | 0 |
| 476 | 19 | 96 | 9 | 2 | 9 | + 2 | 20 | |
| 497 | 6 | 92 | 3 | 3 | 9 | + 2 | 16 | |
| 498 | 5 | 24 | 3 | 14 | 2 | +12 | 92 | |
| 499 | 13 | 40 | 8 | 15 | 4 | +12 | 70 | |
| 500 | 3 | 14 | 2 | 1 | 25 | −20 | 4 | +8 |

*during* the course of a game. If we divide by 469 the sum of the products of 39 and 1, 49 and 2, 30 and 3, and . . . 1 and 30, we find that the actual average number of returns to equilibrium *during* each game is 7.516. This figure should be compared to that of Table 3 (p. 3), which gives 6.978 returns in a theoretical coin-tossing game where $n=100$.

'Column 2 of Table 27 (p. 59) lists the specific spin at which the *last* return to equilibrium occurs *during* each game of 100 spins. We

TABLE 28

| Number of returns | | Number of games | | Total of returns | | |
|---|---|---|---|---|---|---|
| 0 | × | 30 | = | 0 | | |
| 1 | × | 39 | = | 39 | | |
| 2 | × | 49 | = | 98 | | |
| 3 | × | 30 | = | 90 | | |
| 4 | × | 39 | = | 156 | | |
| 5 | × | 35 | = | 175 | | |
| 6 | × | 42 | = | 252 | | |
| 7 | × | 33 | = | 231 | | |
| 8 | × | 38 | = | 304 | | |
| 9 | × | 19 | = | 171 | | |
| 10 | × | 15 | = | 150 | | |
| 11 | × | 24 | = | 264 | | |
| 12 | × | 24 | = | 288 | | |
| 13 | × | 21 | = | 273 | | |
| 14 | × | 16 | = | 224 | | |
| 15 | × | 12 | = | 180 | | |
| 16 | × | 10 | = | 160 | | |
| 17 | × | 3 | = | 51 | | |
| 18 | × | 6 | = | 108 | | |
| 19 | × | 7 | = | 133 | | |
| 20 | × | 3 | = | 60 | | |
| 21 | × | 2 | = | 42 | | |
| 23 | × | 2 | = | 46 | | |
| 30 | × | 1 | = | 30 | | |
| | | 469 | | (3525/469)=7.516 | | |

observe that the last return occurs at the 100th (last) spin of the 1st game, at the 36th spin of the 2nd game, at the 36th spin again of the 3rd, and so on.

'Table 29 (p. 73) lists the distribution of these *last* returns to equilibrium *during* the 500 games. Thus in 17 of the 500 games the last return occurs at the 2nd spin, in 14 of the 500 games the last return occurs at the 4th spin, in 11 of the 500 games the last return occurs at the 6th spin ... and in 39 of the 500 games the last return occurs at the 100th spin. The sum of 17+14+11 ... +39=469 games containing a return to equilibrium *during* the course of a game. If we divide by 469 the sum of the products of 17 and 2, 14 and 4, 11 and 6 ... and 39 and 100, we find that during each game 100 spins long the actual average returns occurs at the 53.254th spin.

'Besides a return to equilibrium *during* a game, I mentioned that in 40 of the games a return to equilibrium occurs *at the end* of the game 100 spins long. Ever betting on the red, before reaching the 100th spin we shall find that the average plus digression *during* each game is 5.93 units, and the average minus digression *during* each game is 5.73 units.

'Column 3 of Table 27 (p. 59) lists the number of changes of lead during each game of 100 spins. I include this column as being of interest to mathematicians: unlike the other columns, column 3 is of no particular aid to gamblers. The number of changes of lead

TABLE 29

| Spin number | Number of games | | Total number of returns | Spin number | Number of games | | Total number of games |
|---|---|---|---|---|---|---|---|
| 2 | × 17 | = | 34 | 52 | × 8 | = | 416 |
| 4 | × 14 | = | 56 | 54 | × 4 | = | 216 |
| 6 | × 11 | = | 66 | 56 | × 5 | = | 280 |
| 8 | × 18 | = | 144 | 58 | × 6 | = | 348 |
| 10 | × 8 | = | 80 | 60 | × 6 | = | 360 |
| 12 | × 13 | = | 156 | 62 | × 10 | = | 620 |
| 14 | × 10 | = | 140 | 64 | × 7 | = | 448 |
| 16 | × 7 | = | 112 | 66 | × 6 | = | 396 |
| 18 | × 6 | = | 108 | 68 | × 5 | = | 340 |
| 20 | × 17 | = | 340 | 70 | × 8 | = | 560 |
| 22 | × 7 | = | 154 | 72 | × 4 | = | 288 |
| 24 | × 7 | = | 168 | 74 | × 8 | = | 592 |
| 26 | × 5 | = | 130 | 76 | × 5 | = | 380 |
| 28 | × 5 | = | 140 | 78 | × 7 | = | 546 |
| 30 | × 11 | = | 330 | 80 | × 8 | = | 640 |
| 32 | × 6 | = | 192 | 82 | × 6 | = | 492 |
| 34 | × 8 | = | 272 | 84 | × 5 | = | 420 |
| 36 | × 8 | = | 288 | 86 | × 11 | = | 946 |
| 38 | × 7 | = | 266 | 88 | × 7 | = | 616 |
| 40 | × 10 | = | 400 | 90 | × 7 | = | 630 |
| 42 | × 7 | = | 294 | 92 | × 11 | = | 1012 |
| 44 | × 7 | = | 308 | 94 | × 13 | = | 1222 |
| 46 | × 8 | = | 368 | 96 | × 19 | = | 1824 |
| 48 | × 7 | = | 336 | 98 | × 24 | = | 2352 |
| 50 | × 5 | = | 250 | 100 | × 39 | = | 3900 |
| | | | | | 469 | | 24976 |

$(24976/469) = 53.254$

73

equals roughly on average 1/2 the number of returns to equilibrium during a game 100 spins long.

'And now, Mr Optimist, come the 4th and 5th columns, which are especially interesting to gamblers.'

'Why?' asks Mr Optimist.

'You're gambling along on an even-money chance and want to know the extent of the winning and losing streaks. Column 4 of Table 27 (p. 59) lists the extent of the *largest plus* digression in units *during* each game of 100 spins. We note that the largest plus digression during the 1st game is 8 units, the largest plus digression during the 2nd game is 3 units, the largest plus digression during the 3rd game is again 3 units, and so on.'

'I admit plus digressions gladden me!' exclaims Mr Optimist.

'Table 30 (p. 75) lists the distribution of the average plus digression *during* a game of 100 spins. Thus the 1st column lists the value in *plus* units *at the end* of a game 100 spins long. The 2nd column lists the number of games where this occurs. Hence 40 games end in a plus digression of 2 units, 37 end in a plus digression of 4 units, 26 end in a plus digression of 6 units ... and 1 game ends in a plus digression of as much as 32 units.'

'I remember you told me that at the end of these 500 games 40 end in a return to equilibrium, 187 end in a plus digression, and 273 end in a minus digression,' comments Mr Optimist. 'So obviously the sum of the number of games at the bottom of the 2nd column equals the winning 187 games.'

'Right. The 3rd column lists the average *plus* digression in units *during* the games listed on the left. Thus the average plus digression *during* the 40 games ending in a gain of 2 units is 7.35 units, the average plus digression *during* the 37 games ending in a gain of 4 units is 8.98 units, the average plus digression *during* the 26 games ending in a gain of 6 units is 10.23 units ... and the average plus digression the 1 game ending in a gain of 32 units is 32.00 units.'

'And I see from the long division at the bottom of Table 30 (p. 75,' says Mr Optimist, 'that the result is the *actual* average *plus* digression in units *during* a game of 100 spins, which is 12.17 units. What does theory give us?'

'The *theoretical* average *plus* digression in units *during* a fair game 100 spins long is 13.46,' I reply. 'So theory is $13.46 - 12.17 = 1.29$ units larger than actuality.'

'Pretty close,' says Mr Optimist.

74

TABLE 30

| Value of plus digression at the end of 100 spins | Number of games | | Average plus digression during the game | | Total units for a particular plus digression |
|---|---|---|---|---|---|
| 2 | 40 | × | 7.35 | = | 294.00 |
| 4 | 37 | × | 8.98 | = | 332.26 |
| 6 | 26 | × | 10.23 | = | 265.98 |
| 8 | 15 | × | 13.10 | = | 196.50 |
| 10 | 18 | × | 12.97 | = | 233.46 |
| 12 | 17 | × | 14.24 | = | 242.08 |
| 14 | 10 | × | 17.80 | = | 178.00 |
| 16 | 8 | × | 17.88 | = | 143.04 |
| 18 | 3 | × | 20.00 | = | 60.00 |
| 20 | 3 | × | 20.67 | = | 62.01 |
| 22 | 3 | × | 23.00 | = | 69.00 |
| 24 | 3 | × | 27.00 | = | 81.00 |
| 26 | 1 | × | 26.00 | = | 26.00 |
| 30 | 2 | × | 30.00 | = | 60.00 |
| 32 | 1 | × | 32.00 | = | 32.00 |
| | 187 | | | | 2275.33 |

$(2275.33/187)=12.17$
the *actual* average *plus* digression
in units *during* 100 spins

'But remember what I've said earlier about averages: in a real game there are significant digressions or fluctuations therefrom.'

'If Table 30 (p. 75) tells us about the digressions *during* a game of 100 spins, how about the digressions *at the end* of 100 spins?' asks Mr Optimits.

'Table 31 (p. 76) gives us the answers,' I reply. 'As you see, we take merely the first two columns of the preceding table, Table 30 (p. 75), and multiply them together.'

'And again I see from the long division at the bottom of Table 31 (p. 76),' continues Mr Optimist, 'that the result is the *actual* average *plus* digression in units *at the end* of a game of 100 spins, which is 8.16 units. What does theory give us?'

'The *theoretical* average *plus* digression in units *at the end* of a fair game 100 spins long is 8.20 units,' I reply. 'So theory is 8.20−8.16=0.04 units larger than actuality.'

'This time it's almost identical,' says Mr Optimist.

TABLE 31

| Value of plus digressions at the end of 100 spins | | Number of games | | Total units for a particular plus digression |
|:---:|:---:|:---:|:---:|:---:|
| 2 | × | 40 | = | 80 |
| 4 | × | 37 | = | 148 |
| 6 | × | 26 | = | 156 |
| 8 | × | 15 | = | 120 |
| 10 | × | 18 | = | 180 |
| 12 | × | 17 | = | 204 |
| 14 | × | 10 | = | 140 |
| 16 | × | 8 | = | 128 |
| 18 | × | 3 | = | 54 |
| 20 | × | 3 | = | 60 |
| 22 | × | 3 | = | 66 |
| 24 | × | 3 | = | 72 |
| 26 | × | 1 | = | 26 |
| 30 | × | 2 | = | 60 |
| 32 | × | 1 | = | 32 |
| | | 187 | | 1526 |

$(1526/187)=8.16$
the *actual* average *plus* digression
in units *at the end* of 100 spins

'Now before gathering all this together in conclusions let's discuss *minus* digressions in exactly the same way we have plus digressions.

'Column 5 of Table 27 (p. 59) lists the extent of the *largest minus* digression in units *during* each game of 100 spins. We note that the largest minus digression during the 1st game is 4 units, the largest minus digression during the 2nd game is 24 units, the largest minus digression during the 3rd game is 12 units, and so on.'

'Thank heavens I wasn't playing in that 2nd game!' exclaims Mr Optimist. 'I think I could ride out fluctuations of 4 or even 12 units, but 24 units in one game is pretty severe.'

'Yes, and remember we're betting only 1 unit per spin,' I add. 'Table 32 (p. 77) lists the distribution of the average minus digression *during* a game of 100 spins. The 1st column lists the value in *minus* units *at the end* of a game 100 spins long. The 2nd column lists the number of games where this occurs. Hence 43 games end

76

in a minus digression of 2 units, 40 in a minus digression of 4 units, 33 end in a minus digression of 6 units . . . and 1 game ends in a minus digression of as much as 36 units.'

'Again, I recall you're telling me that at the end of these 500 games 40 end in a return to equilibrium, 187 end in a plus digression, and 273 end in a minus digression,' comments Mr Optimist. 'So obviously this time the sum of the number of games at the bottom of the 2nd column equals the 273 losing games.'

'Again you're absolutely correct. The 3rd column lists the average *minus* digression in units *during* the games listed on the left. Thus the average minus digression *during* the 43 games ending in a loss of 2 units is 7.04 units, the average minus digression *during* the 40 games ending in a loss of 4 units is 8.08 units, the average minus digression *during* the 33 games ending in a loss of 6 units is 9.40 units . . . and the average minus digression during the 1 game ending in a loss of 36 units is 37.00 units.'

TABLE 32

| Value of minus digression at the end of 100 spins | Number of games | | Average minus digression during the game | | Total units for a particular minus digression |
|---|---|---|---|---|---|
| 2 | 43 | × | 7.04 | = | 302.72 |
| 4 | 40 | × | 8.08 | = | 323.20 |
| 6 | 33 | × | 9.40 | = | 310.20 |
| 8 | 38 | × | 10.96 | = | 416.48 |
| 10 | 20 | × | 11.85 | = | 237.00 |
| 12 | 28 | × | 14.36 | = | 402.08 |
| 14 | 20 | × | 15.75 | = | 315.00 |
| 16 | 20 | × | 18.00 | = | 360.00 |
| 18 | 12 | × | 19.15 | = | 229.80 |
| 20 | 4 | × | 23.00 | = | 92.00 |
| 22 | 5 | × | 23.20 | = | 116.00 |
| 24 | 3 | × | 24.00 | = | 72.00 |
| 26 | 4 | × | 28.75 | = | 115.00 |
| 32 | 2 | × | 32.50 | = | 65.00 |
| 36 | 1 | × | 37.00 | = | 37.00 |
| | 273 | | | | 3393.48 |

(3393.48/273)=12.43
the *actual* average *minus* digression
in units *during* 100 spins

77

'And once more I see from the long division at the bottom of Table 32 (p. 77),' says Mr Optimist, 'that the result is the *actual* average *minus* digression in units *during* a game of 100 spins, which is 12.43 units. Again what does theory give us?'

'The *theoretical* average *minus* digression in units *during* a fair game 100 spins long is 13.46 units,' I reply. 'So theory is 13.46−12.43=1.03 units larger than actuality.'

'Once more pretty close,' says Mr Optimist.

Again if Table 32 (p. 77) tells us about the digressions *during* a game of 100 spins, Table 33 (p. 78) tells us about the digressions *at the end* of 100 spins. As before, we take merely the first two columns of the preceding table, Table 32 (p. 77), and multiply them together.'

TABLE 33

| Value of minus digression at the end of 100 spins | | Number of games | | Total units for a particular minus digression |
|---|---|---|---|---|
| 2 | × | 43 | = | 86 |
| 4 | × | 40 | = | 160 |
| 6 | × | 33 | = | 198 |
| 8 | × | 38 | = | 304 |
| 10 | × | 20 | = | 200 |
| 12 | × | 28 | = | 336 |
| 14 | × | 20 | = | 280 |
| 16 | × | 20 | = | 320 |
| 18 | × | 12 | = | 216 |
| 20 | × | 4 | = | 80 |
| 22 | × | 5 | = | 110 |
| 24 | × | 3 | = | 72 |
| $\frac{26}{32}$ | × | 4 | = | 104 |
| | × | 2 | = | 64 |
| 36 | × | 1 | = | 36 |
| | | 273 | | 2566 |

(2566/273)=9.40
the *actual* average *minus* digression
in units *at the end* of 100 spins

'And, as before, I see from the long division at the bottom of Table 33 (p. 78),' continues Mr Optimist, 'that the result is the *actual* average *minus* digression in units *at the end* of a game of 100 spins, which is 9.40 units. Once more what does theory give us?'

'The *theoretical* average *minus* digression in units *at the end* of a fair game 100 spins long is 8.20 units,' I reply. 'So actuality is 9.40−8.20=1.20 units larger than theory.'

'Once more almost identical!' exclaims Mr Optimist.

TABLE 34

Summary of Tables 30, 31, 32, and 33.

Average *plus* digression in units

|  | Theory | Actuality | Difference |
|---|---|---|---|
| At the end: | 8.20 | 8.16 | −0.04 |
| During: | 13.46 | 12.17 | −1.29 |

Average *minus* digression in units

|  | Theory | Actuality | Difference |
|---|---|---|---|
| At the end: | 8.20 | 9.40 | +1.20 |
| During: | 13.46 | 12.46 | −1.03 |

'Now let's summarize the preceding 4 tables in Table 34 (p. 79), whose lesson for the gambler is extremely important and not to be forgotten: the average *plus* or *minus* digression *during* a game of *n* trials – spins, dice throws, card hands, etc. – is always *larger* than the average *plus* or *minus* digression *at the end* of the same game. Table 10 (p. 15) gave us this theory for an imaginary coin-tossing game. Table 34 (p. 79) gives us both theory and actuality for a *real* roulette or crap game, excluding the difference between 2.70 per cent of Table 34 (p. 79) and 1.41 per cent, which we calculated and discussed earlier in this chapter.

'And now let's finish up,' I continue. 'Column 6 of Table 27 (p. 59) lists the extent of the *largest plus* or *minus* digression in units *at the end* of each game of 100 spins. We observe that we break even at the end of the 1st game, that we lose 24 units at the end of the 2nd game, that we lose 12 units at the end of the 3rd, and so on.'

'I suppose that the Bank's advantage of 2.70 per cent results in most of the games ending up minus?' asks Mr Optimist without great enthusiasm.

'I regret to say so,' I reply. 'Remember what we found: in 40 games we break even, in 187 we win, and in 273 we lose.

'Column 7 of Table 27 (p. 59) lists the number of spins during which the red is in the lead during each game of 100 spins. Like those of column 3 of this same table, the figures of column 7 are of greater interest to mathematicians than to gamblers.

'And lastly column 8 of Table 27 (p. 59) summarizes the results of column 6 in groups of *five* 100-spin game figures. In other words, with our always starting anew, column 8 lists the extent of the *largest plus* or *minus* digression in units that occurs *at the end* of each *500*-spin game. Thus we observe that we lose 34 units at the end of the 1st game, that we win 2 units at the end of the 2nd, that we lose 4 units at the end of the 3rd, and so on. Naturally the sum of the 1st, 2nd, 3rd, 4th, and 5th 100-spin game of column 6 equals the 1st *500*-spin figure of column 8. Thus $0-24-12-2+4=-34$ units. If you want, of course, you may sum the figures of column 8 in groups of *ten* 500-game figures to get 10 games 5,000 spins long, and that's how I constructed Table 26 (p. 56) of this chapter. Thus if we take column 8 and sum $2+6+18+8$ we get 34 units won at the end of the 1st 5,000-spin game, the total listed for the 1st game, units won, Table 26 (p. 56). And if we take column 8 and sum $34+4+34+14+12+12$ units we get 110 units lost at the end of the same 1st 5,000-spin game, the total listed for the 1st game, units lost, Table 26 (p. 56).'

'And as you've told me before, I know what you're going to say,' asserts Mr Optimist. '"No matter how we divide up a large game into a number of smaller games, whether in 500 100-spin games (column 6, Table 27, p. 59), or in 10 5,000-spin games (Table 26, p. 56), or in 1 50,000-spin game, we always win or lose the same amount."'

'Very true – in the Hartman sample, I mentioned at the start of this chapter, that amount – a loss, alas – is 1,040 units. The reason I've summed the results of the Hartman sample in three different ways is to show gamblers this very important conclusion: the gain or loss is the same *no matter how many ways* we may divide up the sample or pie, and I've done this for the very reason that so many gamblers don't believe it or are unsure about it.'

'So if we divide the Hartman sample into 50,000 games each only 1 spin long, *at the end* of the 50,000-spin game we still lose *actually* 1,040 units,' says Mr Optimist.

'Yes.'

'But given a PC of 1.41 per cent rather than 2.70 per cent, our *theoretical* final loss at the end of 50,000 spins is only 705 units.'

'Right.'

'Well, 705 units at the end of almost three months isn't too great,' continues Mr Optimist.

'Not exorbitant, I suppose.'

'Then will you please tell me,' asks Mr Optimist rather testily, 'at either Monte-Carlo roulette on the even chances or on the Pass or Don't Pass line at craps, why are the losses I've witnessed *so damn large*?'

'And sometimes *gains so damn large*!' I counter.

'I myself have lost many times 705 units *in only one hour*!' exclaims Mr Optimist.

'Part of the answer lies in the tables in this and the last chapter, the other part lies in the discussion of staking systems in a subsequent chapter, plus the discussion of conclusions in the last chapter. Let's concern ourselves here only with the conclusions in this chapter.

'In a sense there are two main tables in this book. The first is Table 21 (p. 42), showing how *violent* may be the actual fluctuations on a single number at roulette i.e., a bet on a *long shot*. The second is Table 27 (p. 59), showing that, though usually calmer, the actual fluctuations on an even chance at roulette or craps may also *sometimes be violent*, and such a bet we may call a *short shot*.'

'For a gambler what are the most important columns to study in Table 27 (p. 59)?' asks Mr Optimist.

'Columns 1, 2, 4, 5, and 6.'

'Why?'

'Remember column 1 lists the number of returns to equilibrium *during* a game 100 spins long. Glance with me down the 1st column. If we're using a system requiring a lot of returns to equilibrium, we do just fine in the 1st game of 100 spins: there occur as many as 23 returns. But we soon run into trouble. In the 2nd game there occur only 6 returns, in the 3rd only 12, and in the 4th only 1 return.

'If we could count on only *one* return occurring on the *last* spin, we'd be able to construct all kinds of winning staking systems. Recall again that column 2 lists the specific spin at which the *last* return occurs *during* a game 100-spins long. Again glance with me down the 2nd column. In the 1st game the last return does indeed occur at the 100th or last spin – but in the 2nd game the last return occurs at the 36th spin. We glance over to column 6 and notice that the whole 100-spin game ends in a *minus* digression (of 24 units). This means that from the 37th through the 100th or last spin a

81

system player is betting more and more in the vain hope of encountering enough winning spins to enable him to decrease his bets from whatever awesome heights his system has pushed him. So he went broke on that game. In the 3rd game the last return occurs again at the 36th spin. Once more we glance over to column 6 and notice that the whole 100-spin game ends in another *minus* digression (of 12 units). This means that from the 37th through the 100th or last spin a system player who keeps increasing his bets in the vain hope of encountering enough winning spins to allow him to recoup his losing ones again goes broke. In the 4th game the last return occurs at the 16th spin – but as column 6 indicates a final loss (of 2 units), once more the progressive system player doesn't end up a winner.'

'I notice that in the 5th game the last return occurs at the 52nd spin,' interrupts Mr Optimist. 'And with this 100-spin game ending in a gain (or 4 units), this time the progressive system player must win!' asserts Mr Optimist.

'That's right – but does he *win enough* to cancel out the three previous losing games? Remember – there is always the Bank's maximum allowable stake, and once a player's progression hits that maximum, his bets must remain flat, so that even if the 100-spin does end in a *plus* digression, he might not be able to recoup enough winning bets to cover his past losses.'

'All right, I see how I'm to use columns 1, 2, and 6,' says Mr Optimist. 'I must admit they're going to save me a lot of money as I try out one staking system after another.'

'Before we do, wait until after our discussion of staking systems in a later chapter. Then we'll have even more knowledge and thus be able to select the system most appropriate to our purpose,' I recommend.

'Good enough,' agrees Mr Optimist. 'Now what about the other two columns you mentioned as especially useful to the gambler – columns 4 and 5?'

'Let's say we want to play it safe instead of adopting a staking system. Let's say then we're going to bet just flat stakes. Glance down column 4 and, from one 100-spin game to the next, note what the *largest plus* digression is *during* any given game. Then glance down column 5 and note the corresponding *largest minus* digression *during* the same given game. For 500 games, each 100 spins long, this comparison will give us a perfect picture of the *extent* of the flat-bet fluctuations. Again I must mention modestly that this comparison of flat bets won and lost on *paper* will save us an awful lot of money at the roulette or crap table.'

'I appreciate it,' says Mr Optimist.

'But ultimately column 6 tells us the final story for each 100-spin game – whether we win or lose *at the end* of a game, and by exactly how much,' I caution.

'Do you know of any game in town at the moment?' asks Mr Optimist.

# CHAPTER VIII

# The Result of Three Months: 48,128 Spins: The Theory of Runs on Even-Money Chances

'I remember the subject of *winning* and *losing* runs when we were betting on one number – zero – at roulette,' says Mr Optimist. 'You summed it up for one number in Tables 17 (p. 37) through 21 (p. 42). 'Is there something new?'

'Nothing. Now all we do is apply the same theory of runs to the even-money chances, i.e., to the red and black.'

'Again, will this apply to the Pass and Don't Pass line bets at craps, and to the regular bet at blackjack?' asks Mr Optimist.

TABLE 35

Theoretical number of *Winning* runs on red (or *Losing* runs on black) *at the end* of 1,024 winning spins (zero excluded).

| Exactly r | Number of runs | | (again) r | | Number of spins absorbed | |
|---|---|---|---|---|---|---|
| 1 | 256 | × | 1 | = | 256 | 512 reds (or blacks) |
| 2 | 128 | × | 2 | = | 256 | |
| 3 | 64 | × | 3 | = | 192 | |
| 4 | 32 | × | 4 | = | 128 | |
| 5 | 16 | × | 5 | = | 80 | |
| 6 | 8 | × | 6 | = | 48 | 512 reds (or blacks) |
| 7 | 4 | × | 7 | = | 28 | |
| 8 | 2 | × | 8 | = | 16 | |
| 9 | 1 | × | 9 | = | 9 | |
| 10 | 1 | × | 11 | = | 11 | |
| | 512 | | | | 1024 | reds (or blacks) |

'It most certainly does. And gamblers typically think of betting on runs on some even-money chance – say red. In Table 35 (p. 84) you'll find set forth the theoretical number of *winning* runs on red.'

'But why does Table 35 (p. 84) refer also to *losing* runs on black?' inquires Mr Optimist.

'For the simple reason that, without change, the contents of the whole Table apply equally to black as well. Arbitrarily we've made up our mind to think of a bet on *red* as a *win* – and consequently *black* as a *loss*,' I reply. 'Now as a casino's maximum bet doesn't usually allow doubling our bet more than 9 *times in a row*, I haven't extended the contents of the table beyond this number – which you see listed in the 1st column under *r*, signifying, as before, the number of reds in a row, i.e., the length of the *winning* runs. For convenience the 3rd column repeats this 1st column.'

'From the numbers in the 2nd column I notice that the length of every run is exactly *one half* that of its predecessor,' comments Mr Optimist.

'Right you are. From the first two columns we see that, *at the end* of every 1,024 spins, there occur 256 *winning* runs of exactly 1 red, 128 *winning* runs of exactly 2 reds, 64 *winning* runs of exactly 3 reds . . . and 1 *winning* run of exactly 9 reds. And as you see below the dotted line, there occurs always exactly 1 *winning* run longer than 9 reds.'

'What do the numbers in the 4th and last column mean?' asks Mr Optimist.

'These numbers consist simply of the red *spins* absorbed by the corresponding *winning runs*. Thus the 256 runs of 1 red absorb 256 red spins, and 128 runs of 2 reds absorb another 256 red spins. Notice that the sum of all the runs of exactly 1 and 2 reds equals exactly *half* of the total number of winning spins, i.e., 256+256=512 red spins, and 2×512=1024=red spins.'

'Is this always true?' asks Mr Optimist. 'I'm already beginning to think up a staking system based on this average.'

'Yes, this is *always* true for an even-money chance regardless of the size of the sample, i.e., length of the game. But we're not yet quite ready for constructing staking systems,' I caution. 'now to finish up with the red *spins* absorbed by the corresponding *winning runs*. The 4th and last column of Table 35 (p. 84) shows us that 64 runs of 3 reds absorb 192 red spins, 32 runs of 4 reds absorb 128 red spins . . . and 1 run of 9 reds absorb 9 red spins.'

'And as I see below the dotted line, the 1 winning run longer than

9 reds is, on average, 11 reds long – and absorbs 11 red spins,' comments Mr Optimist.

'Yes, and this illustrates another fact about the number of *winning* runs on red: the length of that very last *winning* run on red is, on average, always *two* reds longer than the next-to-the-last run. Thus the 1 winning run 11 reds long is *two* reds longer than the 1 winning run of 9 reds,' I reply.

'Does this always hold true?' asks Mr Optimist.

'Yes – again this is *always* true for an even-money chance no matter what the size of the sample, i.e., length of the game,' I add. 'And now we're ready to apply the *theoretical* averages of Table 35 (p. 84) to the *actual* averages of the whole first three months or 48,128 spins of the Hartman sample – excluding zero. Table 36 (p. 86) lists the results of the 47, consecutive games each 1,024 spins long.'

'And what do the 6 columns of figures signify in the lower part of Table 36 (p. 86)?' enquires Mr Optimist.

### TABLE 36

Actual runs of *red* and *black* in 47 consecutive games each 1024 spins long.

| Runs: | 1 | 2 | 3 | 4 | 5 | 6 | 7 | 8 | 9 | 10 | 11 | 12 | 13 | 14 | 15 |
|---|---|---|---|---|---|---|---|---|---|---|---|---|---|---|---|
| Theory: | 256 | 128 | 64 | 32 | 16 | 8 | 4 | 2 | 1 | 1/2 | 1/4 | 1/8 | 1/16 | 1/32 | 1/64 |
| Game | | | | | | | | | | | | | | | |
| 1 | 251 | 132 | 51 | 35 | 26 | 5 | 1 | 1 | 0 | 3 | 1 | 0 | 0 | 0 | 0 |
| 2 | 253 | 147 | 72 | 26 | 13 | 6 | 5 | 0 | 1 | 0 | 0 | 1 | 0 | 0 | 0 |
| 3 | 236 | 148 | 68 | 28 | 12 | 6 | 3 | 1 | 2 | 1 | 1 | 1 | 0 | 0 | 0 |
| 4 | 219 | 124 | 64 | 27 | 25 | 6 | 9 | 0 | 1 | 1 | 0 | 0 | 0 | 1 | 0 |
| 5 | 235 | 123 | 64 | 35 | 21 | 7 | 4 | 2 | 0 | 2 | 0 | 0 | 0 | 0 | 0 |
| 6 | 226 | 121 | 75 | 32 | 11 | 14 | 6 | 1 | 0 | 0 | 0 | 0 | 0 | 1 | 0 |
| 7 | 248 | 112 | 64 | 35 | 17 | 11 | 6 | 1 | 1 | 1 | 0 | 0 | 0 | 0 | 0 |
| 8 | 243 | 128 | 60 | 28 | 21 | 13 | 3 | 1 | 0 | 1 | 1 | 0 | 0 | 0 | 0 |
| 9 | 251 | 139 | 73 | 37 | 12 | 1 | 4 | 2 | 2 | 0 | 0 | 0 | 0 | 0 | 0 |
| 10 | 255 | 122 | 70 | 34 | 15 | 6 | 5 | 3 | 1 | 0 | 0 | 0 | 0 | 0 | 0 |
| 11 | 271 | 115 | 61 | 35 | 10 | 10 | 7 | 4 | 1 | 0 | 0 | 0 | 0 | 0 | 0 |
| 12 | 270 | 128 | 63 | 34 | 10 | 11 | 4 | 1 | 0 | 1 | 1 | 0 | 0 | 0 | 0 |
| 13 | 271 | 136 | 67 | 25 | 16 | 10 | 2 | 1 | 2 | 0 | 0 | 0 | 0 | 0 | 0 |
| 14 | 290 | 114 | 62 | 28 | 12 | 9 | 8 | 1 | 0 | 3 | 0 | 0 | 0 | 0 | 0 |
| 15 | 266 | 133 | 61 | 30 | 16 | 8 | 5 | 2 | 0 | 1 | 0 | 0 | 0 | 0 | 0 |
| 16 | 249 | 130 | 63 | 35 | 22 | 6 | 1 | 3 | 1 | 0 | 0 | 0 | 0 | 0 | 0 |
| 17 | 216 | 130 | 63 | 31 | 20 | 7 | 8 | 2 | 0 | 1 | 1 | 0 | 0 | 0 | 0 |
| 18 | 265 | 135 | 69 | 33 | 6 | 6 | 4 | 7 | 0 | 0 | 0 | 0 | 0 | 0 | 0 |
| 19 | 276 | 121 | 63 | 33 | 14 | 9 | 1 | 3 | 1 | 1 | 1 | 0 | 0 | 0 | 0 |
| 20 | 262 | 111 | 62 | 28 | 19 | 11 | 5 | 4 | 0 | 0 | 0 | 0 | 0 | 1 | 0 |
| 21 | 269 | 112 | 67 | 42 | 10 | 10 | 2 | 2 | 1 | 0 | 0 | 0 | 1 | 0 | 0 |

TABLE 36 (continued)

| Runs: | 1 | 2 | 3 | 4 | 5 | 6 | 7 | 8 | 9 | 10 | 11 | 12 | 13 | 14 | 15 |
|---|---|---|---|---|---|---|---|---|---|---|---|---|---|---|---|
| Theory: | 256 | 128 | 64 | 32 | 16 | 8 | 4 | 2 | 1 | 1/2 | 1/4 | 1/8 | 1/16 | 1/32 | 1/64 |
| 22 | 239 | 135 | 61 | 28 | 24 | 5 | 1 | 1 | 1 | 2 | 1 | 0 | 0 | 0 | 1 |
| 23 | 245 | 142 | 59 | 34 | 18 | 6 | 3 | 2 | 1 | 1 | 0 | 0 | 0 | 0 | 0 |
| 24 | 237 | 117 | 72 | 35 | 18 | 8 | 4 | 0 | 0 | 2 | 1 | 0 | 0 | 0 | 0 |
| 25 | 255 | 134 | 66 | 30 | 14 | 9 | 2 | 2 | 2 | 0 | 1 | 0 | 0 | 0 | 0 |
| 26 | 254 | 123 | 53 | 34 | 16 | 7 | 7 | 3 | 0 | 1 | 1 | 0 | 1 | 0 | 0 |
| 27 | 292 | 117 | 55 | 36 | 13 | 8 | 6 | 3 | 0 | 1 | 0 | 0 | 0 | 0 | 0 |
| 28 | 264 | 122 | 66 | 27 | 17 | 12 | 4 | 2 | 1 | 0 | 0 | 0 | 0 | 0 | 0 |
| 29 | 255 | 134 | 61 | 33 | 16 | 5 | 6 | 2 | 2 | 0 | 0 | 0 | 0 | 0 | 0 |
| 30 | 255 | 133 | 59 | 24 | 13 | 12 | 6 | 1 | 1 | 1 | 0 | 2 | 0 | 0 | 0 |
| 31 | 254 | 124 | 60 | 29 | 22 | 8 | 4 | 1 | 2 | 0 | 0 | 0 | 0 | 1 | 0 |
| 32 | 269 | 147 | 54 | 39 | 16 | 8 | 1 | 1 | 0 | 0 | 0 | 0 | 0 | 0 | 0 |
| 33 | 271 | 124 | 65 | 40 | 10 | 9 | 4 | 0 | 2 | 0 | 0 | 0 | 0 | 0 | 0 |
| 34 | 234 | 121 | 54 | 34 | 17 | 10 | 9 | 3 | 2 | 0 | 0 | 0 | 0 | 0 | 0 |
| 35 | 222 | 155 | 72 | 23 | 15 | 4 | 3 | 3 | 2 | 0 | 2 | 0 | 0 | 0 | 0 |
| 36 | 245 | 130 | 52 | 34 | 18 | 7 | 3 | 4 | 2 | 1 | 0 | 0 | 0 | 1 | 0 |
| 37 | 236 | 129 | 61 | 35 | 17 | 9 | 5 | 3 | 1 | 0 | 0 | 0 | 0 | 0 | 0 |
| 38 | 265 | 141 | 70 | 30 | 9 | 11 | 2 | 0 | 0 | 1 | 0 | 1 | 0 | 0 | 0 |
| 39 | 264 | 135 | 62 | 30 | 18 | 7 | 6 | 0 | 0 | 1 | 0 | 0 | 0 | 0 | 0 |
| 40 | 271 | 114 | 61 | 35 | 21 | 11 | 3 | 0 | 0 | 1 | 0 | 0 | 0 | 0 | 0 |
| 41 | 245 | 124 | 74 | 28 | 9 | 10 | 4 | 4 | 1 | 0 | 1 | 1 | 0 | 0 | 0 |
| 42 | 257 | 118 | 70 | 37 | 16 | 4 | 7 | 0 | 1 | 0 | 1 | 0 | 0 | 0 | 0 |
| 43 | 236 | 116 | 59 | 45 | 17 | 11 | 4 | 0 | 1 | 0 | 1 | 0 | 0 | 0 | 0 |
| 44 | 255 | 131 | 61 | 34 | 13 | 9 | 3 | 0 | 3 | 1 | 1 | 0 | 0 | 0 | 0 |
| 45 | 263 | 115 | 67 | 27 | 27 | 7 | 4 | 1 | 1 | 0 | 0 | 0 | 0 | 0 | 0 |
| 46 | 244 | 134 | 79 | 23 | 16 | 8 | 3 | 2 | 2 | 0 | 0 | 0 | 0 | 0 | 0 |
| 47 | 269 | 127 | 74 | 32 | 15 | 5 | 0 | 2 | 1 | 1 | 1 | 0 | 0 | 0 | 0 |

| 1 | 2 | 3 | 4 | | 5 | 6 |
|---|---|---|---|---|---|---|
| Runs | | Theory | Actuality | | | |
| 1 | (47)(256=12032 | | 11918 | −114 | | 253.58 |
| 2 | (47)(128)= | 6016 | 6003 | − 13 | | 127.72 |
| 3 | (47)(64)= | 3008 | 3009 | + 1 | | 64.02 |
| 4 | (47)(32)= | 1504 | 1507 | + 3 | | 32.06 |
| 5 | (47)(16)= | 752 | 753 | + 1 | | 16.02 |
| 6 | (47)(8)= | 376 | 382 | + 6 | | 8.13 |
| 7 | (47)(4)= | 188 | 197 | + 9 | | 4.19 |
| 8 | (47)(2)= | 94 | 82 | − 12 | | 1.75 |
| 9 | (47)(1)= | 47 | 43 | − 4 | | 0.915 |
| 10 | (47)(1/2)= | 23.5 | 30 | + 6.5 | | 0.638 |
| 11 | (47)(1/4)= | 11.75 | 17 | + 5.25 | | 0.362 |
| 12 | (47)(1/8)= | 5.88 | 6 | + 0.125 | | 0.128 |
| 13 | (47)(1/16)= | 2.94 | 2 | − 0.938 | | 0.043 |
| 14 | (47)(1/32)= | 1.47 | 5 | + 353 | | 0.106 |
| 15 | (47)(1/64)= | 0.73 | 1 | + 0.266 | | 0.021 |

'Those figures, my friend, show how closely *actuality* accords with *theory*,' I reply. 'But first let's read across the top of the table where it says *theory*. As you may note, the *number* of runs are identical to those of the 2nd column of Table 35 (p. 84) – 256 runs of 1, 128 runs of 2, 64 runs of 3 . . . and 1 run of 9.'

'You'll recall my saying just now,' interjects Mr Optimist, getting into the intellectual swim again, 'that the length of every run is exactly *one half* that of its predecessor. So after 1 run of 9 we have to descend into 1/2 a run of 10, 1/4 a run of 11 . . . and 1/64th of a run of 15 – in *theory*.'

'Yes – whereas in *actuality*, of course, a real run in the whole 48,128 spins either really occurs or it doesn't. As we note from the 4th vertical column in the lower part of Table 36 (p. 86), there occur *actually* 11,918 runs of 1, 6,003 runs of 2, 3,009 runs of 3 . . . and 43 runs of 9, 30 runs of 10, 17 runs of 11 . . . and 1 run as long as 15,' I remark.

'Where does this run of 15 occur?' asks Mr Optimist.

'Look again at the upper part of Table 36 (p. 86) under the word *game* in the 1st column. Then glance down to the 22nd game – and across the horizontal row of actual runs – you'll find the 1 run of 15 there,' I conclude.

'Is it a run of red or black?' asks Mr Optimist.

'It happens to be a run of 15 black. Although I separate ordinarily the winning runs from the losing ones, in this one table I added them both together to firm up the results. If you count up a game *twice* as long, i.e., $2 \times 48,128 = 96,256$ spins long, then you could count *just* the reds *or* the blacks – but it wouldn't change anything one whit,' I reply.

'In Table 36 (p. 86) why have you *underlined*, in the upper part of the table, *two* runs in every column?' asks Mr Optimist.

'In every column I've underlined the extent of the *largest* and *smallest* fluctuation from theory. Thus *theory* gives 256 runs of 1, while *actuality* gives 292 runs of 1 in the 27th game and 216 runs of 1 in the 17th game. And *theory* gives 128 runs of 2, while *actuality* gives 155 runs of 2 in the 35th game and 111 runs of 2 in the 20th game. I continue arbitrarily to underline these two fluctuations of runs through 7 runs long. After 7 runs the number of runs becomes too tenuous.'

'All right, the two tables in this chapter give me a picture of the average number of runs *exactly r* spins long *at the end* of a theoretical game 1,024 spins long and an actual game 48,128 spins long –

the Hartman sample,' continues Mr Optimist. 'But if I'm going to try out various staking systems, or even stick conservatively to flat stakes, when I walk up to a roulette, craps, or blackjack table, I'd like to know for the even-money chances the *probability* of a run of *r* wins in a row. I suppose that the mathematical formula, however, would be too complicated – especially for me to use during real gaming conditions.'

'No, I'm happy to say such a formula exists,' I respond. 'And it's so simple you may easily memorize it – either at home while figuring systems or at the gaming table under pressure.'

'Marvellous! And you say it's really simple?' asks Mr Optimist.

'The formula for runs is valid for all values of *p* and *q*. As we recall from the discussion of Table 1 (p. 2), Chapter I, and the general discussion of the Bank's Percentage in Chapter II, the value of *p* signifies the probability of a chosen event's occurring in a *single* trial, i.e., the probability of a *win* in one spin, one dice toss, or one card hand. And the value of *q* signifies the probability of the said event's *not* occurring in a single trial, i.e., the probability of a *loss* in one spin, one dice toss, one card hand.'

'And I recall that $p+q=1$ or certainly,' adds Mr Optimist. 'Thus for one number at roulette, $p=1/37$ and $q=36/37$, and $(1/37)+(36/37)=37/37)=1$. And similarly for an even-money chance like red at roulette, excluding zero, $p=1/2$ and $q=1/2$, and $(1/2)+(1/2)=1$. Am I ready now for the formula for runs?'

'Follows the formula for a *winning* run:

Formula for the probability of the occurrence in a single trial of *r* (or more) *wins* in a row on a chosen event =

$$qp^r$$

'And for an even-money chance the above reduces to:

$$(1/2)^{r+1}$$

'Thus the probability of a *winning* run of 1 (or more), 2 (or more), 3 (or more) ... etc. reds or Passes in a row is respectively 1/4, 1/8, 1/16 ... etc.,' I conclude.

'But I thought that if I go to the crap table and plunk all my money down on, say, Pass, in the hope of exactly *one* win's occurring the probability is just 1/2,' objects Mr Optimist.

'If you exclude the matter of the PC, you're absolutely right,' I continue.

89

'But your answer above for a run of 1 (or more) *wins* is 1/4 – not 1/2,' he reposts.

'*For practical gambling purposes* don't think in terms of 1/2, for, say an even-money chance. Think in terms of 1/4, 1/8, 1/16, etc. as I mentioned.'

'Why?'

'You've just bet all your money on Pass, and if you win *just once*, you intend to take your own bet, your winnings, and cash in all your chips, right?' I ask.

'Right,' says Mr Optimist.

'Let's say the shooter throws the dice and the result is a total of 7 on the come out, so you win,' I continue.

'That's the spirit – I win!' cries Mr Optimist. 'Now I take all my money and cash in my chips as you say. And walk away from the crap table.'

'Right. But the dice are *inanimate* objects. They don't *know* you've just walked away. They *continue* to follow the laws of chance for runs as outlined in Table 35 (p. 84). While you're walking happily out of the casino as a winner, the same shooter throws the dice, say, 4 more times before losing on the 5th throw. Now isn't it true that you won, not on *one* throw, but on a *winning run* of 1 (*or more*) throws? The "or more" part of the formula's definition turned out to be exactly 4, but naturally we couldn't know that until it had occurred. In other words if you bet just once and win, that win may not be an isolated event but the beginning of a *winning run* of 1, 2, 3 ... or 9 (or more) Passes. After you walked away from the crap table, for all you knew the shooter may have thrown, say, 10 more Passes, in which case the "or more" of a *winning run* of 1 (or more) would be 9,' I conclude. 'In the following diagram let's look at the formula for a *winning run* of *r* (or more) reds or Passes:'

Probability on an even-money chance for a *winning run* of:

|  | |
|---|---|
| run: | 1 (or more) |
| symbol: | *w* (plus wwwwwwww) etc. – to infinity) |
| probability: | 1/4 |

|  | |
|---|---|
| run: | 2 (or more) |
| symbol: | *ww* (plus wwwwwwww) etc. – to infinity) |
| probability: | 1/8 |

90

      run:   3 (or more)
   symbol:   *www* (plus wwwwwwwww) etc. – to infinity)
probability:   1/16

'I see,' says Mr Optimist. 'May I try using the formula?'

'Give it a whirl. As I said, it's very simple,' I respond.

'You last said that in the case of an even-money chance the formula is $(1/2)^{r+1}$. So whether I'm using a staking system or just flat stakes, let's say I'm hoping, at the crap table, for a *winning run* of 3 (or more) Passes – which is the last example of your diagram. So $(1/2)^{r+1}$ equals $(1/2)^{3+1}$ or $(1/2)^4$, which equals 1/16. How am I doing?'

'Perfectly. Now was that so difficult?'

'As I like betting on even-money chances, I might as well just memorize the answers to the shorter *winning* runs. As you said, *for practical gambling purposes* the probability of a *win* of ONE is 1/4, a *win* of TWO is 1/8, a win of THREE is 1/16 ... I just keep multiplying the denominator by the number 2?'

'That's all you do. And the formula for the probability of a *winning run* of $r$ (or more) wins *not* beginning in a single trial is ...

$$1-(qp^r)$$

'Thus again *for practical gambling purposes* the probability of a *winning* run of 1 (or more) wins *not* occurring is $1-(1/4)=3/4$, of 2 (or more) wins *not* occurring is $1-(1/8)=7/8$, of 3 (or more) wins *not* occurring is $1-(1/16)=15/16$, and so on,' I add.

'I notice,' remarks Mr Optimist somewhat grimly, 'that the probability of a *winning* run *not* beginning grows large very quickly – 3/4, 7/8, 15/16, etc. Not that I haven't experienced my share of such a negative situation at the gaming table. But at least I know now how easy it is to calculate it – and as I prefer, to memorize its answers before going to the gaming table.'

'You know, Mr Optimist, the formula for the *average number* of *winning* runs *at the end* of a game *n* trials long is ...

$$NPQ^r$$

'And for an even-money chance like the red or Pass the above formula reduces to ...

$$n(1/2)^{r+1}$$

'So, for example, the average number of *winning* runs of, say, 2 (or more) reds or Passes *at the end* of a game, say, 1,024 trials long is $(1024)\,(1/2)^{2+1}$, which gives $(1024)\,(1/2)^3$, which gives in turn

91

(1024) (1/16), which gives lastly 64 winning runs of 2 (or more) reds or Passes.'

'Let me try it,' asks Mr Optimist. '*At the end* of a roulette or crap game, of say, 128 trials the average number of *winning* runs of, say, 3 (or more) reds or Passes is $n(1/2)^{r+1}$, which gives $(128)(1/2)^{3+1}$, which gives in turn $(128)(1/2)^4$, which gives in its turn $(128)(1/32)$, which gives lastly 4 winning runs of 3 (or more) reds or Passes. How am I doing?'

'A prodigy. You should go on the stage,' I respond. 'Now you may predict future *winning* (or *losing*) runs that begin at any chosen trial. I bet hardly any croupier or dealer knows how to do this.'

'I'm not going on the stage. I'm going to the crap table!' exclaims Mr Optimist happily. 'Now am I ready for staking systems on runs?'

'Just continue reading,' I conclude.

# CHAPTER IX

# Staking Systems Based on Winning and Losing Runs on the Even-Money Chances

'How about a staking system where we keep doubling our bet after every win?' asks Mr Optimist.

'As a matter of fact that's one of the better systems,' I reply. 'It's called the ...

## Simple Paroli

'Let's also call this system a *pro* system, i.e., one in which we *increase our bet after a winning trial*,' I continue. 'To use the simple paroli we may pick any even-money chance – Heads versus Tails, Red versus Black, Pass versus Don't Pass, the regular bets at blackjack, baccara, chemin-de-fer, and so on. For our discussion let's use Heads, signified by H, and Tails, signified by T.

'Now, as you'll see in a moment, because of what we learned in the last chapter, everything about the simple paroli is so easy, it may be calculated in the head.'

'And wasn't I good at that?' asks Mr Optimist enthusiastically.

'The progression of, say, a maximum of 9 bets for the simple paroli is ...

$$1+2+4+8+16+32+64+128+256, \text{ etc.}$$

'Following the above, we double our stake after every win. After every loss we go back to a stake of 1 unit. We win as gross profit 1 unit for every Heads that actually occurs, or 1/2 a unit per trial, as one will.'

'Do I have to double as far as 256 units?' asks Mr Optimist apprehensively. 'I don't know if I can afford that much.'

'Of course not. We may pick from the progression any figure or amount we want. Go ahead. You pick the maximum you can afford.'

'I can afford a top bet of, say, 8 units,' declares Mr Optimist.

'Okay, that means we want to win consecutively the first 4 figures in the progression, which are ... 1+2+4+8, and their sum is 15 units. To achieve this we hope to encounter in our game as many runs of 4 (or more) Heads as possible. As usual the letter $r$ signifies the length of the run – here 4. And $r$ signifies also the number of figures in the progression. Now from the last chapter we use the formula for a *winning* run on an even-money chance, which was ...

$$(1/2)^{r+1}$$

'And in the present case of a *winning* run of 4 (or more) Heads we get ...

$$(1/2)^{4+1}=(1/2)^5=1/32$$

'Which means that we have one chance out of 32 – or as they say, a probability of 1/32 – of winning 1+2+4+8=15 units at any designated trial. And we have simultaneously a probability of $1-(1/32)=31/32$ of losing *roughly* 1/2 a unit at any designated trial.'

'How do you know we lose about 1/2 a unit per trial? Is that some sort of average?' asks Mr Optimist.

'It is an average. If at any trial we have a probability of 1/32 of winning 15 units, and one of 31/32 of losing on an *average z* units, then we may calculate $z$ by the equation ...

$$(1/32)15=(31/32)z$$

'Which reduces to $(15/32)=31z)$ (32), or $0.46875=0.96875z$, or $(0.46875/0.96875)=z$, and $z=0.4839$, or about 0.50, i.e., 1/2 a unit.'

'How does the simple paroli of 4 look *at the end* of a cycle of say, 64 trials?' asks Mr Optimist.

'Your question is answered in Table 37 (p. 95). As it is noted at the top of the table, $n=64$. In other words the contents of the table apply only to a game 64 trials long, neither fewer nor more. The 1st column lists the consecutive numbers of the run, i.e., exactly 1, 2, 3, and 4 Heads long. Or $r$ equals exactly 1, 2, 3, and 4 Heads. The 2nd column lists the corresponding probabilities of these runs, i.e., the probability of a run of exactly 1 H is 1/8, of 2 H's is 1/16, of 3 H's is

### Table 37

Simple Paroli of 4 (or more) H's

$n=64$

| exactly r | probability | bet | average number of H runs | cw | | tcw |
|---|---|---|---|---|---|---|
| 1 | 1/8 | 1 | 8 | × 1 = | | 8 |
| 2 | 1/16 | 2 | 4 | × 3 = | | 12 |
| 3 | 1/32 | 4 | 2 | × 7 = | | 14 |
| 4 | 1/64 | 8 | 1 | × 15 = | | 15 |
| 4 | 1/64 | 8 | 1 | × 15 = | | 15 |
| | | | 16 | | | 64 units won |

1/32, and of *4 H's (or more)* is $(1/64)+(1/64)=(2/64)=1/32$, which is precisely identical to the answer we calculated just now far more easily via the formula for a *winning* run on an even-money chance, which we know is ...

$$(1/2)^{r+1}$$

The 3rd column lists the consecutive figures or bets of the simple paroli progression, i.e. 1, 2, 4, and 8 units. The 4th column lists the average number of runs of Heads corresponding to the length of the run listed in the 1st column. Thus *at the end* of 64 trials there occur 8 runs of 1 H, 4 runs of 2 H's, 2 runs of 3 H's, plus 1 run of 4 H's and 1 run of 4 H's which equal 2 runs of 4 H's. There is also, of course, a relation between the figures of the 3rd and 4th columns. Thus on 8 runs we bet and win 1 unit, on 4 runs we bet and win 2 units, on 2 runs we bet and win 4 units, and on 1 run we bet and win 8 units and on another 1 run we bet and win 8 units. The 5th column lists the cumulative gross win (*cw*) in units. Thus after a run of 1 H we have won 1 unit, after a run of 2 H's we double up and win 3 units, after a run of 3 H's we double up and win 7 units. From the 1 run of 4 H's we win 15 units, and from the 2nd run of 4 H's we win another 15 units – and to win 15 units twice in 64 trials is identical to winning 15 units once in 32 trials, i.e. we have a probability of 1/32 of winning 15 units at any designated trial, exactly the answer we got in the first place so easily.'

'And now I know what the simple paroli of 4 looks like *at the end* of a cycle of 64 trials,' agrees Mr Optimist. 'By the way what are the figures in the 6th column?'

'The 6th and last column lists the *total cumulative gross win* (*tcw*) in units for the corresponding runs,' I conclude.

'By the way, come to think of it, what happened to all the Tails – the T's?' asks Mr Optimist.

'The probability of Heads and Tails is identical, right?'

'Yes, each is 1/2,' replies Mr Optimist.

'If we bet on Tails, the result would consequently be identical to that of Table 37 (p. 95). All that we should have to do would be to think in terms of Tails rather than Heads, and to substitute T's for all the H's. But we can't bet at the same time on both Heads and Tails *to win*. We have to choose one or the other. Let's say, as we have been doing, that we pick Heads to bet on *to win*. In that case we consequently pick Tails to bet on *to lose*. And as there are as many losing runs as winning ones – 16 of each in 64 trials – we win no more runs than we lose. Thus if we win, as we've calculated, 15 units in 32 trials, we lose an identical 15 units in the following 32 trials. And 32 trials of Heads plus 32 trials of Tails equals one cycle of 64 trials of both.'

'What if I feel I can afford a top bet of, say, 128 units instead of the modest 8 units?' asks Mr Optimist.

'Then the progression of the simple paroli is ...

$$1+2+4+8+16+32+64+128 \ldots$$

'Remember the letter *r* signifies both the length of the run – here

TABLE 38

Simple Paroli of 8 (or more) H's
$n=1024$

| exactly r | probability | bet | average number of H runs | cw | | | tcw |
|---|---|---|---|---|---|---|---|
| 1 | 1/8 | 1 | 128 | × | 1 | = | 128 |
| 2 | 1/16 | 2 | 64 | × | 3 | = | 192 |
| 3 | 1/32 | 4 | 32 | × | 7 | = | 224 |
| 4 | 1/64 | 8 | 16 | × | 15 | = | 240 |
| 5 | 1/128 | 16 | 8 | × | 31 | = | 248 |
| 6 | 1/256 | 32 | 4 | × | 63 | = | 252 |
| 7 | 1/512 | 64 | 2 | × | 127 | = | 254 |
| 8 | 1/1024 | 128 | 1 | × | 255 | = | 255 |
| 8 | 1/1024 | 128 | 1 | × | 255 | = | 255 |
| | | | 256 | | | | 2048 units won |

8 – and also the number of figures in the progression – again 8. We ask the question: what is the probability in a single trial of a *winning* run of 8 (or more) heads? We have ...

$$(1/2)^{8+1}=(1/2)^9=1/512$$

'Hence at any designated trial we have a probability of 1/512 of winning $1+2+4+8+16+32+64+128=255$ units. And we have simultaneously at any designated trial a probability of $1-(1/512)=511/512$ of losing *roughly* again 1/2 a unit per trial.'

'How does the simple paroli of 8 look *at the end* of a cycle of, say, 1,024 trials?' asks Mr Optimist.

'Your question is answered in Table 38 (p. 96). As the figures in the 6 columns follow identically the definitions of those in the 6 columns of Table 37 (p. 95), we needn't go through them all again,' I respond.

'Very good. By the way, when I bet a simple paroli of 4, my top bet is 8 units, and when I bet a simple paroli of 8, my top bet is 128 units, but what are my respective *average* bets?' asks Mr Optimist.

'In Table 39 (p. 97) I list the average bet for every simple paroli – from a progression of 1, i.e. flat stakes, to a progression of 128, i.e. a run of 8 (or more) Heads. At the beginning of this chapter I mentioned that a simple paroli, where we double our bet after every win, is one of the better staking systems. One of the reasons for this claim is that in the simple paroli, as we shall see anon when comparing it to other staking systems, the average amount bet is *very small*. And this is a most important advantage, because as we remember from Chapter III (p. 17), the Bank's percentage is taken from this very same average amount bet. So from this standpoint,

TABLE 39

$n=1024$

| Simple Paroli of r | bet | average bet |
|---|---|---|
| 1 | 1 | 1.000 |
| 2 | 2 | 1.333 |
| 3 | 4 | 1.774 |
| 4 | 8 | 2.133 |
| 5 | 16 | 2.581 |
| 6 | 32 | 3.048 |
| 7 | 64 | 3.528 |
| 8 | 128 | 4.016 |

the lower the latter the better the system. And secondly, as we have seen, the amount we may expect to win or lose on any designated trial of the simple paroli system is easily calculated. We may easily find out where we stand with any simple paroli progression. But this is unfortunately not true of many other systems, whose rules are so chaotic that we simply can't figure out, except very roughly indeed, where we stand.'

'You know, I was just thinking that in the case of the simple paroli we could change the progression from just doubling our stake after every win,' comments Mr Optimist.

'What would you suggest?' I ask curiously.

'First we should follow the progression of the simple paroli – doubling our stake after every win. Then we should *add* to our stake, after every win, *one* unit of our *own* capital,' explains Mr Optimist. 'Wouldn't such a system be the next simplest and logical step? And careful and conservative too!'

'Ah yes, that's a progression only slightly more complicated than the simple paroli, and it has a name,' I reply. 'And the name is . . .

### Great Paroli

'Like the simple paroli, the great paroli is also a *pro* system, i.e. one in which we *increase our bet after a winning trial*,' I continue. 'The progression of, say, a maximum of 9 bets for the great paroli is . . .

$$1+3+7+15+31+63+127+255+511$$

'As you can see, Mr Optimist, in the great paroli progression each stake, after a win, is *double* the preceding one *plus one* unit of our own capital. Then we return to a bet of 1 unit. As before, after every loss we continue to bet only 1 unit. We win as gross profit 2 units for every Heads that actually occurs, or 1 unit per trial, as one will.'

'And once more the letter $r$ signifies both the length of the run – the number of H's of which it's composed – and the number of figures in the progression. And lastly we use the same formula as before, the formula for a *winning* run on an even-money chance, which is . . .

$$(1/2)^{r+1}$$

'May I pick from the progression one of the bets?' asks Mr Optimist.

'Please do.'

'I think I can afford a top bet of, say, 15 units. What are my chances of winning and losing?' asks Mr Optimist.

'Exactly the same as your chances for the first example of the simple paroli, which as you remember, was a probability of 1/32 for a run of 4 (or more) H's.'

'But how can that be? The progression for the great paroli is obviously very different – instead of $1+2+4+8$ units for the simple paroli we have $1+3+7+15$ units for the great paroli,' objects Mr Optimist.

'Ah yes, the *progressions* are indeed quite different,' I concede, 'but the mathematical *chances* for the simple and great paroli are identical. Only the *figures* we're adding up differ, not the underlying *number of heads* that we hope will occur, i.e. in this case 4 (or more) H's – whose probability, as we know, is 1/32,' I reply. 'Look at Table 40 (p. 99), which gives all the information for a great paroli of 4 (or more) H's, and compare it to Table 37 (p. 95), which gives all the information for a simple paroli of 4 (or more) H's. As you'll note, the 1st, 2nd, and 4th columns of the two tables are identical, for these pertain to our *chances* of winning. On the other hand the 3rd, 5th, and 6th columns are different, for these pertain to the two *progressions*, each unlike the other as you say.'

'What if I pick from the great paroli progression a top bet of, say, 255 units?' asks Mr Optimist. 'Now what are my chances of winning and losing?'

'Exactly the same as your chances for the second example of the simple paroli, which as you remember, was a probability of 1/512 for a run of 8 (or more) H's. Thus at any designated trial, for the

TABLE 40

Great Paroli of 4 (or more) H's
$n=64$

| exactly r | probability | bet | average number of H runs | cw | | tcw |
|---|---|---|---|---|---|---|
| 1 | 1/8 | 1 | 8 | × 1 | = | 8 |
| 2 | 1/16 | 3 | 4 | × 4 | = | 16 |
| 3 | 1/32 | 7 | 2 | × 11 | = | 22 |
| 4 | 1/64 | 15 | 1 | × 26 | = | 26 |
| 4 | 1/64 | 15 | 1 | × 26 | = | 26 |
| | | | $\overline{16}$ | | | $\overline{98}$ units won |

99

simple paroli we have a probability of 1/512 for a run of 8 or more H's. Thus at any designated trial, for the simple paroli we have a probability of 1/512 of winning, as you'll recall, 1+2+4+8+16+32+64+128=255 units as gross profit, the sum listed at the bottom of the *cw* or cumulative gross *w*in column of Table 38 (p. 96). By contrast in the present case of the great paroli, at any designated trial we have the *same* probability of 1/512 of winning 1+3+7+15+31+63+127+255=502 units as gross profit, the sum listed at the bottom of the *cw* or cumulative gross *w*in column of Table 41 (p. 100). Look at this latter table, which gives all the information for a great paroli of 8 (or more) H's, and compare it to Table 38 (p. 96), which gives all the information for a simple paroli of 8 (or more) H's. Once more as you'll note, the 1st, 2nd, and 4th columns of the two tables are identical, and pertain to our *chances* of winning. By the same token the 3rd, 5th, and 6th columns are different, for these pertain to the two *progressions*, each unlike the other.'

'Again very good,' interjects Mr Optimist, 'And again, when I bet a great paroli of 4, my top bet is 15 units, and when I bet a great paroli of 8, my top bet is 255 units, but what are my respective *average* bets?'

'In Table 42 (p. 101) I list the average bet for every great paroli – from a progression of 1, i.e. flat stakes, to a progression of 255, i.e. a run of 8 (or more) Heads,' I reply.

TABLE 41

Great Paroli of 8 (or more) H's
$n=1024$

| exactly r | probability | bet | average number of H runs | cw | | tcw |
|---|---|---|---|---|---|---|
| 1 | 1/8 | 1 | 128 | × 1 | = | 128 |
| 2 | 1/16 | 3 | 64 | × 4 | = | 256 |
| 3 | 1/32 | 7 | 32 | × 11 | = | 352 |
| 4 | 1/64 | 15 | 16 | × 26 | = | 416 |
| 5 | 1/128 | 31 | 8 | × 57 | = | 456 |
| 6 | 1/256 | 63 | 4 | × 120 | = | 480 |
| 7 | 1/512 | 127 | 2 | × 247 | = | 494 |
| 8 | 1/1024 | 255 | 1 | × 502 | = | 502 |
| 8 | 1/1024 | 255 | 1 | × 502 | = | 502 |
| | | | 256 | | | 3586 units won |

TABLE 42

$n=1024$

| Great Paroli of r | bet | average bet |
|---|---|---|
| 1 | 1 | 1.000 |
| 2 | 3 | 1.667 |
| 3 | 7 | 2.429 |
| 4 | 15 | 3.207 |
| 5 | 31 | 4.161 |
| 6 | 63 | 5.095 |
| 7 | 127 | 6.055 |
| 8 | 255 | 7.031 |

'You know, a comparison of Table 39 (p. 97), giving the average bets for the simple paroli with Table 42 (p. 101) giving the average bets for the great paroli, helps me to choose between these two *pro* staking systems, i.e. systems where we increase our bet after a win,' declares Mr Optimist.

'Which system do you prefer?' I ask.

'Frankly, I'll pick the simple paroli. Under the stress of a real gambling table I want to keep everything I think and do as uncomplicated as possible. No matter how tired I may become, for example, I can always remember just to double my bet – but to have to remember to add even one unit after every win – well after a couple of hours at the tables I might begin to forget. And is the great paroli worth it?' asks Mr Optimist.

'When you win, you obviously win more, but when you lose, by the same token you obviously lose more. And as the average bet of the simple paroli is considerably smaller than the corresponding bet of the great paroli, when you use the simple paroli, the Bank's percentage, which as we know keeps gnawing away at the *average amount we bet*, is significantly smaller – and that's a very important goal for any staking system,' I reply. 'And now let's finish up with the ...

*Simple Martingale*

'This is an *anti* staking system, i.e. one in which we *increase our bet after a LOSING trial*,' I continue. 'Had we not already examined the simple paroli, where we double our bet after every *win*, the simple martingale, where we double our bet after every *LOSS*, would require an equal length of time to examine. As it is, the

101

discussion and tables of this whole chapter allow us to dispose of the simple martingale, which is probably the most famous staking system in the world, in a relatively short space of time. The main thing to grasp is that the simple martingale is the *REVERSE* or *MIRROR IMAGE* of the simple paroli.

'Thus the progression we adopt for the simple martingale is ...

$$1+2+4+8+16+32+64+128+256, \text{ etc.}$$

'Which is the same as for the simple paroli,' declares Mr Optimist.

'Identical. The simple martingale is the opposite of the simple paroli, however, in the respect just mentioned: if in the simple paroli we double our stake after every *win*, in the simple martingale we double our stake after every *LOSS*. In addition if in the simple paroli after every loss we go back to a stake of 1 unit, in the simple martingale after every *WIN* we go back to a stake of 1 unit.

'On the other hand in both these staking systems we win as gross profit 1 unit for every Heads that actually occurs, or 1/2 a unit per trial, as one will.'

'If we toss a coin three times in a row, so that $r=n=3$, there are a total of 8 possible permutations or arrangements of the H's and T's. Table 43 (p. 103) repeats twice these 8 possible permutations, once for a simple paroli of 3 H's, and once for a simple martingale of 3 T's. As usual, in *both* staking systems we are betting on *Heads to win*. And in both systems we adopt the same double-up progression – $1+2+4=7$ units.

'Using the simple paroli, we win these 7 units on the run of 3 H's as shown by the 1st permutation. We get started again and win 2 units on the run of 2 H's as shown by the 4th permutation. We break even on the 3rd permutation. We lose either 1, 2, or 3 units on the 5 other permutations. But the end result is the same: all told we win 8 units gross and lose 8 units gross so our net is 0.

'By the same token using the simple martingale, we lose these 7 units on the run of 3 T's as shown by the 8th permutation. We get started again and lose 2 units on the run of 2 T's as shown in the 5th permutation. We break even on the 6th permutation. We win either 1, 2, or 3 units on the 5 other permutations. But as in the simple paroli the end result for the simple martingale is the same: all told we win 8 units gross and lose 8 units gross so our net is 0.

'So based on Table 43 (p. 103) the simple paroli and simple martingale are really the same?' asks Mr Optimist.

TABLE 43

*Simple Paroli of 3 H's*
Betting on Heads to win (Tails to lose)
Progression: $1+2+4=7$ units *WIN*
probability (exactly) – $r=n=3$: $(1/2)^r=(1/2)^3=1/8$
Hence exactly 8 permutations or arrangements of H & T

| 1 | 2 | 3 | 4 |
|---|---|---|---|
| win | lose | win | win |

| | | | | | | | |
|---|---|---|---|---|---|---|---|
| H | 1 | H | 1 | H | 1 | T | −1 |
| H | 2 | H | 2 | T | −2 | H | 1 |
| H | 4 | T | −4 | H | 1 | H | 2 |
| $(\overline{7})$ + | | $(-\overline{1})$ + | | $(\overline{0})$ + | | $(\overline{2})$ | =win 8 units (gross) |

| 5 | 6 | 7 | 8 |
|---|---|---|---|
| lose | lose | lose | lose |

| | | | | | | | |
|---|---|---|---|---|---|---|---|
| H | 1 | T | 1 | T | 1 | T | 1 |
| T | −2 | H | 1 | T | − | T | −1 |
| T | −1 | T | −2 | H | 1 | T | −1 |
| $(-\overline{2})$ + | | $(-\overline{2})$ + | | $(-\overline{1})$ + | | $(-\overline{3})$ | =lose 8 units (gross) |
| | | | | | | | $\overline{0}$ units (net) |

*Simple Martingale of 3 T's*
Betting on Heads to win (Tails to lose)
Progression: $1+2+4=7$ units *LOSE*
probability (exactly) – $r=n=3$: $(1/2)^r=(1/2)^3=1/8$
Hence exactly 8 permutations or arrangements of H & T

| 1 | 2 | 3 | 4 |
|---|---|---|---|
| win | win | win | win |

| | | | | | | | |
|---|---|---|---|---|---|---|---|
| H | 1 | H | 1 | H | 1 | T | −1 |
| H | 1 | H | 1 | T | −1 | H | 2 |
| H | 1 | T | −1 | H | 2 | H | 1 |
| $(\overline{3})$ + | | $(\overline{1})$ + | | $(\overline{2})$ + | | $(\overline{2})$ | =win 8 units (gross) |

| 5 | 6 | 7 | 8 |
|---|---|---|---|
| lose | lose | win | lose |

| | | | | | | | |
|---|---|---|---|---|---|---|---|
| H | 1 | T | −1 | T | −1 | T | −1 |
| T | −1 | H | 2 | T | −2 | T | −2 |
| T | −2 | T | −1 | H | 4 | T | −4 |
| $(-\overline{2})$ + | | $(\overline{0})$ + | | $(+\overline{1})$ + | | $(-\overline{7})$ | =lose 8 units (gross) |
| | | | | | | | $\overline{0}$ units (net) |

103

'No, my friend, *they are not at all the same*, for the simple reason that at the gaming table you never actually play all 8 permutations of either system – or of any system for that matter,' I continue.

'What do I play?' asks Mr Optimist rather eagerly.

'Table 43 (p. 103) gives us 8 permutations for each system. Thus each permutation should occur, so to speak, once every 8 times. But at the gaming table the god of chance acts very differently. He puts an infinite, or if you want, very large number of these permutations into a large box and, after shaking them up thoroughly in the box, dumps blindly *SOME* of the permutations out on to the crap, roulette, and blackjack table. But *which* permutations have fallen out of the box? With almost certainty the pile before us will contain *more* of *some* permutations and *fewer* of *others*. And will there be *more* permutations ending in a *plus* and *fewer* permutations ending in a *minus* – or sadly, vice versa? If there be more *plus* ones, then if we play on all the permutations in the pile we'll end up a net *winner*. But if there be more *minus* ones, then we'll end up a net *loser*.' I conclude.

'I see,' replies Mr Optimist, 'but doesn't what you've just said apply equally to both systems?'

'Yes, it does.'

'Then why do you claim that the simple paroli and simple martingale *are not at all the same*?' asks Mr Optimist.

'I said earlier that the simple martingale is the *reverse* of the simple paroli. The *crux* of this reversal is illustrated in Table 43 (p. 103). Compare the 1st permutation of the paroli with the 8th permutation of the martingale. From the former we *win* from HHH the *largest* sum of the game – $1+2+4=7$ units, whereas from the latter we *lose* from TTT the *largest* sum of the game – $1+2+4=7$ units.

'In other words in a perfectly balanced situation, in the paroli we encounter a lot of small losses and then one large gain, whereas in the martingale we encounter a lot of small gains and then one large loss. But as you'll recall, Mr Optimist, the god of chance doesn't allow us to play a perfectly balanced situation. The pile of permutations he dumps out before us to play may have, in the paroli, an excess of small losses and *omit entirely* the permutation HHH of our *one* large gain, and in the martingale, a deficiency of small gains and *more than one* permutation TTT of our *large* loss.

'But the impact of Table 43 (p. 103) isn't borne home to us, because in a real gambling situation we don't usually play such a small progression of $1+2+4=7$ units, whose top bet is only 4 units. At a real crap, roulette, or blackjack table too many gamblers play a progression of $1+2+4+8+16+32+64+128=255$ units, i.e. in the paroli a *winning* run of 8 (or more) H's, or in the martingale a *losing* run of 8 (or more) T's, both with a top bet of 128 units. With such *long* runs fluctuations become very violent – and thus *ruinous!*' I warn.

'Very well,' exclaims Mr Optimist getting angry, 'I'll adopt a progression on a run requiring *only 2 wins in a row*. You can't say that's a dangerous system!'

'Would you be willing to try out this "safe" system over the first 1,024 spins of the Hartman sample?'

'Of course!' cries Mr Optimist confidently.

'Very well. Table 44 (p. 106) shows the *consecutive* results. We count each run of *exactly 2 reds* as a *win*, signified by the letter *w*, and each black and zero as a loss. A run of exactly 1 red is counted also as a loss for the following reason: we have adopted a very modest paroli progression of $1+2=3$ units won on a run of exactly 2 reds. Let's say we come upon a single red, i.e. the permutation *black, red, black*. After we get to the single red, we double our bet of 1 unit to 2 units, but we lose it on the following black. Hence the combination of a single red followed by a black loses us 2 units on these 2 trials, or an average loss of 1 unit on the single red and another on the black. Table 45 (p. 107) shows the *total* results.

'As we note from the figure at the bottom of the last column of Table 44 (p. 106), there occur 170 *w*'s or *wins* or runs of exactly 2 reds. From each win receive $1+2=3$ units. As there occur 170 such wins, our gross gain is $170\times3=510$ units. As we note from the figure at the bottom of the 3rd column of Table 45 (p. 107), there occur 684 losing spins, and as we lose one unit from each spin, our gross loss is $684\times1=684$ units. In addition there occur 162 odd-number winning spins, whence we lose 1/2 unit per spin, or $(162/2)=81$ units lost. Hence $684-81=603$. So total units lost is 603, total units won is 510, and $603-510=93$ units, our final net loss.

'By the way, where is the longest losing run in the game?' inquires Mr Optimist.

'You'll find it in the 6th column of Table 44 (p. 106) – a losing run of exactly 30 spins, which starts at the 623rd spin, for 118 wins plus 505 losses equals 623 spins. If you look at the last three figures of the 1st column of Table 45 (p. 107)), you'll note that the two

## TABLE 44

*Winning* and *Losing* runs during the 1st 1,024 spins of the Hartman sample: *w* signifies a win of exactly 2 reds.

| | | | | | | | |
|---|---|---|---|---|---|---|---|
| 6 | w | w | 1 | w | w | w | w |
| w | 17 | w | w | 2 | w | 2 | w |
| 4 | w | 6 | 1 | w | 2 | w | 3 |
| w | 5 | w | w | 13 | w | 10 | w |
| w | w | 1 | 1 | w | 2 | w | 3 |
| w | w | w | w | 3 | w | 6 | w |
| 3 | 23 | 3 | w | w | (30) | w | w |
| w | w | w | 5 | 1 | w | 5 | 3 |
| w | 5 | 5 | w | w | 7 | w | w |
| 6 | w | w | 3 | 4 | w | 4 | w |
| w | 2 | 6 | w | w | w | w | w |
| 7 | w | w | w | 8 | 1 | w | 8 |
| w | 8 | 1 | 4 | w | w | 3 | w |
| 14 | w | w | w | 11 | 2 | w | w |
| w | w | 3 | w | w | w | 10 | 2 |
| 2 | 4 | w | 16 | w | 5 | w | _w_ |
| w | w | w | w | 16 | w | w | 296 runs |
| 15 | 8 | 7 | 1 | w | 2 | 7 | 170 w's |
| w | w | w | w | w | w | w | & |
| 5 | w | 4 | 6 | 1 | 6 | 2 | 126 l's |
| w | 9 | w | w | w | w | w | |
| 2 | w | 1 | 2 | 6 | 7 | w | |
| w | 12 | w | w | w | w | 3 | |
| 1 | w | 2 | w | w | 4 | w | |
| w | 18 | w | w | 14 | w | 7 | |
| 5 | w | 7 | 2 | w | 2 | w | |
| w | 3 | w | w | w | w | w | |
| 20 | w | 1 | w | 2 | 4 | 2 | |
| w | 12 | w | 7 | w | w | w | |
| 2 | w | 1 | w | 13 | 3 | 5 | |
| w | w | w | 3 | w | w | w | |
| w | 1 | 1 | w | w | 9 | 1 | |
| 2 | w | w | 5 | 1 | w | w | |
| w | 3 | 4 | w | w | 1 | 4 | |
| 3 | w | w | 6 | 7 | w | w | |
| w | 15 | w | w | w | w | w | |
| 11 | w | 5 | 3 | 6 | 1 | 3 | |
| w | w | w | w | w | w | w | |
| w | w | 5 | 2 | w | 1 | 1 | |
| 5 | 4 | w | w | w | w | w | |

TABLE 45

Total number of spins absorbed by the
126 *Losing* runs exactly 2 reds long during the 1st 1,024 spins of the Hartman
sample

| *Length of* Losing *run* | | *Number of* Losing *runs* | | *Spins* *absorbed* |
|---|---|---|---|---|
| 1 | × | 20 | = | 21 |
| 2 | × | 20 | = | 40 |
| 3 | × | 17 | = | 51 |
| 4 | × | 11 | = | 44 |
| 5 | × | 13 | = | 65 |
| 6 | × | 10 | = | 60 |
| 7 | × | 9 | = | 63 |
| 8 | × | 4 | = | 32 |
| 9 | × | 2 | = | 18 |
| 10 | × | 2 | = | 20 |
| 11 | × | 2 | = | 22 |
| 12 | × | 2 | = | 24 |
| 13 | × | 2 | = | 26 |
| 14 | × | 2 | = | 28 |
| 15 | × | 2 | = | 30 |
| 16 | × | 2 | = | 32 |
| 17 | × | 1 | = | 17 |
| 18 | × | 1 | = | 18 |
| 20 | × | 1 | = | 20 |
| 23 | × | 1 | = | 23 |
| 30 | × | 1 | = | 30 |
| | | 126 | | 684 losing spins |

There occur 170 winning runs, each 2
reds long; and 126 losing runs; hence
170+126=296 runs; 170×2=340 winning spins; and as there occur 684 losing
spins, we have 340+684=1024 spins in
the whole game.

losing runs shorter than 30 spins were respectively 23 and 20 spins
long. Thus even when we're betting on only 2 reds in a row, in a
game 1,024 spins long it is quite normal to encounter such long
losing runs. I might add that during the 2nd and 3rd games 1,024
spins long of the Hartman sample there occur two losing runs

respectively 29 and 37 spins long, if we adopt the same very modest paroli progression of doubling *only once* on 2 reds in a row.

'By the way, how much of our loss of 93 units owes itself to the inclusion of zero in the 1st game?' asks Mr Optimist.

'Following the method of calculating the Bank's percentage explained in Chapter III, we have *any* equals $(1)(1024) \times (0.027027) = 27.68$ units, very roughly,' I reply. 'Thus if we had omitted zero, we should have lost only $93 - 27.68 = 65.32$ units. But we must always face the reality of the Bank's percentage. So let's leave zero in.'

'Well, I must say having lost 93 units on doubling only once on a run of 2 reds does give me a lot to think about,' comments Mr Optimist.

'Well, I must say having lost 174 units on doubling only once on a run of 2 reds does give me a lot to think about,' comments Mr Optimist.

'Now let's consider briefly the ...

### Great Martingale

'We may dispose of this monster quickly. The great martingale is to the small martingale what the great paroli is to the small paroli,' I remark. 'After every *loss* we double our stake and add one unit of our own capital to form the progression ...

$$1 + 3 + 7 + 15 + 31 + 63 + 127 + 255 + 511$$

'And after every win we revert to a stake of 1 unit. We win as gross profit 2 units for every Heads that actually occurs, or 1 unit per trial, as one will. The great martingale is, of course, an *anti* staking system, i.e. we increase our bet after every *losing* trial.'

'And after the *losing* run above of 9 (or more) Tails, how much is our loss?' asks Mr Optimist.

'The sum of the $r = 9$ figures in the great martingale progression, which comes to 1,013 units,' I reply.

'Forget it!' exclaims Mr Optimist. 'What's next?'

'We have a few ...

### Variations on the Paroli and Martingale

'So far we have examined only the two most famous progressions, viz. $1 + 2 + 4 + 8 + 16$, etc. and $1 + 3 + 7 + 15 + 31$, etc.

'One variation is $1+1+2+4+8+16$ etc., i.e. we repeat the first bet *once* before starting the usual doubling-up progression.

'Another staking system is the short progression $1+2+3+6$. If we win either of the first two bets, we win 1 unit. If we win either of the second two, we break even. When we lose all four bets, of course, we lose $1+2+3+6=12$ units, whose probability at any designated trial is 1/32, following the formula for a run of $r$ (or more) losses given earlier. We're assuming this to be an *anti* progression, but it may be used just as well, of course, as a *pro* one. Let us remember the simple rule: any progression may be reversed from a *pro* to an *anti* one, or vice versa.

'Another progression is $1+1+2+2+3+3+4+4+5+5$ etc. Another is $1+1+2+2+4+4+8+8$ etc. An even slower one is $1+2+2+3+3+3+4+4+4+4+5+5+5+5+5$. And still another is $1+2+3+5+8+13+21+34+55+89+144$ etc., where each subsequent figure is the sum of the two preceding ones (the celebrated Fibonacci series.)

'But however complicated or intellectually amusing such progressions may be, none of them offers any practical advantage over either the simple paroli – or even the simple martingale.

'And we close with a staking system which, however amusing superficially, has brought ruin to a great number of gamblers ...

## Permutation System

'Although any progression on Heads or Win may be used with this system, the simple or great martingale have been traditionally popular, At any rate we adopt some sort of *anti* progression.

'Prior to going to the casino we mix in an opaque urn, or in any suitable receptacle, a small, arbitrary number of pellets, half marked *Win*, half *Loss*. Let's say, Mr Optimist, that there are 8 pellets. Reaching inside, we remove a random pellet and place it to our left on a table. We repeat this operation until all 8 pellets have been placed on the table in a row in the particular random order of their appearance. After noting down this order on a sheet of paper, we go to the casino and select any game offering an even-money chance.

'Let's say we pick roulette, and exclude the matter of zero. We decide to play on red, rather than black, and call red a *win*, black a *loss*. Now we remove from our pocket the sheet of paper. We adopt an *anti* progression, betting that *during the very next r* spins of the wheel the particular order, arrangement, or *permutation* of *wins* and *losses*, just as written down on the paper, *will not occur at all*.

'Let's say the permutation we pulled out from the urn is … WLWLLWLW. Now we place our first wager on red. Let's say we follow the simple martingale. Regardless of the actual order of the reds and blacks produced in the very next $r=8$ spins of the wheel, we place our bets strictly according to the theoretical order of the *wins* and *losses* on our sheet of paper, remembering $w$ stands for *red*, $l$ for black. This is how we bet. We wager 1 unit on red, 1 unit on black, 2 units on red, 1 unit on black, 2 units on black, 4 units on red, 1 unit on black, and finally 2 units on red. In other words we simply double our bet after every *loss* or black, returning to the basic wager of 1 unit after every *win* or red, strictly following the order of $w$'s and $l$'s represented by the permutation on the paper.

'We repeat this particular order or permutation of 8 wagers as often as we wish.

'Until the roulette wheel produces an order of reds and blacks exactly *opposite* to that on our sheet of paper, we *win* about 1/2 a unit per spin. When the *exact opposite* order of our permutation occurs, however, then we lose $1+2+4+8+16+32+64+128=255$ units, a gross loss.

'The theory, or more properly, the delusion behind this system is that it is possible to vanquish chance by chance itself. For would it not be excessively improbable, reason the adherents of the system, that during an actual game of roulette spins a permutation of reds and blacks, arranged by pure chance in that *exact* order, should be repeated by pure chance in the *exact opposite* order?

'The answer is unfortunately – no. Let $r$ signify the number of both *wins* and *losses* comprising the permutation we took out of the urn and wrote down. In the case at hand the sum of the *wins* and *losses* is $r=8$. The probability that the *exact opposite* of the order of our own permutation of *wins* and *losses* should be repeated by an actual roulette wheel is simply …

$$(1/2)^{r+1}$$

'And consequently the probability of the "excessively improbable" disastrous exact opposite order is $(1/2)^{8+1}=(1/2)^{9}=1/512$.

'Using some simple mathematical calculations, Mr Optimist, we may predict the "excessively improbable" permutation will have the following chances of occurring …

110

| | | |
|---|---|---|
| 10 per cent chance at least once *before* the | 54th spin. | |
| 25 | 147th | |
| 50 | 355th | |
| | | |
| 75 | 708th | |
| 90 | 1,178th | |
| 95 | 1,533th | |
| 99 | 2,385nd | |

'And naturally when it does occur, we shall lose the 255 units. Do you want to try the permutation system in reality at the gaming tables, Mr Optimist?'[1]

'Thanks a lot, but I think I'll leave all progressive staking systems to somebody else,' responds Mr Optimist, 'But there must be other systems, less dangerous, less costly, cleverer, more successful ...'

'Then have the kindness to continue reading,' I reply.

[1] For method of calculation see Appendix p. 221.

# CHAPTER X

# Staking Systems Based Ordinarily on a Plus Digression on the Even-Money Chances

'Although not so simple – or nearly so desirous – as staking systems based on runs, staking systems based *ordinarily* on a plus digression *at the end* of *n* trials, Mr Optimist, tend to be intellectually ingenious and consequently oftentimes hypnotize their users into thinking that they, the users, have acquired some unusual, even mysterious, advantage over adverse chance,' I declare to our interested friend.

'No system is going to hypnotize me!' exclaims Mr Optimist. 'By the way why do you use the word "ordinarily" in your chapter heading?'

'As you recall, the simple martingale requires only 1 H to recoup all previous losses and gain 1 unit. The progressions we're going to examine now, however, require for success not only more than a single H but an excess of H's over T's, i.e. the systems are based *ordinarily* on a plus digression *at the end* of *n* trials. I say *ordinarily* because from time to time they may succeed on the basis of even a minority of H's although, as we'll see, this is exceptional. But first I want to explain the simplest system in the world – so simple you'll probably laugh at it. Yet in the future whenever you become even a little confused about a staking system, Mr Optimist, think back over "the simplest system" and your confusion should clear up almost instantly.'

'Okay – bring on the world's "simplest system",' agrees our friend.

'Let's say you and I are tossing a coin for Heads and Tails.'

'Just don't bring on Peter and Paul,' grumbles Mr Optimist.

'We'll play two games. The first game will be for you, the second for me. In both games Heads wins, Tails loses. In both games each of us must use the *pro* system called the simple paroli, which we examined at length. And each game lasts for exactly two tosses. Now we hand the coin to the god of chance to toss,' I conclude.

'Betting 1 unit on Heads to win, I use the simple paroli,' announces Mr Optimist. 'What comes up?'

'Heads,' I declare.

'All right, now doubling my bet to 2 units, what comes up on the second and last toss of my game?' asks Mr Optimist.

'Tails, so you lost your original stake of 1 unit,' I respond. 'Now it's my turn. The god of chance tosses the coin. The reverse takes place: Tails comes up so I lose my original stake of 1 unit. He tosses the coin for the second and last time for my game: Heads comes up so I win a stake of 1 unit. The result of each of our games follows:

> Your game: HT    net: you lose 1 unit
> My game: TH    net: I break even'

'Wait a minute!' cries Mr Optimist. 'Your permutations are unfair to me and fair to you!'

'That's right – your game *ends* in a Tails, a *minus* digression. On the other hand my game *ends* in a Heads, a *plus* digression,' I reply. 'And yet as in *each* game the number of H's and T's is *equal*, both games end in a return to equilibrium. So why do you complain?' I ask.

'Well, it's obvious enough – you bribed the god of chance to end your game in a *plus* digression and to end mine in a *minus* digression. Why couldn't you have switched the results the other way around?' asks Mr Optimist, both angry and hurt.

'Because I wanted to use "the simplest system" – two games of only two tosses – to illustrate perhaps the most important pitfall of a progressive betting system: if it *ends* in a *plus* digression, you can hardly fail to win, but if it *ends* in a *minus* digression, you'll most certainly lose. And 50 per cent of the time, as it were, you'll end in a minus digression – look at the two games we just played,' I mention. 'And these two games of Heads and Tails were mathematically *fair* games too. May I recall your attention to the results of the 500 mathematically *unfair* games, each 100 spins long, of the Hartman sample, as examined in Chapter VII, Table 27, p. 59, 6th column. *At the end* of these 500 games 40 result in a return to

113

equilibrium, 187 result in a plus digression, and 273 result in a minus digression.'

'So a progressive system would succeed 187 times and fail 273 times,' declares Mr Optimist somewhat sorrowfully. 'Or in other words, all else being equal, using a progressive system I'd lose my shirt 273−187=86 times?'

'I'm afraid so. And the returns to equilibrium don't do you any good, because of the 40 games ending in a return to equilibrium, in theory half or 20 end in a plus digression but the other half or 20 end in a minus digression. So these games cancel each other out,' I conclude. 'At any rate, Mr Optimist, as we begin examining one famous staking system after another, always keep in the back of your mind the *simple* lesson of the "simplest system in the world"', which we've just played – and the actual results of the 500 games of the Hartman sample, which we've just recalled: if a game *ends* in a *minus* digression, a progressive staking system will most likely fail, whereas if a game *ends* in a *plus* digression, a progressive staking system will most likely succeed. And given that *actual* casino games are almost always mathematically unfair, i.e. usually *end* in a *minus* digression, in practice we should run into bad if not very bad trouble more than half the time. Were I not to explain this before our discussing various systems, I should be doing you an extreme injustice. But having done so, we may now proceed to examine the staking system called the . . .

*Labouchere*

'Along with the progressions to follow, we play the Labouchere system over the random sample of 100 coin tosses represented by Table 46 (p. 115), always betting on Heads (H) to win, Tails (T) to lose. Although there occur 50 H's and 50 T's *at the end* of the $n=100$ trials, the fact that this ultimate return to equilibrium *ends* in a *plus* digression PLACES THE LABOUCHERE AND ANY PROGRESSIVE SYSTEM IN AN UNDESERVEDLY FAVORABLE LIGHT, but for the purpose of *comparing* one system to another, I choose to play each over the same permutation or arrangement of 100 trials which ends in a return to equilibrium. In addition the game of Table 46 (p. 115) contains all told 11 returns to equilibrium, as indicated by the horizontal black lines. Notice that, following the evidence as presented by Professor William Feller in Table 7 (p. 7), the returns to equilibrium tend to

114

TABLE 46          TABLE 47

## TABLE 46

| n | H | T | n | H | T |
|---|---|---|---|---|---|
| 1 | H |   | 51 | H | H |
| 2 |   | T | 52 |   | T |
| 3 |   | T | 53 |   | T |
| 4 |   | T | 54 | H |   |
| 5 | H |   | 55 | H |   |
| 6 |   | T | 56 |   | T |
| 7 |   | T | 57 | H |   |
| 8 |   | T | 58 | H |   |
| 9 | H |   | 59 |   | T |
| 10 |   | T | 60 | H |   |
| 11 | H |   | 61 |   | T |
| 12 |   | T | 62 |   | T |
| 13 |   | T | 63 | H |   |
| 14 | H |   | 64 |   | T |
| 15 |   | T | 65 | H |   |
| 16 | H |   | 66 |   | T |
| 17 |   | T | 67 | H |   |
| 18 | H |   | 68 | H |   |
| 19 |   | T | 69 | H |   |
| 20 |   | T | 70 | H |   |
| 21 |   | T | 71 | H |   |
| 22 |   | T | 72 |   | T |
| 23 | H |   | 73 |   | T |
| 24 | H |   | 74 | H |   |
| 25 |   | T | 75 |   | T |
| 26 |   | T | 76 | H |   |
| 27 |   | T | 77 | H |   |
| 28 | H |   | 78 | H |   |
| 29 | H |   | 79 |   | T |
| 30 |   | T | 80 |   | T |
| 31 |   | T | 81 |   | T |
| 32 |   | T | 82 | H |   |
| 33 | H |   | 83 |   | T |
| 34 | H |   | 84 | H |   |
| 35 |   | T | 85 |   | T |
| 36 | H |   | 86 | H |   |
| 37 | H |   | 87 | H |   |
| 38 | H |   | 88 | H |   |
| 39 | H |   | 89 |   | T |
| 40 |   | T | 90 |   | T |
| 41 | H |   | 91 |   | T |
| 42 |   | T | 92 |   | T |
| 43 |   | T | 93 | H |   |
| 44 |   | T | 94 |   | T |
| 45 |   | T | 95 |   | T |
| 46 | H |   | 96 |   | T |
| 47 | H |   | 97 | H |   |
| 48 | H |   | 98 | H |   |
| 49 | H |   | 99 | H |   |
| 50 | H |   | 100 | H |   |

## TABLE 47

| n | w | l | cwl | n | w | l | cwl |
|---|---|---|---|---|---|---|---|
| 1 | 5 | + | 5 | 51 | 5 | + | 10 |
| 2 |   | 5 | 0 | 52 |   | 5 | − 5 |
| 3 |   | 7 | − 7 | 53 |   | 6 | − 11 |
| 4 |   | 9 | − 16 | 54 | 7 |   | − 4 |
| 5 | 11 |   | − 5 | 55 | 7 |   | + 3 |
| 6 |   | 10 | − 15 | 56 |   | 7 | − 4 |
| 7 |   | 13 | − 28 | 57 | 10 |   | + 6 |
| 8 |   | 16 | − 44 | 58 | 4 |   | + 10 |
| 9 | 19 |   | − 25 | 59 |   | 5 | − 5 |
| 10 |   | 17 | − 42 | 60 | 6 |   | + 1 |
| 11 | 22 |   | − 20 | 61 |   | 6 | − 5 |
| 12 |   | 20 | − 40 | 62 |   | 8 | − 13 |
| 13 |   | 27 | − 67 | 63 | 10 |   | − 3 |
| 14 | 34 |   | − 33 | 64 |   | 9 | − 12 |
| 15 |   | 30 | − 63 | 65 | 12 |   | 0 |
| 16 | 40 |   | − 23 | 66 |   | 10 | − 10 |
| 17 |   | 33 | − 56 | 67 | 14 |   | + 4 |
| 18 | 46 |   | − 10 | 68 | 6 |   | + 10 |
| 19 |   | 20 | − 30 | 69 | 5 |   | + 5 |
| 20 |   | 40 | − 70 | 70 | 5 |   | + 10 |
| 21 |   | 60 | − 30 | 71 | 5 |   | + 5 |
| 22 |   | 80 | − 210 | 72 |   | 5 | 0 |
| 23 | 100 |   | − 110 | 73 |   | 7 | − 7 |
| 24 | 80 |   | − 30 | 74 | 9 |   | + 2 |
| 25 |   | 40 | − 70 | 75 |   | 8 | − 6 |
| 26 |   | 80 | − 150 | 76 | 11 |   | + 5 |
| 27 |   | 120 | − 270 | 77 | 5 |   | + 10 |
| 28 | 160 |   | − 110 | 78 | 5 |   | + 5 |
| 29 | 120 |   | + 10 | 79 |   | 5 | 0 |
| 30 |   | 5 | − 5 | 80 |   | 7 | − 7 |
| 31 |   | 6 | − 11 | 81 |   | 9 | − 16 |
| 32 |   | 7 | − 18 | 82 | 11 |   | − 5 |
| 33 | 8 |   | − 10 | 83 |   | 10 | − 15 |
| 34 | 8 |   | − 2 | 84 | 13 |   | − 2 |
| 35 |   | 8 | − 10 | 85 |   | 12 | − 14 |
| 36 | 11 |   | + 1 | 86 | 17 |   | + 3 |
| 37 | 9 |   | + 10 | 87 | 7 |   | + 10 |
| 38 | 5 |   | + 5 | 88 | 5 |   | + 5 |
| 39 | 5 |   | + 10 | 89 |   | 5 | 0 |
| 40 |   | 5 | − 5 | 90 |   | 7 | − 7 |
| 41 | 6 |   | + 1 | 91 |   | 9 | − 16 |
| 42 |   | 6 | − 5 | 92 |   | 11 | − 27 |
| 43 |   | 8 | − 13 | 93 | 13 |   | − 14 |
| 44 |   | 10 | − 23 | 94 |   | 12 | − 26 |
| 45 |   | 12 | − 35 | 95 |   | 15 | − 41 |
| 46 | 14 |   | − 21 | 96 |   | 18 | − 59 |
| 47 | 13 |   | − 8 | 97 | 21 |   | − 38 |
| 48 | 12 |   | + 4 | 98 | 20 |   | − 18 |
| 49 | 6 |   | + 10 | 99 | 19 |   | + 1 |
| 50 | 5 |   | + 5 | 100 | 9 |   | + 10 |

cluster although as no one may predict *where* they may cluster, whether at the beginning, middle, or end of the game, *no staking system may be based on the clustering.* Notice that from the 1st to the 69th trial there occurs *only 1* return to equilibrium, *all the remaining 10 returns* occurring from the 70th to the 100th trial.

'The adjacent Table 47 (p. 115) shows the results of the Labouchere system played over the random permutation or game of H's and T's comprising Table 46 (p. 115).'

'Would you mind telling me,' breaks in Mr Optimist, 'why the system is called the "Labouchere"?'

'Well, its name comes from its popularizer, the Rt Hon. Henry Labouchere, M.P., British journalist and liberal parliamentarian (1831–1912), but he himself read it in a book by the Marquis de Condorcet, the French philosopher and mathematician (1743–1794). Although Labouchere himself used the system a few times with great success, the system itself is very bad. I regret to say he was just lucky, i.e. the few times he used it, at Bad Homburg v. d. Höhe in Germany and at Monte Carlo in Monaco, his games could only have fortunately *ended* in *plus* digressions. But for this *anti* system here are the rules he followed.

'On a sheet of paper we write down a small, arbitrary number of figures, such as 1–2–3, 1–2–3–4, 3–4–5–6–7, 1–2–3–4–5–6–7–8–9–10–11–12, or whatever, keeping in mind that the greater the number of figures, and the larger they are in amount, the larger is the risk we're taking. As the eventual figures of the progression differ from permutation to permutation, or game to game, as it were (reflecting varying ratios of H's to T's), we unfortunately can't lay down a rule, as we did for the paroli and martingale, for the amount we must wager at any given trial. Just the same after every win we bet either the same amount or, usually, less on the next trial, and after every loss we increase our bet a small, medium, or even large amount on the next trial. Assuming we don't run into the more-than-likely minus digression that fluctuates on and on, we win as net profit the sum of the original figures written before any cancellation of figures began. Thus if the original figures be 1–2–3–4, our net profit *at the end* of a *finished game* will be 1+2+3+4=10 units.

'Let's say we'll be conservative and play the figures 1–2–3–4. The mechanics of the Labouchere, or *Labby*, comprise the following three steps.

116

'(1) At any given trial the amount of our bet equals the sum of the *two uncancelled outside figures* of whatever series of figures appear on our sheet of paper. If no uncancelled outside figures remain, then we have *won* the sum of the original series of figures written down before the first cancellation, and the game has ended.

'(2) If the previous trial was a *loss*, then prior to the next bet we *add* this amount to the righthand end of the series.

'(3) If the previous trial was a *win*, then prior to the next bet we *cancel* the two uncancelled outside figures of the series.

'In addition, the following four points, though not essential, might also be remembered. During the game the gross gain equals the sum of all the cancelled figures. The gross loss equals the sum of all the figures excluding the original ones. The net gain or loss equals the difference between these two sums. And at any given trial the sum of all the uncancelled figures equals the amount which must be won in order to complete the game, i.e. to win the sum of the original figures written down.

'As we know, we have chosen, for our original figures, the series 1–2–3–4 and have so written them on our sheet of paper. According to step (1) our wager equals the sum of the two uncancelled outside figures, i.e. $1+4=5$ units. As we note in Table 46 (p. 115), the first trial is an H. Hence in Table 47 (p. 115) the first figure in the *w*(*win*) column is 5. Thus according to (3) we cancel the two uncancelled outside figures, leaving our series . . . 1–2–3–4. Again according to (1) our wager now equals $2+3=5$ units. As we observe in Table 46 (p. 115), the second trial is a T. Hence in Table 47 (p. 115) the first figure in the *l* (*loss*) column is 5, and the *cwl* (cumulative net *w*in or *l*oss) has decreased from +5 to 0. According to (2) we add the amount of our losing wager (5 units) to the righthand end of the series, leaving the latter as . . . 1–2–3–4–5. Once more according to (1) our bet equals the sum of the two uncancelled outside figures, i.e. $2+5=7$ units. As we observe, the third trial is another T – hence the second figure in the *l* column is 7, and *cwl* is now −7. According to (2) again, we add the amount of our losing wager (7 units) to the righthand end of the series, leaving it . . . 1–2–3–4–5–7. Once more according to (1) our bet equals the sum of the two uncancelled outside figures, i.e. $2+7=9$ units. As we observe, the fourth trial is another T – hence the third figure in the *l* column is 9 units, and *cwl* is now −16. According to (2) again, we add 9 to the righthand end of the series, leaving it as . . . 1–2–3–4–5–7–9. According to (1) our next bet is $2+9=11$ units.

117

As we note, the fifth trial is an H – hence the second figure in the $w$ column is 11 units, and $cwl$ has decreased from $-16$ to $-5$. According to (3) we cancel the two uncancelled outside figures, leaving our series as .... $1$-$2$-3-$4$-5-7-$9$. And again according to (1) our wager now equals $3+7=10$ units.

'The horizontal black lines of Table 47 (p. 115) indicate that during the 100-trial session we are able to complete 11 *winning* games, each yielding $1+2+3+4=10$ units net profit. And 10 $\times 11=110$ units net profit for the whole session.

'Is the number 11 games above or below the theoretical average number of *winning* games *at the end* of 100 trials?

'In the case of the Labouchere progression the probability at any given trial of completing the cancellation of the series of $f$ *original* figures is ... $(1/2f)$ .... and the theoretical average number of such completed series of *winning* games *at the end* of $n$ trials is ... $(1/2f) (n)$.

'In the session comprising Table 47 (p. 115), before any cancellation begins our *original* series is composed of 4 figures: hence $f=4$. Thus the probability at any given trial of our finishing the cancellation of all four figures is ... $(1/2\times4)=1/8$ ... and the theoretical average number of such completed series *at the end* of 100 trials ... $(1/8) (100)=12.5$. Hence the actual number of 11 winning games is only slightly below average.

'It is the length of the first winning game of Table 47 (p. 115) that should serve as a grave warning to any prospective player of the Labouchere progression. What if we had not won the 120 units on the 29th trial? And would that have been so unlikely? It would have been no more improbable, of course, than the occurrence of a T rather than an H. Had this misfortune occurred, our first game would have lasted as long as 37 trials. Table 48 (p. 118) lists the disturbing results. Instead of our largest wager being "only" 160 units it would have become as much as 400.

TABLE 48

| $n$ | $w$ | $l$ | $cwl$ |
|-----|-----|-----|-------|
| 29 |     | 120 | $-230$ |
| 30 |     | 160 | $-390$ |
| 31 |     | 200 | $-590$ |
| 32 |     | 240 | $-830$ |
| 33 | 280 |     | $-550$ |
| 34 | 280 |     | $-270$ |
| 35 |     | 280 | $-550$ |
| 36 | 400 |     | $-150$ |
| 37 | 160 |     | $+ 10$ |

Instead of our largest cumulative net loss being "only" 270 units it would have become as much as 830! And let's remember that such

118

a "conservatively" short series of only 4 figures *occurs quite frequently*.

'According to Professor Louis Bachelier, the probability of there occurring a certain ratio of H's to T's (or the reverse) *during* a game is *twice* the probability of there occurring this same ratio of H's to T's *at the end* of the same game.

'We are playing the Labouchere over the 100 coin tosses of Table 46 (p. 115) and the result is listed in Table 47 (p. 115).

'What is the probability of a losing streak like the first 28 tosses by the end of which the ratio of T's to H's has reached the alarming ratio of 18 T's to "only" 10 H's? If we look at Table 9 (p. 13), we multiply the *at end* probability value of Q/2 by 2 and get, of course, the *during* probability value of simply Q itself, whose values for a game of 100 tosses are listed under the latter letter. Thus for a game 100 trials long the probability of a digression of (more than) 18 T's to "only" 10 H's *during* the game is the 5th value down the Q column – 0.3730. In other words were we to play 3 sessions, each 100 trials long, an adverse digression *worse* than that of the first game of Table 47 (p. 115) would occur theoretically sometime *during* one of the 3 sessions.

'And what if the 29th trial had just happened to be after all a T rather than an H, i.e. that matters had turned out like the disaster of Table 48 (p. 118)? In this case the ratio is 23 T's to only 13 H's, yet again looking down the Q column of Table 9 (p. 13), we note that the probability of an adverse digression of (more than) 23 T's to "only" 13 H's *during* the game is the 6th value down the Q column – 0.2762. In other words were we to play 4 sessions, each 100 trials long, an adverse digression *worse than that of the* first game of Table 48 (p. 118) would occur theoretically sometime *during* one of the 4 sessions.

'As I've mentioned before, however, few gamblers are content to play one game only 100 trials long. So what happens if we play the Labouchere over the first 1,024 spins of the Hartman sample? As I noted in Chapter VII (p. 55), the last return to equilibrium during the 50,000-spin Hartman sample occurs at the 136th spin. Let us assume that up to this spin, betting on Red (Heads), we have won neither more nor fewer than the theoretical average number of *winning* games, to be exact, $(1/2f)$ $(n)=(1/8)$ $(136)=17$ games, for $17\times10=170$ units.

'At the 136th spin we begin the 18th game. How does it eventuate in actuality? Although at the 217th spin we do succeed in

119

finally winning the game, i.e. our 10 units, let us note the grave implications of the following facts. The game itself lasts as long as 71 spins. *During* its course there occurs an adverse ratio of 33 Blacks (Tails) to only 13 Reds (Heads). The largest cumulative net loss is the enormous sum of 5,165 units. The largest bet is the equally enormous sum of 1,765 units. The average wager is 370 units. And following the method of calculating the Q column of Table 9 (p. 13), except that instead of a game of 100 trials we're playing one of 1,024, the probability of the occurrence of the mentioned adverse digression is as large as 0.52.'

'And where do these gigantic paper losses leave us?' asks Mr Optimist, mopping the cold sweat from his brow.

'They leave us, Mr Optimist, with the . . .

*Reverse Labouchere*

'Oh, I think I've read about this one!' exclaims Mr Optimist happily.

'Indeed you have,' I reply. 'You read about it in *Thirteen Against the Bank*, by Norman Leigh (N.Y., 1976), a doughty Englishman who, in 1966, took with him to the French Riviera a dozen of his countrymen and won considerable sums of money. As Mr Leigh mentions, the Reverse Labouchere was invented and described by another of his countrymen, the Hon. S. R. Beresford (1868–1928), in his delightful book, *Beresford's Monte-Carlo* (Nice, 1926). Unfortunately neither of these two gentlemen had the vaguest notion of the pitfalls of the Reverse Labouchere, let alone the Labouchere itself.

'Well now, just as the simple martingale is an *anti* system which is the reverse or mirror image of the simple paroli, so the Reverse Labouchere is a *pro* system which is the reverse or mirror image of the Labouchere. In other words while in the Labouchere we tend to increase our bet after a *loss*, so in the Reverse Labouchere we tend to increase our bet after a *win*. In addition although Table 43 (p. 109) shows that the simple paroli and simple martingale have the identical expectation of zero – *if we play all possible permutations*, WHICH THE GOD OF CHANCE NEVER LETS US DO – just the same I should like to go on record now as advising all gamblers that, assuming all else equal, it is ALWAYS better to adopt a *pro* system rather than an *anti* one, i.e. it is always preferable to bet progressively large sums with money *already won* rather than with one's own capital. To be sure, this isn't an original gambling concept, but it is nonetheless a worthwhile one always to follow. Will you always bear in mind this positive concept, Mr Optimist?'

'Always!' agrees our friend.

'Very well, here then are the three steps of the Reverse Labouchere:

'(1) At any given trial the amount of our bet equals the sum of the *two uncancelled outside figures* of whatever series of figures appears on our sheet of paper. If no uncancelled outside figures remain, then we have *lost* the sum of the original series of figures written down before the first cancellation, and the game has ended.

'(2) If the previous trial was a *win*, then prior to the next bet we *add* this amount to the righthand end of the series.

'(3) If the previous trial was a *loss*, then prior to the next bet we *cancel* the two uncancelled outside figures of the series.

'The following three points might also be remembered although they're not essential. During the game the gross gain equals the sum of all the figures excluding the original ones. The gross loss equals the sum of all the cancelled figures. And the net gain or loss equals the difference between these two sums.

'As we went carefully through the steps for the regular Labouchere, even though those for the Reverse Labouchere are indeed "the reverse", just the same, Mr Optimist, I believe that the application of the above three steps to the random permutation or game of Table 46 (p. 115) needs no further elucidation. The results of the Reverse Labouchere are shown in Table 49 (p. 122).

'As we observe, as in all *pro* systems we keep reinvesting our gains in the hope of eventually piling up enough in one long game of winning trials to wipe out the cumulative net losses from all the shorter losing games. Not surprisingly, therefore, you'll note in Table 49 (p. 122) that by the 45th trial we've lost 8 consecutive games of 10 units each for a total *cwl* of (8) (10)=80 units. And for the same reasons that matters could have been much worse, over the same permutation, for the regular Labouchere – worse in the sense of a violently adverse digression *during* the 100 trials – so we could have easily collected a cumulative net loss much larger than 80 units. And as you'll further note, *as much as 99 per cent of our total winnings* are gained during *only the last 5* trials of the winning game, which lasts from the 46th trial to the 71st. At the 66th trial we have still only 1 unit profit – yet just 5 trials later 166

## TABLE 49

| n | w | l | cwl |
|---|---|---|-----|
| 1 | 5 | + | 5 |
| 2 |  | 6 − | 1 |
| 3 |  | 6 − | 7 |
| 4 |  | 3 − | 10 |
| 5 | 5 | + | 5 |
| 6 |  | 6 − | 1 |
| 7 |  | 6 − | 7 |
| 8 |  | 3 − | 10 |
| 9 | 5 | + | 5 |
| 10 |  | 6 − | 1 |
| 11 | 6 | + | 5 |
| 12 |  | 8 − | 3 |
| 13 |  | 7 − | 10 |
| 14 | 5 | + | 5 |
| 15 |  | 6 − | 1 |
| 16 | 6 | + | 5 |
| 17 |  | 8 − | 3 |
| 18 | 7 | + | 4 |
| 19 |  | 10 − | 6 |
| 20 |  | 4 − | 10 |
| 21 |  | 5 − | 5 |
| 22 |  | 5 − | 10 |
| 23 | 5 | + | 5 |
| 24 | 6 | + | 11 |
| 25 |  | 7 + | 4 |
| 26 |  | 7 − | 3 |
| 27 |  | 7 − | 10 |
| 28 | 5 | + | 5 |
| 29 | 6 | + | 11 |
| 30 |  | 7 + | 4 |
| 31 |  | 7 − | 3 |
| 32 |  | 7 − | 10 |
| 33 | 5 | + | 5 |
| 34 | 6 | + | 11 |
| 35 |  | 7 + | 4 |
| 36 | 7 | + | 11 |
| 37 | 9 | + | 20 |
| 38 | 11 | + | 31 |
| 39 | 13 | + | 44 |
| 40 |  | 15 + | 29 |
| 41 | 14 | + | 43 |
| 42 |  | 17 + | 26 |
| 43 |  | 15 + | 11 |
| 44 |  | 14 − | 3 |
| 45 |  | 7 − | 10 |
| 46 | 5 | + | 5 |
| 47 | 6 | + | 11 |
| 48 | 7 | + | 18 |
| 49 | 8 | + | 26 |
| 50 | 9 | + | 35 |
| 51 | 10 | + | 45 |
| 52 |  | 11 + | 34 |
| 53 |  | 11 + | 23 |
| 54 | 11 | + | 34 |
| 55 | 14 | + | 48 |
| 56 |  | 17 + | 31 |
| 57 | 15 | + | 46 |
| 58 | 19 | + | 65 |
| 59 |  | 23 + | 42 |
| 60 | 20 | + | 62 |
| 61 |  | 25 + | 37 |
| 62 |  | 21 + | 16 |
| 63 | 18 | + | 34 |
| 64 |  | 25 + | 9 |
| 65 | 19 | + | 28 |
| 66 |  | 27 + | 1 |
| 67 | 11 | + | 12 |
| 68 | 22 | + | 34 |
| 69 | 33 | + | 67 |
| 70 | 44 | + | 111 |
| 71 | 55 | + | 166 |
| 72 |  | 5 − | 5 |
| 73 |  | 5 − | 10 |
| 74 | 5 | + | 5 |
| 75 |  | 6 − | 1 |
| 76 | 6 | + | 5 |
| 77 | 8 | + | 13 |
| 78 | 10 | + | 23 |
| 79 |  | 5 − | 5 |
| 80 |  | 5 − | 10 |
| 81 |  | 5 − | 5 |
| 82 | 5 | − | 0 |
| 83 |  | 7 − | 7 |
| 84 | 3 | − | 4 |
| 85 |  | 6 − | 10 |
| 86 | 5 | + | 5 |
| 87 | 6 | + | 11 |
| 88 | 7 | + | 18 |
| 89 |  | 8 + | 10 |
| 90 |  | 8 + | 2 |
| 91 |  | 8 − | 6 |
| 92 |  | 4 − | 10 |
| 93 | 5 | − | 5 |
| 94 |  | 6 − | 1 |
| 95 |  | 6 − | 7 |
| 96 |  | 3 − | 10 |
| 97 | 5 | + | 5 |
| 98 | 6 | + | 11 |
| 99 | 7 | + | 18 |
| 100 | 8 | + | 26 |

units! So far as *pro* systems go, the simple paroli is far better.

'As for the frequency of occurrence of a *losing* game, it is identical to that of a winning game of the regular Labouchere, i.e. the probability at any given trial of our completing the cancellation of the series of *f original* figures is ... (1/2f) ... and the theoretical average number of such completed *losing* games *at the end* of *n* trials is ... (1/2f) (n). Hence at the end of the present game of 100 trials the theoretical average number is ... (1/8) (100)=12.5, whereas actuality gives us 16−3=13 losing games.

'If we glance at the 16 games of Table 49 (p. 122) underlined by horizontal lines, we note from the *cwl* column that 13 of them end in a loss of 10 units and 3 – the 9th, 11th, and 16th – end in various gains – 166, 23, and 26 units respectively. Thus the gross loss is (13) (10)=130 units, the gross gain 166+23+26=215 units, and the net gain consequently 215−130=85 units.'

'Those are a lot of harrowing ups and downs for just 85 units,' comments Mr Optimist.

'I should think so. One of the main troubles with either the Labouchere or Reverse Labouchere is that there is no *predetermined top bet*, whereas with the simple paroli we can pick out *ahead of time* that our top bet will be either 2, 4, 8, 16, etc. units. And take the matter of the average amount bet. For the 100 trials of Table 47 (p. 115) the average wager of the Labouchere is as large as 10.91 unts, and for the long losing game itself the average wager is 43.6 units. As you may easily calculate from Table 49 (p. 122), the comparable bets for the Reverse Labouchere are 6.68 units for the whole session and as much as 18.69 units for the long winning game. On the other hand from Table 39 (p. 97) we see that the average wager for the simple paroli varies from only 1.3 to 4.0 units, both favorably low figures.

'Yes, but we can easily raise the average wager of the simple paroli by choosing a much higher top bet,' objects Mr Optimist.

'Agreed, my friend, but we *don't have* to choose a much higher top bet in the case of the simple paroli, whereas in the case of either the Labouchere or the Reverse Labouchere we are *forced* up into large top bets,' I reply. 'At any rate, Mr Optimist, although you may render a contrary judgment, in my own opinion, based on what we have seen of the Labouchere and the Reverse Labouchere, they are very bad systems. As I've mentioned, I consider the simple paroli infinitely better. This leaves us to consider ...

## Variations on the Labouchere and Reverse Labouchere

'Just as the simple paroli and simple martingale have spawned variations of themselves, so have the Labouchere and Reverse Labouchere. In the case of the latter two, gamblers have altered the *f original* figures from, say, $1+2+3$, $3+4+5$, $7+8+9$, or whatever, to $1+2+1$, $2+3+2$, or even $1+1+1$ to prevent the bet at any given trial from becoming very large. It goes without saying that if we reduce the original three figures from, say, $7+8+9$ to $1+1+1$ we proportionately reduce our risk – just as it's undeniable that in a single toss of a coin it's less risky to wager 1 unit than 2, or 2 units than 10, etc. What gamblers are trying to do here, of course, is reduce their losses, i.e. their risk, *without* proportionately reducing their gains. But the impossibility of this is self-evident.

'Another way of keeping the original figures of the Labouchere – or the Reverse Labouchere – from ballooning into enormous bets was invented by a third Britisher, the Hon. Victor Bethell (1864–1927), who proposed his "solution" to the problem in his own delightful book, *Monte Carlo Anecdotes and Systems of Play* (London, 1927). For the Labouchere in particular Bethell's way of reducing a gambler's risk is to subdivide a series of figures into several smaller ones whenever the gross loss, which always equals the sum of the uncancelled figures, approximates some moderate predesignated amount. Let's fix the latter at an arbitrary 40 units. We go to the gaming table, play the Labouchere, and after a moderate length of time our series of 4 original figures has developed into . . . $\cancel{1}$–$\cancel{2}$–3–4–5–$\cancel{6}$–7–$\cancel{9}$–10–13, and the sum of the uncancelled figures is 42, a reasonable approximation of 40 units. Instead of continuing with this series and perhaps being forced into dangerously large stakes we now subdivide the gross loss of 42 units into, say, 4 smaller *f original* figures, of which three are . . . $1+2+3+4=10$ units . . . and the fourth . . . $1+2+3+6=12$ units. Returning to the gaming table, we now play one of these series after another. Let's imagine that we manage to cancel out the three identical series but that the fourth has developed into . . . $\cancel{1}$–$\cancel{2}$–3–$\cancel{6}$–5–7–$\cancel{9}$–10–13 . . . and the sum of the uncancelled figures is 38, a reasonable approximation to 40 units. To avoid continuing on to possibly unacceptable large stakes, once more we subdivide the gross loss, here 38, into 4 smaller series, of which three are again . . . $1+2+3+4=10$ units . . . and the fourth . . . $1+2+3=8$ units. Naturally $(3)(10)=30$, $(1)(8)=8$, and

124

30+8=38. Returning once more to the table, we again play one of these series of *f original* figures after another. Let's imagine that this time we manage to cancel out *all four* series of figures before again reaching a gross loss approximating the predesignated limit of 40 units. In this case our final cumulative net gain, or *cwl*, is the difference between the gross gain and loss of all 9 completed series, or 104−80=24 units.'

'Then by following Victor Bethell's method of continually sub-dividing a Labouchere series whenever the figures become excessively large we have solved the inherent weakness of the Labouchere?' asks Mr Optimist.

'We haven't "solved" anything, I regret to say, Mr Optimist. All we're doing is burdening ourselves at the gaming table with even more arithmetical juggling. Again, *whether we win or lose* with the Labouchere, the Reverse Labouchere, or Bethell's continual sub-division of a large series into any number of smaller ones depends as always on whether the god of chance throws at us randomly more *plus* digressions than *minus* ones. It's just as simple as that. I recommend again your examining the 8 possible permutations of Table 43 (p. 103) and its discussion. The latter table compares, over 3 trials, the simple paroli and simple martingale, and *whether we win or lose* depends on whether the god of chance throws at us randomly more *winning* runs than *losing* runs than average dictates. So again it's all one and the same thing – "luck". And this being the case, I may only repeat, Mr Optimist, exactly what I said before. If we're going to pick out some sort of progression – and a *pro* one, where we keep reinvesting our winnings, is always better than an *anti* one *in an actual gambling situation* – then we might as well stick to the simple paroli, which involves no tedious and confusing cancellations, whose top wager may be predetermined by us, whose simplicity militates against costly errors, and whose average wager tends to be favorably low.'

# CHAPTER XI

# Miscellaneous Staking Systems for the Even-Money Chances

'You know, I was thinking,' comments Mr Optimist.

'A very precarious occupation,' I reply.

'I think there's a system even simpler than the "world's simplest system" that you played with me in the last chapter,' continues our friend, still somewhat hurt and irritable that he wasn't the winner at the end of our mentioned game of four tosses using the simple paroli.

'What's on your mind?' I ask curiously.

'Instead of playing the simple paroli or simple martingale over a game of *3* tosses, which you illustrated on Table 43 (p. 103), or playing the simple paroli over *4* tosses, which we did in the last chapter to *my* loss,' continues Mr Optimist, as I say, still hurt and irritable, 'why don't we play a game over just *1* toss?' A nefarious gleam appears in his eye.

'Okay – what do I do?'I ask. 'What is the system?'

'As I say, we'll play the game over just 1 toss. You'll bet 1 unit on Heads, while I'll bet 1 unit on Tails. Fair enough?' asks Mr Optimist, producing from his pocket a purportedly honest penny.

'Fair enough,' I reply.

'All right, now I'll give the coin its one and only toss,' he declares, matching deed to word.

'Tails!' I exclaim.

'Exactly!' cries out Mr Optimist exultantly. 'In only one toss you lost your 1 unit to me, and the game is finished. Now isn't *that* the "simplest system in the *universe*"?'

'It certainly is,' I reply. 'And I must confess that your "universal system", Mr Optimist, 'brilliantly illustrates the very core of all

126

gambling systems we have been talking about and shall talk about.'

'I thought you'd like it!' exclaims Mr Optimist, beaming, 'even though you lost. After all, there was a fifty–fifty chance that it could have been the other way around, so in a single toss you could have won my 1 unit.'

'Do you mind if I use your "universal system" to comment on gambling systems in general?' I ask.

'Not at all.'

'Let's pretend we're at the gaming tables in the middle of some system, and whether it's simple or complicated – whether the simple paroli, great martingale, Labouchere, etc. – makes *no difference*. Whether it's the toss of a penny, the spin of a roulette wheel, the throw of a pair of dice, etc. *every trial* is physically and therefore mathematically *independent* of all past trials and all future ones. In especial *for practical gambling purposes* the *past* permutation, order, or arrangement of trials of a game of any length may NOT be used to predict the *future* permutation, order, or arrangement of trials. Take, for example, the problem of runs, which we examined in Chapter VIII. All we know is that on average a certain number of winning and losing runs will occur by the end of a game. But as Table 36 (p. 86) of the Hartman sample definitely shows, the *actual* number of runs invariably fluctuates from game to game around the *theoretical average* number of runs. In one game we'll encounter fewer plus – or minus – runs, while in another we'll encounter more plus – or minus – runs. It's really all up to our friend the god of chance. The whole matter may be summed up by your "universal system". Whether in the *next trial* the permutation, order, or arrangement will be Heads or Tails no gambler *can ever tell*, and this is so whether he *has* or *has not* been tossing that coin and counting up the ratio of Heads to Tails already fallen.'

'It's a bitter pill to realize that 1 *game* of, say, 50,000 *tosses* is without the slightest doubt merely my "universal system" of 50,000 *games* of 1 *toss*, and that we can't predict in any way the outcome from one game to another,' says Mr Optimist with a sigh.

'Yes, it is. But if we could predict, then there wouldn't be any gamble, and all the casinos would have to close down. Even the dealers and croupiers would be betting on the *known order and number* of future events. The casinos would go bankrupt,' I point out. 'Now that your "universal system" has helped us to grasp this

127

absolutely fundamental basis for all casino gambling games – with the exception of blackjack, which we'll examine anon – let's look into several other popular staking systems, such as the . . .'

### D'Alembert

'Where have I heard this name before?' asks Mr Optimist.

'Although popular tradition attributes this *anti* progression to the celebrated French mathematician and philospher, Jean le Rond d'Alembert (1717?–1783), the real inventor remains anonymous. Before its simple description, however, I should like to repeat, Mr Optimist, the *strong warning* first stated in my introduction to the Labouchere system. As we shall play the D'Alembert over the same random permutation or game of Table 46 (p. 115), and as the latter ends in a *return to equilibrium* achieved by a *plus digression*, this places the D'Alembert progression IN AN UNDESERVEDLY FAVORABLE LIGHT. In other words with the D'Alembert – and with the progressions to follow – we may make a parallel with my "world's simplest system", described in Chapter X (pp. 112–114). If our game results in a return to equilibrium *ending* in a *plus* digression, the system will work, but if there is a return to equilibrium *ending* in a *minus* digression, it won't work. You'll recall that in my "world's simplest system" my permutation or game of 2 tosses resulted in TH, and the H favored me, while in your permutation or game of 2 tosses resulted in HT, and the T brought you a net loss, *even though both games* – TH and HT – *resulted in a return to equilibrium*,' I conclude.

'Can't you say anything hopeful about the D'Alembert?' asks Mr Optimist somewhat peevishly.

'Yes I can,' I respond. 'With the D'Alembert and subsequent progressions our stakes *increase very slowly*. Hence our average stake is very small – until we encounter a minus digression which may continue to infinity, in which case our average stake as well as cumulative net loss will be very large. So until disaster strikes, the D'Alembert is a very safe system. If this is paradoxical, at least I'm warning you ahead of time with the truth.'

'All right, all right,' interrupts Mr Optimist, torn between hope and fear, 'how do I play the D'Alembert?'

'As I mentioned, the D'Alembert is a very slow progression. Betting on Heads (H) to win, we increase our stake 1 unit after every loss and decrease our stake 1 unit after every win,' I reply.

128

TABLE 50

| n | w | l | cwl |   | n | w | l | cwl |
|---|---|---|---|---|---|---|---|---|
| 1 | 1 | + | 1 |   | 51 | 6 | + | 13 |
| 2 |  | 1 − | 1 |   | 52 |  | 5 + | 8 |
| 3 |  | 2 − | 3 |   | 53 |  | 6 + | 2 |
| 4 |  | 3 − | 6 |   | 54 | 7 | + | 9 |
| 5 | 4 | − | 2 |   | 55 | 6 | + | 15 |
| 6 |  | 3 − | 5 |   | 56 |  | 5 + | 10 |
| 7 |  | 4 − | 9 |   | 57 | 6 | + | 16 |
| 8 |  | 5 − | 14 |   | 58 | 5 | + | 21 |
| 9 | 6 | − | 8 |   | 59 |  | 4 + | 17 |
| 10 |  | 5 − | 13 |   | 60 | 5 | + | 22 |
| 11 | 6 | − | 7 |   | 61 |  | 4 + | 18 |
| 12 |  | 5 − | 12 |   | 62 |  | 5 + | 13 |
| 13 |  | 6 − | 18 |   | 63 | 6 | + | 19 |
| 14 | 7 | − | 11 |   | 64 |  | 5 + | 14 |
| 15 |  | 6 − | 17 |   | 65 | 6 | + | 20 |
| 16 | 7 | − | 10 |   | 66 |  | 5 + | 15 |
| 17 |  | 6 − | 16 |   | 67 | 6 | + | 21 |
| 18 | 7 | − | 9 |   | 68 | 5 | + | 26 |
| 19 |  | 6 − | 15 |   | 69 | 4 | + | 30 |
| 20 |  | 7 − | 22 |   | 70 | 3 | + | 33 |
| 21 |  | 8 − | 30 |   | 71 | 2 | + | 35 |
| 22 |  | 9 − | 39 |   | 72 |  | 1 − | 1 |
| 23 | 10 | − | 29 |   | 73 |  | 2 − | 3 |
| 24 | 9 | − | 20 |   | 74 | 3 | | 0 |
| 25 |  | 8 − | 28 |   | 75 |  | 2 − | 2 |
| 26 |  | 9 − | 37 |   | 76 | 3 | + | 1 |
| 27 |  | 10 − | 47 |   | 77 | 2 | + | 3 |
| 28 | 11 | − | 36 |   | 78 | 1 | + | 1 |
| 29 | 10 | − | 26 |   | 79 |  | 1 − | 1 |
| 30 |  | 9 − | 35 |   | 80 |  | 2 − | 3 |
| 31 |  | 10 − | 45 |   | 81 |  | 3 − | 6 |
| 32 |  | 11 − | 56 |   | 82 | 4 | − | 2 |
| 33 | 12 | − | 44 |   | 83 |  | 3 − | 5 |
| 34 | 11 | − | 33 |   | 84 | 4 | − | 1 |
| 35 |  | 10 − | 43 |   | 85 |  | 3 − | 4 |
| 36 | 11 | − | 32 |   | 86 | 4 | | 0 |
| 37 | 10 | − | 22 |   | 87 | 3 | + | 3 |
| 38 | 9 | − | 13 |   | 88 | 2 | + | 5 |
| 39 | 8 | − | 5 |   | 89 |  | 1 − | 1 |
| 40 |  | 7 − | 12 |   | 90 |  | 2 − | 3 |
| 41 | 8 | − | 4 |   | 91 |  | 3 − | 6 |
| 42 |  | 7 − | 11 |   | 92 |  | 4 − | 10 |
| 43 |  | 8 − | 19 |   | 93 | 5 | − | 5 |
| 44 |  | 9 − | 28 |   | 94 |  | 4 − | 9 |
| 45 |  | 10 − | 38 |   | 95 |  | 5 − | 14 |
| 46 | 11 | − | 27 |   | 96 |  | 6 − | 20 |
| 47 | 10 | − | 17 |   | 97 | 7 | − | 13 |
| 48 | 9 | − | 8 |   | 98 | 6 | − | 7 |
| 49 | 8 | | 0 |   | 99 | 5 | − | 2 |
| 50 | 7 | + | 7 |   | 100 | 4 | + | 2 |

'Table 50 (p. 129) shows how we fare over the 100 trials of Table 46 (p. 115).'

'As usual the horizontal black lines indicate completed games?' asks Mr Optimist.

'Yes indeed.'

'So we've won 5 completed games for a profit of 1 unit for every Heads that occurs, or about 1/2 a unit for every trial. We complete a game on the 1st, 71st, 77th, 78th, and 88th trial, giving us a total net profit (*cwl*) of . . . 1+35+3+1+5=45 units. Not bad!' exclaims Mr Optimist.

'Until the 89th trial, which remains an *uncompleted* game even though on the 100th and last trial we win 2 units, giving us a net profit of 45+2=47 units. Our gross profit is 312 units, our gross loss 265 units, and the difference gives us the mentioned net win of 312−265=47 units. I might add that the average wager is 5.77 units,' I reply.

'I like the D'Alembert system!' exclaims Mr Optimist. 'It's slow and stately.'

'So is atherosclerosis. Let's see how well the D'Alembert does over the 50,000 spins of the Hartman sample,' I suggest. 'Let's divide the 50,000 spins into 5 games each 10,000 spins long. Remember here we're betting on Red to win against Black and zero to lose, i.e. the PC against us is 2.70 per cent. Table 51 (p. 130) sets out the results. The *ses.* column lists the consecutive numbers of the 5 sessions, the *ret.* column the total number of returns to equilibrium *during* each session which *end* in the necessary *plus* digression, and the *last* column the specific spin at which the last favorable return to equilibrium occurs.

TABLE 51

| ses. | ret. | last |
|------|------|------|
| 1 | 29 | 136 |
| 2 | 51 | 2,486 |
| 3 | 10 | 148 |
| 4 | 6 | 34 |
| 5 | 52 | 1,456 |

If we win about 1/2 a unit for every trial that occurs, then at the end of the 1st session we win (136/2)=68 units, but as there occurs no positive return to equilibrium after the 136th spin, our actual loss is *much more* than the extent of the minus digression that sets in at the 137th spin and continues to the 10,000th spin, the end of the game, and such a loss will be actually *enormous*, for let's remember that during this entire minus digression, in the manner of all *anti* progressions we're *increasing* our bet after every loss, i.e. after every Black and Zero. A similar comment may be made on

130

the results of the 2nd through 5th game each 10,000 spins long. So again I must repeat about the D'Alembert – our average stake is very small – until we encounter the inevitable minus digression, and in Table 51 (p. 130) the figures in the *last* column, when such digressions begin, indicate how dangerous the D'Alembert really is. If the figures in the *last* column could only be quite close to the *end* of each game, i.e. close to 10,000, we could have considerable faith in the system, but even the largest "last" return – the 2,486th spin of the 2nd game – is so far from the 10,000th spin that we realize the D'Alembert is a disastrous dream. All of which brings us to the ...'

*Cover*

'This is to some extent an *anti* system, and the progression we use on Heads (H) is even slower than that of the D'Alembert. Although both systems involve the simple arithmetical progression of $1-2-3-4-5-6$, in the Cover the rate of increase is much slower, and the rate of decrease is nil. As in the Labouchere systems we must write down figures on a sheet of paper and cancel them out according to the following rules:

'(1) At any given trial the amount of our bet equals *1 unit more* than the *smallest uncancelled* figures of whatever series of figures appears on our sheet of paper.

'(2) If the previous trial was a *loss*, then prior to the next bet we *add* this amount to the righthand end of the series.

'(3) If the previous trial was a *win*, then prior to the next bet we *cancel* the smallest uncancelled figure of the series.

'The following four points might also be remembered. During the game the gross gain equals the sum of all the cancelled figures plus a figure equaling their number. The gross loss equals the sum of all figures cancelled or uncancelled. And the net gain or loss equals the difference between these two sums. In addition at any given trial the sum of all the uncancelled figures plus a figure equaling their number comprises the amount which must be won in order to complete the game, i.e. to win 1 unit for every Head (H) that has occurred, or 1/2 a unit per trial, as one will.

'If we apply the system, like all the others, over the random permutation of H's and T's of Table 46 (p. 115), Mr Optimist, we'll find that the result is almost identical to that of the D'Alembert, Table 50 (p. 129), assuming again that every initial H is a plus

131

game, every initial T the start of a minus one. Thus according to the black horizontal lines of Table 50 (p. 129) we win 5 completed games using the Cover (or D'Alembert) progression. Of these 5 games 3 are minus (more than 1 trial) and 2 plus (exactly 1 trial – an H). As with the D'Alembert, so with the Cover it is the minus games which worry a player, for they may eventuate in an uncompleted game, and the *last* column of Table 51 (p. 130) shows how soon and easily one of these endless minus digressions may begin.

'If we follow the three-step instruction as enumerated above for the Cover, Mr Optimist, the cancellations on our sheet of paper for the 3 minus games of the Cover appear as in Table 52 (p. 132).

TABLE 52

COVER MINUS GAMES

1. 1̶–2̶–2̶–3̶–3̶–3̶–3̶–4–4–4–4–4–4–4–4–5̶–5̶–5̶–
   5̶–5̶–5̶–5̶–6̶–6̶–6̶–6̶–6̶–7–7–7–8̶–8̶–8̶–8̶–8

2. 1̶–2̶–3̶

3. 1̶–2̶–2̶–3̶–3̶

'The first minus game has, not surprisingly, exactly 35 cancelled figures, for each figure represents *two* completed bets. A figure *before* cancellation represents a loss (Tails) to that amount, and the same figure *after* cancellation represents a win (Heads) to that amount *plus 1 unit*. Hence 35 cancelled figures represent $2\times35=70$ bets, of which 35 are H's and 35 are T's.

'The second minus game is only 3 figures long, indicating the length of the game is $2\times3=6$ trials. If we artificially divest the second series of its cancellation, we have the series of actual losing bets, whose sum is . . . . $1+2+3=6$ units. And if we replace the cancellation, we have the series of actual winning bets, whose sum is . . . $2+3+4=9$ units. And $9-6=3$ units net profit, i.e. 1 unit for each of the 3 H's that have occurred, or 1/2 unit per trial, as one will.

'If the number of completed and uncompleted games are identical for both the D'Alembert and the Cover, and occur also at identical trials, and earn the same 1/2 unit per trial, what is the difference between the two systems?' inquiries Mr Optimist with impeccable logic.

'The difference is that as the stakes rise more slowly in the Cover it is, if only from this standpoint, a safer system. Thus in the game of

Table 50 (p. 129) the D'Alembert has a gross gain of 312 units, a gross loss of 265 units, and a difference or net gain of 47 units, whereas the Cover has a gross gain of 253 units, a gross loss of 209 units, and a difference or net gain of 44 units – the slight discrepancy owing itself only to the irrelevant matter of the H's of the last few trials of the session. Thus the average bet of the D'Alembert here is 5.77 units, of the Cover 4.62 units – a difference of $5.77 - 4.62 = 1.15$ units.

'Consequently my opinion, Mr Optimist, is that if you like fussing around with the intrigue of cancelling figures on a sheet of paper, pick the Cover. On the other hand if you want the same result but are willing to pay for mechanical simplicity with a larger average bet and therefore proportionately greater risk, pick the D'Alembert. Which would you choose?

'Frankly, I don't like either of them,' comments our friend. 'Why not just use the simple paroli?'

'That's what I feel. On the other hand perhaps you'll be bewitched by the whole process of the . . .'

*Blundell*

'Who was Blundell?' asks Mr Optimist.

'All we know is that Wilfred Blundell, another Britisher, was a resident of Monte Carlo in the 1880s, and he revealed his curious system to his countryman the Hon. Victor Bethell (1864–1927), who wrote it up in his amusing book, *Ten Days at Monte Carlo at the Bank's Expense* (London, 1898).

'The essence of the Blundell is that we play a series of games of *flat stakes* starting with *1* unit and not returning to a bet of 1 unit until we've wiped out all past losses, if any. Only after recouping all past losses may we start again with a bet of 1 unit. The Blundell is a very slow progression indeed. First we wager on Heads 1 unit for a certain number of trials, then 2 units for a certain number of trials, then 3 units for a certain number of trials, and so forth. Table 53 (p. 134) shows how the progression accelerates.

'Under the heading *Trials*, the *win* and *lose* columns indicate the rate at which we increase our wager of *only 1 unit* after every *minus* or *losing* game. Thus we bet 1 unit and keep doing so until having won 1 *trial before* having lost 10 *trials*. If the latter, our cumulative net loss (*cwl*) for this completed *minus* game is 10 units. Then we increase our bet to 2 units and keep playing until having won 5

133

TABLE 53

| bet | Trials win before | lose | Trials cwl per game | Units cwl per games |
|-----|-------------------|------|---------------------|---------------------|
| 1 | 1 | 10 | 10 | 10 |
| 2 | 5 | 10 | 20 | 30 |
| 3 | 10 | 10 | 30 | 60 |
| 4 | 15 | 10 | 40 | 100 |
| 5 | 20 | 10 | 50 | 150 |

*trials before* having lost 10 more *trials*. If the latter, our cumulative net loss (*cwl*) for the second completed *minus* game is 20 units. Then we increase our bet to 3 units and keep playing until having won 10 *trials before* having lost 10 more *trials*. If the latter, our *cwl* for the third completed *minus* game is 30 units. And so on until we've reached the arbitrary largest bet of 5 units and continue playing flat stakes of 5 units and either *recoup all previous losses in units* or suffer a final cumulative net loss (*cwl*) of 150 units for *all five* completed *minus* games.

'On the other hand, upon winning *any* one of the above games, we return immediately to a flat stake of 1 unit, i.e. we start playing the first game again.

'How does the Blundell compare with the other progressions when played over Table 46 (p. 115)?' asks Mr Optimist. 'I must say the system sounds both safe and easy to play.'

'The answer to your question, Mr Optimist, is disclosed by Table 54 (p. 135),' I reply. 'Counting the usual horizontal black lines, we note that there occur 9 completed games – 4 *plus* games and 5 *minus* ones – and 1 uncompleted game, beginning at the 79th trial. Of the completed games we note that only the second ends in a cumulative net loss – of 10 units. All the *plus* games end in a *cwl* of 1 unit except the third, which ends in a gain of 10 units. Hence the gain from all the completed games, *plus* and *minus*, is 17−10=7 units, and if we subtract, as we must the 2 units lost from the uncompleted game, our final profit for the whole session is 5 units.'

'I don't care what you said about comparing the D'Alembert to atherosclerosis,' cries out Mr Optimist in rebellion, 'I like the looks of the Blundell. It's obviously simple, requires no cancellation of a lot of figures, and the average amount staked is kept small.'

'I'm glad it pleases you,' I reply. 'But before we run off to the

TABLE 54

| n | w | l | cwl | | n | w | l | cwl |
|---|---|---|---|---|---|---|---|---|
| 1 | 1 | + | 1 | | 51 | 1 | + | 1 |
| 2 | | 1 − | 1 | | 52 | | 1 − | 1 |
| 3 | | 1 − | 2 | | 53 | | 1 − | 2 |
| 4 | | 1 − | 3 | | 54 | 1 | − | 1 |
| 5 | 1 | − | 2 | | 55 | 1 | | 0 |
| 6 | | 1 − | 3 | | 56 | | 1 − | 1 |
| 7 | | 1 − | 4 | | 57 | 1 | | 0 |
| 8 | | 1 − | 5 | | 58 | 1 | + | 1 |
| 9 | 1 | − | 4 | | 59 | | 1 − | 1 |
| 10 | | 1 − | 5 | | 60 | 1 | | 0 |
| 11 | 1 | − | 4 | | 61 | | 1 − | 1 |
| 12 | | 1 − | 5 | | 62 | | 1 − | 2 |
| 13 | | 1 − | 6 | | 63 | 1 | − | 1 |
| 14 | 1 | − | 5 | | 64 | | 1 − | 2 |
| 15 | | 1 − | 6 | | 65 | 1 | − | 1 |
| 16 | 1 | − | 5 | | 66 | | 1 − | 2 |
| 17 | | 1 − | 6 | | 67 | 1 | − | 1 |
| 18 | 1 | − | 5 | | 68 | 1 | | 0 |
| 19 | | 1 − | 6 | | 69 | 1 | + | 1 |
| 20 | | 1 − | 7 | | 70 | 1 | + | 1 |
| 21 | | 1 − | 8 | | 71 | 1 | + | 1 |
| 22 | | 1 − | 9 | | 72 | | 1 − | 1 |
| 23 | 1 | − | 8 | | 73 | | 1 − | 2 |
| 24 | 1 | − | 7 | | 74 | 1 | − | 1 |
| 25 | | 1 − | 8 | | 75 | | 1 − | 2 |
| 26 | | 1 − | 9 | | 76 | 1 | − | 1 |
| 27 | | 1 − | 10 | | 77 | 1 | | 0 |
| 28 | 2 | + | 2 | | 78 | 1 | + | 1 |
| 29 | 2 | + | 4 | | 79 | | 1 − | 1 |
| 30 | | 2 + | 2 | | 80 | | 1 − | 2 |
| 31 | | 2 | 0 | | 81 | | 1 − | 3 |
| 32 | | 2 − | 2 | | 82 | 1 | − | 2 |
| 33 | 2 | | 0 | | 83 | 1 | − | 3 |
| 34 | 2 | + | 2 | | 84 | 1 | − | 2 |
| 35 | | 2 | 0 | | 85 | | 1 − | 3 |
| 36 | 2 | + | 2 | | 86 | 1 | − | 2 |
| 37 | 2 | + | 4 | | 87 | 1 | − | 1 |
| 38 | 2 | + | 6 | | 88 | 1 | | 0 |
| 39 | 2 | + | 8 | | 89 | | 1 − | 1 |
| 40 | | 2 + | 6 | | 90 | | 1 − | 2 |
| 41 | 2 | + | 8 | | 91 | | 1 − | 3 |
| 42 | | 2 + | 6 | | 92 | | 1 − | 4 |
| 43 | | 2 + | 4 | | 93 | 1 | − | 3 |
| 44 | | 2 + | 2 | | 94 | | 1 − | 4 |
| 45 | | 2 | 0 | | 95 | | 1 − | 5 |
| 46 | 2 | + | 2 | | 96 | | 1 − | 6 |
| 47 | 2 | + | 4 | | 97 | 1 | − | 5 |
| 48 | 2 | + | 6 | | 98 | 1 | − | 4 |
| 49 | 2 | + | 8 | | 99 | 1 | − | 3 |
| 50 | 2 | + | 10 | | 100 | 1 | − | 2 |

gaming table to try it, let's ask ourselves how long can we keep betting the same stake *before* going on to a larger stake. I've taken the liberty of laying out the answers in Table 55 (p. 136).'

TABLE 55

| bet | P | Q |
|-----|------|------|
| 1 | 0.91 | 0.09 |
| 2 | 0.67 | 0.33 |
| 3 | 0.50 | 0.50 |
| 4 | 0.40 | 0.60 |
| 5 | 0.33 | 0.67 |

'The letter $P$ signifies the probability of winning one particular game, while $Q$ signifies the probability of having to go on to the next larger wager.

'Thus we have a 91 per cent chance of winning 1 unit, and a 9 per cent chance of having to go on to bet 2 units. After reaching a bet of 2 units, we have a 67 per cent chance of winning 5 units before having to go on to a bet of 3 units. After reaching a bet of 3 units, we have a 50 per cent chance of winning 10 units before having to go on to a bet of 4 units. After reaching a bet of 4 units, we have a 40 per cent chance of winning 15 units before having to go on to a bet of 5 units. And after having reached 5 units, we have a 33 per cent chance of winning 20 units before losing our last 10 units and ending with a total cumulative net loss of 150 units.

'Remember, however, that the Blundell system as presented in Tables 54 (p. 135) and 55 (p. 136) is calculated on the basis of a mathematically fair game. At the casino . . .'

'I know, I know . . . at the casino we play inevitably an unfair game, with the possible exception of Blackjack,' replies Mr Optimist. 'Still, I like the Blundell.'

'Your preferences are your own,' I respond. 'Now we go on to the . . .'

*Ascot*

'After whom is this system named?' asks Mr Optimist.

'Although the inventor is anonymous, the name refers to the race track at Ascot Heath, England,' I reply.

'How does it work?' asks our ever curious friend. 'I bet it's not so good as the Blundell.'

'First we write down on a sheet of paper a series comprised of an *odd* number of figures, such as 1–2–3, 1–2–3–4–5, or 1–2–3–4–5–6–7, etc.' I explain.

'I prefer the Blundell already,' inserts Mr Optimist.

'The rule is that our *first* bet is the *middle* figure of the series, our *last* either the *smallest* figure at the left or the *largest* figure at the right. For our example let's adopt the series 1–2–3–4–5–6–7. Hence our first wager is 4 units. If we win, our next bet will be 5 units. If we lose, our next bet will be 3 units. After that we continue to wager 1 unit more after every win and 1 unit less after every loss until reaching a bet of either 1 unit or 7 units. Naturally, if we reach a bet of 1 unit, we have lost $1+2+3+4=10$ units, but if we reach a bet of 7 units we have won $4+5+6+7=22$ units. Then we begin again with a bet of 4 units.

'Table 56 (p. 138) summarizes the results of the Ascot played over the session of 100 coin tosses comprising Table 46 (p. 115),' I continue. 'Counting the black horizontal lines, we note that there occur 8 completed games and no uncompleted game. Of these 8 games, 4 are winning ones – by definition ending in a bet of 7 units – and 4 are losing ones – by definition ending in a bet of 1 unit. As the cumulative net gain from all the former is $1+22+14+22=59$ units, and the cumulative net loss from all the latter is $12+15+9+21=57$ units, our final profit for the session is $59-57=2$ units.

'I like the Blundell better,' comments Mr Optimist. 'All that trouble just for 2 units!'

'At any trial the probability of *winning* a game is . . .

$$(1/2)^{r+1}$$

'and by the same token at any trial the probability of *losing* a game is also . . .

$$(1/2)^{r+1}$$

'Hence at the end of the 100 trials of Table 56 (p. 138) there occur $(1/32)(100)=3.14$ winning games and equally $(1/32)(100)=3.14$ losing games, or a total of $(2)(3.14)=6.28$ games all together. As you'll note, there occur in actuality in this session 8 games.

'In Table 57 (p. 139) we may compare the frequency of the

TABLE 56

| n | w | l | cwl | | n | w | l | cwl |
|---|---|---|---|---|---|---|---|---|
| 1 | 4 | + | 4 | | 51 | 4 | + | 4 |
| 2 | | 5 − | 1 | | 52 | | 5 − | 1 |
| 3 | | 4 − | 5 | | 53 | | 4 − | 5 |
| 4 | | 3 − | 8 | | 54 | 3 | − | 2 |
| 5 | 2 | − | 6 | | 55 | 4 | + | 2 |
| 6 | | 3 − | 9 | | 56 | | 5 − | 3 |
| 7 | | 2 − | 11 | | 57 | 4 | + | 1 |
| 8 | | 1 − | 12 | | 58 | 5 | + | 6 |
| 9 | 4 | + | 4 | | 59 | | 6 | 0 |
| 10 | | 5 − | 1 | | 60 | 5 | + | 5 |
| 11 | 4 | + | 3 | | 61 | | 6 − | 1 |
| 12 | | 5 − | 2 | | 62 | | 5 − | 6 |
| 13 | | 4 − | 6 | | 63 | 4 | − | 2 |
| 14 | 3 | − | 3 | | 64 | | 5 − | 7 |
| 15 | | 4 − | 7 | | 65 | 4 | − | 3 |
| 16 | 3 | − | 4 | | 66 | | 5 − | 8 |
| 17 | | 4 − | 8 | | 67 | 4 | − | 4 |
| 18 | 3 | − | 5 | | 68 | 5 | + | 1 |
| 19 | | 4 − | 9 | | 69 | 6 | + | 7 |
| 20 | | 3 − | 12 | | 70 | 7 | + | 14 |
| 21 | | 2 − | 14 | | 71 | 4 | + | 4 |
| 22 | | 1 − | 15 | | 72 | | 5 − | 1 |
| 23 | 4 | + | 4 | | 73 | | 4 − | 5 |
| 24 | 5 | + | 9 | | 74 | 3 | − | 2 |
| 25 | | 6 + | 3 | | 75 | | 4 − | 6 |
| 26 | | 5 − | 2 | | 76 | 3 | − | 3 |
| 27 | | 4 − | 6 | | 77 | 4 | + | 1 |
| 28 | 3 | − | 3 | | 78 | 5 | + | 6 |
| 29 | 4 | + | 1 | | 79 | | 6 | 0 |
| 30 | | 5 − | 4 | | 80 | | 5 − | 5 |
| 31 | | 4 − | 8 | | 81 | | 4 − | 9 |
| 32 | | 3 − | 11 | | 82 | 3 | − | 6 |
| 33 | 2 | − | 9 | | 83 | | 4 − | 10 |
| 34 | 3 | − | 6 | | 84 | 3 | − | 7 |
| 35 | | 4 − | 10 | | 85 | | 4 − | 11 |
| 36 | 3 | − | 7 | | 86 | 3 | − | 8 |
| 37 | 4 | − | 3 | | 87 | 4 | − | 4 |
| 38 | 5 | + | 2 | | 88 | 5 | + | 1 |
| 39 | 6 | + | 8 | | 89 | | 6 − | 5 |
| 40 | | 7 + | 1 | | 90 | | 5 − | 10 |
| 41 | 4 | + | 4 | | 91 | | 4 − | 14 |
| 42 | | 5 − | 1 | | 92 | | 3 − | 17 |
| 43 | | 4 − | 5 | | 93 | 2 | − | 15 |
| 44 | | 3 − | 8 | | 94 | | 3 − | 18 |
| 45 | | 2 − | 10 | | 95 | | 2 − | 20 |
| 46 | 1 | − | 9 | | 96 | | 1 − | 21 |
| 47 | 4 | + | 4 | | 97 | 4 | + | 4 |
| 48 | 5 | + | 9 | | 98 | 5 | + | 9 |
| 49 | 6 | + | 15 | | 99 | 6 | + | 15 |
| 50 | 7 | + | 22 | | 100 | 7 | + | 22 |

138

largest bet of 4 units with that of the smallest one of 1 unit,'
I conclude, 'but I'm sure I needn't warn you, Mr Optimist . . .'

'Oh, I know what you're going to say, as ever!' responds our friend. 'Over a session representing a mathematically unfair game the actuality of Table 57 (p. 139) would be far worse!'

TABLE 57

| bet | Actual | Theory |
|-----|--------|--------|
| 1 | 4 | 1.6 |
| 2 | 7 | 9.4 |
| 3 | 19 | 23.4 |
| 4 | 34 | 31.2 |
| 5 | 23 | 23.4 |
| 6 | 9 | 9.4 |
| 7 | 4 | 1.6 |
| | 100 | 100.0 |

'It most certainly would be!' I exclaim. 'I'm glad you've grasped the essential!'

'Between the Ascot and the Blundell, however, I still prefer the latter,' asserts Mr Optimist.

'Good enough. Then that leads us to the last system, called the . . .'

*Fitzroy*

'Who is Mr Fitzroy?' Inquires Mr Optimist promptly.

'Please, sir – we're speaking again of another aristocrat!' I reply.

'Good heavens, I didn't know!' responds Mr Optimist.

'The system in question was named after the Hon. Fitzroy S. Erskine (1870–1914), although it's sometimes called the *Rosslyn*, however, after Erskine's elder brother, the 5th Earl of Rosslyn (1869–1939). Both gentlemen were frequent visitors to Monte Carlo, and once the Earl of Rosslyn bet Sir Hiram S. Maxim (1840–1916), a native-born American and inventor of the famous Maxim machine gun, that the "Fitzroy" is an infallible system,' I continue.

'Who won?' asks Mr Optimist.

'The casino,' I reply.

'How sad!' exclaims Mr Optimist. 'What are the details?'

'The details are laid bare in Table 58 (p. 140),' I go on. 'The progression is very rapid, for with one exception, we must increase our bet by 1 unit after *every* trial, the exception being the second trial of every minus game – one beginning with a Tails (T) – whose bet is 3 units rather than 2. Thus the progression for every minus game is 1–3–4–5–6–7–8–9 . . . etc., until we've won 2 units for every Heads (H) that occurs, or 1 unit per trial, as one will.

'As usual we'll play the progression over the actual coin tosses

## Table 58

| n | w | l | cwl | | n | w | l | cwl |
|---|---|---|---|---|---|---|---|---|
| 1 | 1 | + | 1 | | 51 | 1 | + | 1 |
| 2 | | 1 − | 1 | | 52 | | 1 − | 1 |
| 3 | | 3 − | 4 | | 53 | | 3 − | 4 |
| 4 | | 4 − | 8 | | 54 | 4 | | 0 |
| 5 | 5 | − | 3 | | 55 | 4 | + | 4 |
| 6 | | 6 − | 9 | | 56 | | 1 − | 1 |
| 7 | | 7 − | 16 | | 57 | 3 | + | 2 |
| 8 | | 8 − | 24 | | 58 | 1 | + | 1 |
| 9 | 9 | − | 15 | | 59 | | 1 − | 1 |
| 10 | | 10 − | 25 | | 60 | 3 | + | 2 |
| 11 | 11 | − | 14 | | 61 | | 1 − | 1 |
| 12 | | 12 − | 26 | | 62 | | 3 − | 4 |
| 13 | | 13 − | 39 | | 63 | 4 | | 0 |
| 14 | 14 | − | 25 | | 64 | | 5 − | 5 |
| 15 | | 15 − | 40 | | 65 | 6 | + | 1 |
| 16 | 16 | − | 24 | | 66 | | 5 − | 4 |
| 17 | | 17 − | 41 | | 67 | 6 | + | 2 |
| 18 | 18 | − | 23 | | 68 | 6 | + | 8 |
| 19 | | 19 − | 42 | | 69 | 1 | + | 1 |
| 20 | | 20 − | 62 | | 70 | 1 | + | 1 |
| 21 | | 21 − | 83 | | 71 | 1 | + | 1 |
| 22 | | 22 − | 105 | | 72 | | 1 − | 1 |
| 23 | 23 | − | 82 | | 73 | | 3 − | 4 |
| 24 | 24 | − | 58 | | 74 | 4 | | 0 |
| 25 | | 25 − | 83 | | 75 | 5 | − | 5 |
| 26 | | 26 − | 109 | | 76 | 6 | + | 1 |
| 27 | | 27 − | 136 | | 77 | 5 | + | 6 |
| 28 | 28 | − | 108 | | 78 | 1 | + | 1 |
| 29 | 29 | − | 79 | | 79 | | 1 − | 1 |
| 30 | | 30 − | 109 | | 80 | | 3 − | 4 |
| 31 | | 31 − | 140 | | 81 | | 4 − | 7 |
| 32 | | 32 − | 172 | | 82 | 5 | − | 2 |
| 33 | 33 | − | 139 | | 83 | | 6 − | 8 |
| 34 | 34 | − | 105 | | 84 | 7 | − | 1 |
| 35 | | 35 − | 140 | | 85 | | 8 − | 9 |
| 36 | 36 | − | 104 | | 86 | 9 | | 0 |
| 37 | 37 | − | 67 | | 87 | 9 | + | 9 |
| 38 | 38 | − | 29 | | 88 | 1 | + | 1 |
| 39 | 39 | + | 10 | | 89 | | 1 − | 1 |
| 40 | | 30 − | 20 | | 90 | | 3 − | 4 |
| 41 | 40 | + | 20 | | 91 | | 4 − | 8 |
| 42 | | 22 − | 2 | | 92 | | 5 − | 13 |
| 43 | | 41 − | 43 | | 93 | 6 | − | 7 |
| 44 | | 42 − | 85 | | 94 | | 7 − | 14 |
| 45 | | 43 − | 128 | | 95 | | 8 − | 22 |
| 46 | 44 | − | 84 | | 96 | | 9 − | 31 |
| 47 | 45 | − | 39 | | 97 | 10 | − | 21 |
| 48 | 46 | + | 7 | | 98 | 11 | − | 10 |
| 49 | 41 | + | 48 | | 99 | 12 | + | 2 |
| 50 | 1 | + | 1 | | 100 | 10 | + | 12 |

listed in Table 46 (p. 115). As I mentioned, the results of the Fitzroy during this session of 100 trials comprises Table 58 (p. 140). Of the 17 games 9 are plus ones – consisting of a single H – and 8 are minus ones – beginning with a T and ending with an H. At the end of any actual session close to half the games will be plus and half minus. As the cumulative net profit from the 9 plus games is naturally 9 units, and that from the 8 minus games is $48+4+2+2+8+6+9+12=91$ units, our final profit for the session itself is $9+91=100$ units, i.e. 2 units for every H that occurs, or 1 unit per trial, as one will.

'Although the Fitzroy is successful over Table 58 (p. 140), the theoretical goal of trying to make as much as 1 unit profit for every trial played reveals it to be a very dangerous system indeed,' I conclude.

'It's quite understandable why Lord Rosslyn lost the bet to Sir Hiram Maxim,' replies Mr Optimist. 'Lord Rosslyn should have tried his system out on paper first.'

'Oh, he did,' I respond, 'but the series of trials was too short and, unlike those from the Hartman sample, evidently didn't take zero into account. Just the same, even in a mathematically fair game, like that of Table 58 (p. 140), it's obviously too dangerous a system. During the long minus game from the 2nd to the 49th trial the average bet of the Fitzroy is as much as 24.42 units! It might be mentioned that for any Fitzroy minus game the average theoretical wager is very roughly $(n/2)+1$ units, with $n$ signifying the length of the minus game.'

'You know, of all the games in this chapter the one I still like best is the . . .'

'Blundell!' I respond. 'Because it's so simple?'

'No, because it's the only one named after a commoner – he has my republican sympathies!' answers Mr Optimist.

# CHAPTER XII

# American Roulette

'Except for the double zero, what is the difference between American roulette and Monte-Carlo or European roulette?' asks Mr Optimist.

'A great deal of difference. Although both games have the 36 numbers from 1 to 36, the zero *plus* the double zero on the American roulette wheel – giving 38 numbers in all – allows the Bank a percentage of $(2/38)(100)=5.26$ per cent on *all* bets except one, which I'll get to in a moment. In contrast, the Monte-Carlo or European roulette has just the *single* zero, allowing the Bank a percentage of $(1/37)(100)=2.70$ per cent on *all* bets except the even-money chances, which again I'll get to in a moment.

'The unique bet at American roulette is the one where we bet precisely on the *five* numbers zero, double zero, 1, 2, and 3. If on the next spin one of these five numbers occurs, then the Bank's pay-off is 5 to 1, resulting in a PC of 7.89 per cent,' I conclude.

'Well then, what's the point of betting on those five particular numbers?' asks Mr Optimist.

'There isn't any point – that's why I brought the matter up,' I reply.

'Well, at American roulette how about the PC for the even-money chances, like red, black, high, low, odd, or even?' asks our friend.

'They have against them the same redoubtable PC as bets on the various numbers, in whatever combination – 5.26 per cent,' I warn.

'Why that's terribly high!' exclaims Mr Optimist. 'I recall from the Hartman sample the adverse effect of even a PC of 2.70 per cent – in the 500 games each 100 spins long, we broke even at the

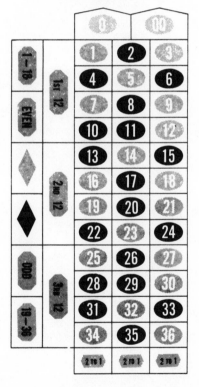

*American Roulette*

end of 40 games, we won something at the end of 187 games, and we lost something at the end of 273 games.'

'That's right – although it's important to remember that, although I referred to the Monte-Carlo "In-Prison rule" in Chapter VII (p. 55), *for the even-money chances alone* this "In-Prison rule", whose mechanics I explain in the Appendix, reduces the PC of 2.70 per cent to the far more reasonable 1.41 per cent,' I conclude.

'All right, given that at American roulette the PC is 5.26 per cent on all bets excepts the one on zero, double zero, 1, 2, and 3, which is 7.89 per cent, and at Monte-Carlo or European roulette the PC is 2.70 per cent on the numbers and 1.41 per cent on the even-money chances, how does a week at American roulette compare with one at Monte-Carlo roulette?' asks Mr Optimist.

'I'm afraid a comparison disfavors American roulette rather badly,' I reply. 'All you have to do is compare the theoretical results of American roulette, laid out in Table 59 (p. 143), to those of Monte-Carlo roulette, laid out in Table 15 (p. 33). Each game is played over the identical theoretical week of 3,862 spins. Although you may profitably compare any two of the eight columns in each table, the far righthand one gives a rough idea of how really invidious is the disadvantage of American roulette compared to its Monte-Carlo cousin,' I declare.

TABLE 59

$n = 3862$

| | 0.25 | 0.25 | | 0.25 | | 0.25 |
|---|---|---|---|---|---|---|
| $P$ | more than | between | | between | | more than |
| 1/38 | −441 | −441 | −203 | −203 | 35 | 35 |
| 2/38 | −370 | −370 | −203 | −203 | −36 | −36 |
| 3/38 | −336 | −336 | −203 | −203 | −70 | −70 |
| 4/38 | −320 | −320 | −203 | −203 | −86 | −86 |
| 5/38 | −409 | −409 | −203 | −203 | −201 | −201 |
| 6/38 | −298 | −298 | −203 | −203 | −108 | −108 |
| 12/38 | −263 | −263 | −203 | −203 | −143 | −143 |
| 18/38 | −246 | −246 | −203 | −203 | −160 | −160 |
| 24/38 | −234 | −234 | −203 | −203 | −172 | −172 |

'Well, after looking over the contents of both tables,' responds Mr Optimist, 'I have only one question. In American gambling casinos is there some game other than roulette, with its terrible PC

143

of 5.26 per cent, that offers a more favorable PC? Is there any American game, for example, that offers the relatively small PC of 1.41 per cent we find on the even-money chances of Monte-Carlo roulette?'

'Indeed there is. The game is craps, and if you'll be so kind as to continue reading, Mr Optimist . . .'

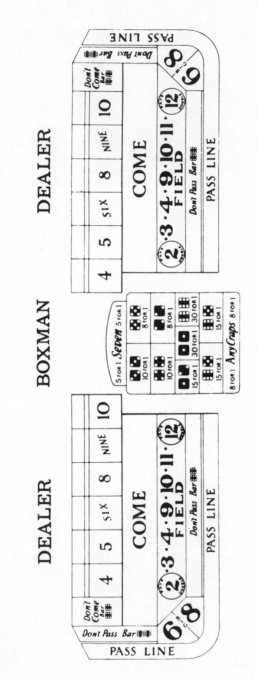

*Craps*

# CHAPTER XIII

# Craps

'This is the game for me!' cries out Mr Optimist. 'I like all the action – the stickman chanting his rigmarole, the players whooping it up, bets constantly coming and going!'

'There are some bets that are relatively worthwhile. Most of them are terrible. All told there are 16 standard bets on a typical craps layout. Here are the rules for each bet including the Bank's percentage. After the rules and PC's we'll see how, *at the end* of a typical theoretical week of 3,862 dice throws, all the bets at craps compare with all those at Monte-Carlo and American roulette. Then we can quickly conclude which games and bets to play and which strategies or systems to adopt. How's that for positive thinking?'

'Lead on!' cries Mr Optimist.

'For clarity I'll explain the bets under two headings, the first concerning wagers won or lost in *one or more* throws of the dice, the second concerning those won or lost in *just one* throw of the dice,' I continue.

I.   Wagers won or lost in *one or more* throws

1. *Pass Line*

'The Pass bet is undoubtedly the most popular bet at craps. It's an even-money chance like the red at roulette, and its PC is the relatively small 1.41 per cent' I comment.

'And as at Monte-Carlo roulette the PC against the even-money chances, like red, is also 1.41 per cent,' interjects Mr Optimist, 'are the two bets absolutely identical in every way?'

'Absolutely identical,' I reply. 'A bet on Pass wins on the first throw, called the *come-out*, if the *shooter*, the player casting the dice, throws a total of 7 or 11 on the first cast, but loses if the player throws either 2, 3, or 12 (craps) on the first cast.'

'Is there any advantage to being the player called the *shooter*?' asks Mr Optimist.

'None whatsoever. If the casino had a machine throwing the pair of dice, it would serve just as well,' I reply. 'To continue. If the shooter doesn't win with an immediate 7 or 11, or lose with an immediate 2, 3, or 12, the only six remaining totals are 4, 5, 6, 8, 9, or 10, called *point numbers*. Whichever one of these is thrown, it becomes the *shooter's point*, and he must continue to throw the dice until throwing either his point again or a 7. If he throws his point *before* throwing a 7, i.e. if he *passes* or *makes* his point, then a bet on the Pass Line wins. On the other hand, if he throws a 7 *before* his point, i.e. if he *sevens out*, a bet on the Pass Line loses. It should also be remembered that once you place a wager on the Pass Line, the bet can't be removed until won, but a player may *add* to it as many more units as he wants at any time. In addition so that all the players will know at all times which *one* of the six point numbers the shooter is trying to throw, one of the *dealers* places a red *dice buck* on the appropriate number among the six numbered squares or *boxes* located on the stickman's and dealer's side of the table. As you'll recall from Chapter III, Mr Optimist, the definitions of the letters $p$, $q$, $b$, and $y$ are as follows. The letter $p$ signifies the probability of winning in one trial, $q$ the probability of losing in one trial, $b$ the Bank's pay-off odds-to-1, and $y$ the Bank's percentage represented as a decimal fraction, which, if multiplied by 100, gives us the Bank's percentage.

'For the Pass Line we have $p=(244/495)=0.492929\ldots$, $q=(251/495)=0.5070707\ldots$, $b=1$ – i.e. the pay-off odds are 1 to 1, i.e. an even-money chance, and $y=(7/495)=0.014141$, and $(0.014141)(100)=1.41$ per cent.

## 2. *Don't Pass Line* (bar 6–6)

'Excluding the matter of the Bank's percentage, just as Heads is to Tails, red is to black, so Pass is to Don't Pass. And as the PC of Don't Pass is 1.40 per cent, for *all practical purposes* the bet is identical to Pass.

'If the shooter on the come-out throws a total of 2 or 3, a bet on Don't Pass wins. If the shooter throws an immediate 7 or 11, however, a Don't Pass bet loses. If the shooter throws a pair of sixes for a total of 12, it's a *stand-off* or tie, and a Don't Pass bet neither wins nor loses.

'If the shooter on the first cast throws neither 2, 3, 7, 11, or 12, then the only six remaining totals are the point numbers 4, 5, 6, 8, 9, and 10.

'If the shooter throws a 7 *before* his point, a bet on Don't Pass wins. But if he throws his point *before* a 7, then a bet on Don't Pass loses. It should also be remembered that once you place a wager on the Don't Pass Line, the bet may be removed at any time, but a player may *never add* to it more units.

'For the Don't Pass Line we have $p=(949/1925)=0.492987$, $q=(976/1925)=0.5070129, b=1$, and $y=(27/1925=0.014025\ldots$ and $(0.014025)(100)=1.40$ per cent.

## 1. *Come*

'This bet is identical in every way, practical and mathematical, with a bet on the Pass Line. A bet on Come may *not* be made, however, until *after* the shooter has established his own point number. Then if the shooter's very next cast is 7 or 11, a Come bet wins. If the shooter's very next bet is 2, 3, or 12, a Come bet loses. If none of these five totals are thrown, then the very next number has to be either 4, 5, 6, 8, 9, or 10. Whichever is thrown, it becomes the private point number of the player who has placed a bet on Come, and the dealer will immediately shift his bet from the Come space to the appropriate number in one of the six numbered squares or boxes located above the Come space. If the shooter throws subsequently the Come player's own point before a 7, then the Come player wins. On the other hand, if the shooter throws a 7 before the Come player's point, the Come player loses. It should be remembered that, once placed on Come, a wager may not be removed until won, but a player may *add* to it as many more units as he wants at any time.

## 2. *Don't Come* (bar 6–6)

'This bet is identical in every way, practical and mathematical, with a bet on the Don't Pass Line. A bet on Don't Come may not be made, however, until after a shooter has established his own point number. Then a bet on Don't Come wins, if the shooter's very next cast is 2 or 3, but if it is a 7 or 11, a bet on Don't Come loses. If the shooter throws a pair of sixes for a total of 12, it's a stand-off or tie, and a Don't Come bet neither wins nor loses.

'If the shooter on the first cast throws neither 2, 3, 7, 11, or 12, then he must throw one of the six remaining totals, i.e. 4, 5, 6, 8, 9, 10, and the number thrown becomes his private point. Henceforth the rules are the same as for Don't Pass.

### 3. *Don't Pass Line* (bar 1–2)

'If the casino bars 1–2 instead of 6–6, this increases the Bank's percentage on the Don't Pass Line from 1.41 per cent to 4.39 per cent because the frequency of the stand-off is doubled.

'What should I do then?' asks Mr Optimist.

'Don't play it. There is no need to. Play the Pass Line instead, for its PC remains always 1.41 per cent,' I reply.

'For the Don't Pass Line (bar 1–2) we have $p=(447/935)=0.4780748$, $q=(488/935)=0.5219251$, $b=1$, $y=(41/935)=0.043850$, and $(0.043850)(100)=4.39$ per cent.

### 4. *Big 6 or Big 8*

'To make this wager just place your bet on either of the spaces marked Big 6 or Big 8. Whichever of the two numbers a gambler may choose, he wins if the shooter throws that number *before* throwing a 7, and conversely loses if the shooter throws a 7 *before* throwing the player's number. In other words, the player has chosen either 6 or 8 as his own private point number.

'For the Big 6 or Big 8 we have $p=(5/11)$ 0.454545 ... $q=(6/11)=0.545454$ ..., $b=1$, $y=(1/11)=0.090909$ ..., and $(1/11)(100)=9.09$ per cent.

### 5. *Place bet: Number 4 or 10*

'After the shooter has thrown his own point, a gambler may ask the dealer to "place" a bet in the square above either the 4 or 10 point number.

'Then if the shooter casts this number *before* a 7, the player wins, but if the shooter throws a 7 *before* the player's own place number, the player loses.

'For the mathematical values we have $p=(1/3)=0.3333$ ..., $q=(2/3)=6666$ ..., $b=1.8$, $y=(1/15)=0.06667$, and $(0.06667)(100)=6.67$ per cent.

148

## 6. *Place bet: Number 5 or 9*

'Same rules as for Place bets 4 or 10.

'For the mathematical values we have $p=(2/5)=0.40$, $q=(3/5)=0.60$, $b=1.4$, $y=(1/25)=0.0400$, and $=(0.0400)(100)$ $=4.00$ per cent.

## 7. *Place bet: Number 6 or 8*

'Same rules as for Place bets 4 or 10.

'For the mathematical values we have $p=(5/11)=0.4545\ldots$, $q=(6/11)=5454\ldots$, $b=1.167$, $y=(1/66)=0.01515\ldots$, and $(0.01515)(100)=1.52$ per cent.

## 8. *Take the Odds*

'Along with Lay the Odds, this is the most favorable bet on the crap table, with a PC of only 0.85 per cent. As most players seem to be ignorant of its existence, Take the Odds is unprofitably neglected.

'The wager is actually a combination of *two bets*, a regular one on the *Pass Line*, with a $p$ value of $(244/495)$ and a PC of 1.41 per cent, and a second one on the *unmarked* green felt next to the Pass Line, with a $p$ value of $(196/495)=0.3959595\ldots$ and a PC of 0 per cent, i.e. the casino has NO advantage whatsoever *individually* over this "side" bet.

'To Take the Odds first place a bet on Pass. Then as soon as the shooter throws a *point*, tell the dealer, "Odds", and place a second wager of the same amount next to your Pass bet.

'As Take the Odds is obviously an advantageous bet for the player, we'll talk more about it anon when we discuss strategies and systems for craps.

'Combining the mathematical values of *both* Pass and Take the Odds, we have $p=(1124/2475)=0.454141\ldots$, $q=(1351/2475)=0.5458585\ldots$, $y=(7/825)=0.00848484\ldots$, and $(0.008484)(100)=0.85$ per cent.

'As for the value of $b$, the Take-the-Odds bet is paid off at *correct* odds, i.e. if the shooter's point is 4 or 10, the Odds bet is paid off at 2 to 1, if 5 or 9, at 3 to 2, and if 6 or 8, at 6 to 5.

## 9. *Lay the Odds*

'The same as Take the Odds except that you place your second bet, whose $p$ value is $(949/1925)=0.492987$ and a PC of 0 per cent,

149

next to a first one on *Don't Pass*. As this is a rather rare bet, ask the dealer for assistance.

'Combining the mathematical values of both Don't Pass and Lay the Odds, we have $p=(689/1353)=0.5092387$, $q=(664/1353)=0.4907612$, $y=(27/3245)=0.0083204$), and $(0.0083204) (100)=0.83$ per cent.

'As for the value of $b$, the Lay-the Odds bet is paid off at *correct* odds, i.e. if the shooter's point is 4 or 10, the Odds bet is paid off at 1 to 2, if 5 or 9, at 2 to 3, and if 6 or 8, at 5 to 6.

## 10. *Hardway 4 or 10*

'Place your bet in the rectangle, in the center of the layout, containing a pair of dice showing two 2's or two 5's, according to your choice. You win if the shooter throws that specific combination of double numbers *before* either a 7 or the same total in any other combination, and conversely you'll lose if the shooter throws either a 7 or the same total in any other combination *before* that specific combination of double numbers.

'For Hardway 4 or 10 we have $p=(1/9)$, $q=(8/9)$, $b=7$, $y=(1/9)=0.1111\ldots$, and $(0.1111) (100)=11.11$ per cent.

## 11. *Hardway 6 or 8*

'Place your bet in the rectangle, in the center of the layout, containing a pair of dice showing two 3's or two 4's, according to your choice. You win if the shooter throws that specific combination of double numbers *before* either a 7 or the same total in any other combination, and conversely you'll lose if the shooter throws either a 7 or the same total in any other combination *before* that specific combination of double numbers.

'For Hardway 6 or 8 we have $p=(1/11)=0.090909$, $q=(10/11)=0.9090909\ldots$, $b=9$, $y=(1/11)=0.09090909$, and $(0.090909) (100)=9.09$ per cent.

## 12. *Hardway 6 or 8*

'Just as some casinos, to increase their PC, bar 1–2 rather than 6–6 (or 1–1) on the Don't Pass Line, so others, to achieve the same goal, pay off on Hardway 6 or 8 only *7 to 1* rather than *9 to 1*.

'Under this unfavorable circumstance we have $p=(1/11)=0.090909$, $q=(10/11)=0.9090909\ldots$, $b=7$,

$y = (3/11) = 0.2727272 \ldots$, and $(0.27272727)(100) = 27.27$ per cent.

## II. Wagers won or lost in *exactly one* throw

### 13. *Field*

'Place your bet in the large rectangle marked *Field*. Your bet wins after the shooter's *very next cast* if he throws a total of either 2, 3, 4, 9, 10, 11, or 12 and conversely loses if he throws a total of either 5, 6, 7, or 8.

'Although the player has 7 numbers in his favor, and only 4 in his disfavor, the probability of the 7 favorable numbers is only $(16/36) = 0.4444 \ldots$, whereas that of the 4 unfavorable numbers is as large as $(20/36) = 0.55555$, and their difference is the PC of 11.11 per cent.

'Hence to make the Field more appealing some casinos pay off at 1 to 1 on 3, 4, 9, 10, and 11 – and 2 to 1 on 2 and 12 – which decreases the PC from 11.11 per cent to $(2/36) = 0.05555$, or 5.56 per cent.

'At any rate for the more unfavorable PC we have $p = 0.472$, $q = 0.528, b = 1, y = (2/36) = 0.05555\ldots$, and $(0.0555)(100) = 5.56$ per cent.

### 14. *Double Aces or Sixes*

'Place your bet in the small rectangle, in the middle of the layout, containing a pair of dice showing two aces or two sixes, according to your choice. Your bet wins after the shooter's *very next cast* if he throws any combination totalling either 2 or 12, and conversely loses if he throws any other total.

'For Double Aces or Sixes we have $p = (1/36) = 0.027777\ldots$, $q = (35/36) = 0.972222 \ldots$, $b = 29$, $y = (1/6) = 0.16666 \ldots$, and $(0.16666)(100) = 16.67$ per cent.

### 15. *Three or Eleven*

'Place your bet in the small rectangle, in the middle of the layout, containing a pair of dice showing a total of either 3 or 11, according to your choice. Your bet wins after the shooter's *very next cast* if he throws either of these totals, and you lose if he throws any other total.

151

'For Three or Eleven we have $p=(1/18)=0.05555$ ..., $q=(17/18)=0.94444$ ..., $b=14$, $y=(1/6)=0.16666$, and $(0.16666)$ $(100)=16.67$ per cent.

## 16. *Seven*

'Place your bet in the small rectangle, in the middle of the layout, containing a pair of dice showing a total of 7. Your bet wins after the shooter's *very next cast* if he throws a total of 7, and you lose if he throws any other total.

'For Seven we have $p=(1/6)=0.16666$ ..., $q=(5/6)=0.83333$ ..., $b=4$, $y=(1/6)=0.16666$ ..., and $(16666)$ $(100)=16.67$ per cent.

## 17. *Any Craps*

'Place your bet in the small rectangle, at the bottom of the middle of the layout, marked *Any Craps*. Your bet wins after the shooter's *very next cast* if he throws a total of either 2, 3 or 12, and conversely you lose if he throws any other total.

'For Any Craps we have $p=(1/9)=0.1111$ ..., $q=(8/9)=0.8888$ ..., $b=7$, $y=(1/9)=0.1111$, and $(0.1111)$ $(100)=11.11$ per cent – or in other words Any Craps and Hardway 4 or 10 are absolutely identical in every way.

\* \* \* \*

'As I mentioned, Mr Optimist, after the foregoing rules and PC's etc. for the 16 different bets at craps come the results in Table 60 (p. 153) for each of these bets *at the end* of a theoretical week of 3,682 dice throws.

'So you may easily compare all the bets at craps with all those at either American or Monte-Carlo roulette, which are sum-marized in exactly the same way in Tables 15 (p. 33) and 59 (p. 143), I've used the same number of trials – 3,862 – for all three games. The only exception is that for crap bets 1 and 2 – the Pass, Come, Don't Pass, and Don't Come bets – I've used 3,702 throws so that you may make an exact comparison between these and any of the six even-money chances – say red – at Monte-Carlo roulette.

'You'll recall, Mr Optimist, how we read this standard table for one week's play at the two other games. I divided the probabilities of winning and losing into quarters, whose results in Table 60 (p. 153) are listed in the usual six columns, which we read horizontally from right to left beginning with the top of the 1st column on the right.

'Thus *at the end* of a week at craps, at bet #1 – Pass or Come – we have a probability of 25 per cent of losing between 15 units and possibly winning some *indefinite* amount, of a second 25 per cent of losing between these 15 units and 52 units, of a third 25 per cent of losing between the latter 52 units and 89 units, and a fourth and final 25 per cent of losing more than the latter 89 units.

'For bet #2 – Don't Pass or Don't Come – we read across the same way beginning again with the righthand column but reading horizontally from right to left along the second row of figures down. As we note, the mathematical results of row #2 are identical with #1, because all the mathematical values of the bets – the PC, $p$, $q$, and $b$ – happen to be identical.

'For bet #3 – Don't Pass (bar 1–2) – we read horizontally across the third row down. As I mentioned, Mr Optimist, this is a bad bet, because barring the 1–2 instead of 1–1 raises the PC from 1.41 per cent to 4.39 per cent. Thus we have a probability of 25 per cent of losing between 127 units and possibly winning some indefinite amount, of a second 25 per cent of losing between these 127 units

TABLE 60

$n=3862$

| | $p$ | 0.25 more than | 0.25 between | | 0.25 between | | 0.25 more than |
|---|---|---|---|---|---|---|---|
| 1 | 244/495 | − 89 | − 89 | − 52 | − 52 | − 15 | − 15 |
| 2 | 949/1925 | − 89 | − 89 | − 52 | − 52 | − 15 | − 15 |
| 3 | 447/935 | −213 | −213 | −170 | −170 | −127 | −127 |
| 4 | 5/11 | −396 | −396 | −351 | −351 | −306 | −306 |
| 5 | 1/3 | −315 | −315 | −258 | −258 | −201 | −201 |
| 6 | 2/5 | −205 | −205 | −155 | −155 | −105 | −105 |
| 7 | 5/11 | −104 | −104 | − 59 | − 59 | − 14 | − 14 |
| 8 | 1124/2475 | − 81 | − 81 | − 35 | − 35 | 11 | 11 |
| 9 | 689/1353 | − 72 | − 72 | − 32 | − 32 | 8 | 8 |
| 10 | 1/9 | −544 | −544 | −429 | −429 | −314 | −314 |
| 11 | 1/11 | −479 | −479 | −351 | −351 | −223 | −223 |
| 12 | 1/11 | −938 | −938 | −810 | −810 | −682 | −682 |
| 13 | 4/9 | −261 | −261 | −215 | −215 | −169 | −169 |
| 14 | 1/36 | −868 | −868 | −644 | −644 | −420 | −420 |
| 15 | 1/18 | −802 | −802 | −644 | −644 | −486 | −486 |
| 16 | 1/6 | −734 | −734 | −644 | −644 | −554 | −554 |

153

and losing 170 units, of a third 25 per cent of losing between the latter 170 units and 213 units, and a fourth and final 25 per cent of losing more than 213 units.'

'Glancing down the very righthand column,' declares Mr Optimist, 'I notice that after the whole week of 3,862 casts only the 8th and 9th bets – Take the Odds and Lay the Odds – show any positive results – a probability of 25 per cent of gaining more than respectively 11 and 8 units. It isn't much, but it's something!'

'That's absolutely correct, and your observation brings me to the general discussion of the best strategies for craps,' I reply. 'Up till now, having calculated the very low PC's of respectively 0.85 per cent and 0.83 per cent at Take the Odds and Lay the Odds, many writers on gambling assert something like, "At craps, or any game, pick the bet with the smallest possible PC against you and just wager on it. There is nothing more to discuss". So far as I'm concerned, there is a great deal more to discuss. Although to avoid repetition most of the discussion on gambling strategy I postpone appropriately until my final chapter, *Conclusions*, in the matter of craps in particular there are several very important points that must be brought up.

'The first point, Mr Optimist, is that as the difference between the PC's of Take the Odds and Lay the Odds is only 0.01604 per cent *for practical gambling purposes* either of these bets is as good as the other one. And as so few gamblers ever bet Lay the Odds, there are some dealers who don't even know what the bet means. So just forget about Lay the Odds. That leaves us with Take the Odds, which we'll get to in a moment.

'If you glance down the righthand column of Table 60 (p. 153), you'll notice quickly that besides the two Odds bets, i.e. #8 and #9, the only *three other bets that a serious gambler should consider are bets* #1, #2, and #7. As we recall, bet #7 is Place bet Number 6 or 8, and the PC is 1.52 per cent. But as the difference between this PC and #1, Pass, is only 0.10101 per cent, again *for practical gambling purposes* just forget about #7, Place bet Number 6 or 8.

'Once more glancing down the righthand column of Table 60 (p. 153), you'll notice how the large PC's of *all* the other bets renders their consideration *simply out of the question* for any gambler trying to make money. The smallest loss is 105 units for Place bet Number 4 or 10, and the largest is 682 units for #12, Hardway 6 or 8.

'That leaves us, Mr Optimist, with #1 – Pass and Come – and #8

– Take the Odds. Now if we go by some other writers, we say to ourselves, "As the PC on #8 is only 0.85 per cent compared to that on #1, which is 1.41 per cent, then we eliminate #1". As I mentioned, my friend, the strategy at craps isn't that simple.

'First of all you'll recall that in my description of #8 – Take the Odds – I said it's really a combination of *two* bets, a regular one of 1 unit on the *Pass Line*, whose PC is 1.41 per cent, and an adjacent one of 1 unit, the *Odds* bet, on the unmarked green felt next to the Pass bet, whose PC is 0 per cent, i.e. over this *side* bet itself the casino has NO PERCENTAGE advantage whatsoever.

'Unfortunately although the combination of the TWO bets lowers the PC for *both* bets together to an average 0.85 per cent, to obtain the latter desirable PC we must bet TWO units every time we make the bet,' I conclude. 'In other words, we're forced to DOUBLE THE SIZE of our bet.'

'Is that bad?' asks Mr Optimist.

'It's not so much that it *is* "bad" as that it might *be* "bad" depending on the *ratio* of the *size* of our bet to the *total* amount of our gambling capital,' I continue.

'To make myself clear, first, let's pretend that instead of betting at a mathematically *unfair* game, whose PC is 0.85 per cent, let's say that we're gambling at a mathematically *fair* game, i.e. where the PC is 0 per cent. Secondly, let's imagine that at every toss of a coin we're betting on Heads to win and Tails to lose, i.e. the casino is betting on Tails to win. Third, let's say that we have a certain gambling capital, either *large* or *small*, and that every time we make a bet we're going to bet either all, 1/2, 1/5, 1/10, 1/20, 1/100 etc. of this same capital,' I continue.

'I'd be too nervous to bet *all*, i.e. 100 per cent of my capital on just one toss!' exclaims Mr Optimist.

'Anybody would be. But at the gaming table haven't you seen foolish and impulsive gamblers do that very thing, i.e. suddenly shove *all* their capital out on to the table for one last do-or-die bet?' I ask.

'I'm afraid I have seen it happen,' responds Mr Optimist.

'For how many tosses can a gambler last if he bets all of his capital at one time?' I ask.

'Not very long,' answers Mr Optimist.

'For how many tosses can he last if he bets only 1/2 of his capital?' I ask.

'I don't know – but a little longer,' responds Mr Optimist.

155

'For how many tosses if he bets only 1/5 of his capital?'

'Not too long – but a little longer,' responds Mr Optimist.

'In other words the *smaller* our bet in ratio to our capital the *longer* we can last before being wiped out or ruined, or expressed the other way round, the *larger* our bet in ratio to our capital the *sooner* we'll be wiped out or ruined,' I declare.

TABLE 61

$p=Q=1/2$

| Q | 1 all | 2 1/2 | 5 1/5 | 10 1/10 | 20 1/20 | 50 1/50 | 100 1/100 | 1000 1/1000 |
|---|---|---|---|---|---|---|---|---|
| 0.01 | | | | 18 | 66 | 390 | 1530 | 150300 |
| 0.05 | | | 9 | 31 | 115 | 676 | 2652 | 260520 |
| 0.10 | | | 13 | 45 | 163 | 962 | 3774 | 370740 |
| 0.25 | | 7 | 27 | 92 | 335 | 1977 | 7753 | 761521 |
| 0.33 | | 9 | 35 | 121 | 441 | 2601 | 10201 | 1002001 |
| 0.50 | 1 | 20 | 78 | 267 | 975 | 5748 | 22544 | 2214422 |
| 0.75 | 28 | 90 | 354 | 1210 | 4410 | 26010 | 102010 | 10020010 |
| 0.90 | 167 | 568 | 2235 | 7637 | 27836 | 164175 | 643887 | 63246303 |
| 0.99 | 32000 | 90000 | 354000 | 1210000 | 4410000 | 26010000 | 102010000 | 10020010000 |

'Yes, I'd say that's true,' agrees Mr Optimist.

'In Table 61 (p. 156) we'll find laid out, in simple arithmetical terms, this ratio of bet size to the probability of ruin,' I continue. 'In the lefthand column under Q are 9 arbitrary probabilities of ruin. In the horizontal double row above the table are, first, numbers signifying the entirety of our imaginary gambling capital – 1, 2, 5, 10, 20 ... 1,000 units, and, second, beneath these, simple fractions signifying the same thing except based on the ratio of bet size to capital, i.e. 1/2 signifies that at each toss we wager 1/2 of our capital, 1/5 signifies that at each toss we wager 1/5 of our capital, and ... 1/1000 signifies that at each toss we bet 1/1000 of our capital. And third, all the figures within the table signify *n* trials or tosses of a coin, *at the end* of which we're wiped out or ruined by an *adverse digression of Tails* and the casino rakes in our last bet. Table 61 (p. 156) may be read either vertically or horizontally.

'Let's assume we're always betting 1 unit per toss. In the lefthand probability-of-ruin column Q let's glance down to, say, the 6th probability value, which is 0.50. Now let's read horizontally from left to right from this 0.50. We note that if we bet all our capital on one toss we have a probability of 0.50 – fifty–fifty – of lasting only 1 toss before being wiped out. On the other hand, if our capital is 2 units and at every toss we again bet 1 unit – 1/2 our capital – we have a probability of 0.50 of lasting as many as 20 tosses. Still reading from left to right, if our capital is 5 units and at every toss we continue betting 1 unit – 1/5 of our capital – we have a probability of 0.50 of lasting for as many as 78 tosses. On the other hand, if we increase our capital to 10 units and for every toss still keep betting 1 unit – 1/10 of our capital – we have a probability of 0.50 of lasting for 267 tosses before being ruined, i.e. before the casino rakes in our last 1-unit bet. And so on if we bet only 1/20, 1/50, 1/100, and 1/1000 of our capital at each toss.

'As for reading Table 61 (p. 156) vertically, if our capital is 1 unit we have a probability of 0.50 of ruin in 1 toss, an increasing probability of 0.75 of ruin at the end of 28 tosses, an increasing probability of 0.90 of ruin at the end of 167 tosses, and by 32,000 tosses it's 99 per cent probable that we'll have lost our entire capital of 1 unit. The rest of the table may be read in the same way,' I conclude.

'Now I understand why you issued a warning about the Take the Odds bet at craps,' declares Mr Optimist. 'Because we're *forced* to DOUBLE the size of our wager – 1 unit on Pass, an adjacent 1 unit for the Odds bet – we may be seriously increasing the probability of ruin as laid out in Table 61 (p. 156).'

'Exactly, my friend. And remember that Table 61 (p. 156) is made out for a game in which the casino, betting on Tails to win, has no *percentage* advantage whatsoever, whereas the PC in Take the Odds, though very small, is still 0.85 per cent, which *decreases* the number of tosses or trials before we're wiped out,' I add.

'I suppose if I were a millionaire it wouldn't make any difference,' asserts Mr Optimist. 'Then the ratio of the size of my bet, instead of being, say, 1 to 1, 1 to 2, 1 to 5, 1 to 10 ... or 1 to 1,000, as in Table 61 (p. 156), would be as large as 1 to 1,000,000 – complete safety.'

'Not really, Mr Optimist. We'd better avoid making such statements. Let's put it this way. How many millionaires take their whole million dollars out of the bank and, *in any one session*, use them to back their bet at any casino gambling game?'

'None that I've heard of,' responds Mr Optimist.

'Exactly. To back their bet *in any one session* they might withdraw from their bank 10,000 units or 1,000 units, and the results for 1,000 units are listed in the righthand column of Table 61 (p. 156). In other words for *practical gambling purposes* the weight of all those million dollars deposited in their bank doesn't really help

157

them. What gambling millionaires do is bring, say, 10,000 units with them into the casino, but as often as not their much larger betting capital doesn't help them at all,' I warn.

'Why not? From what I've learned from Table 61 (p. 156) I should think it would make all the difference in the world,' objects our friend.

'In your thinking you're forgetting one important practical fact,' I declare. 'And *this is one of the most important points in this book*, affecting gamblers with small as well as large capital.

'In discussing the danger of increasing the size of our bet, for purposes of illustration I've always said that we keep betting ONE unit on every toss. But *in practice* most gamblers bet much more than 1 unit per trial. Let's take the two cases. A millionaire will take 10,000 units out of the bank, go to a casino, and step up to a crap table whose maximum bet is 1,000 units, which he proceeds to wager on every cast of the dice. But so far as bet size goes, what is he really doing? The RATIO of 10,000 units to 1,000 units is 10,000/1,000 or just 10 to 1, so the number of dice throws the millionaire can survive is listed in the 4th column – headed by 1/10 – of Table 61 (p. 156). So far as $Q=0.50$ goes, the millionaire can last no more than 267 throws,' I conclude.

'That's not very long,' agrees Mr Optimist shaking his head over the millionaire's plight.

'Let's take the second case,' I continue, 'the more common one of the relatively poor gambler.'

'I'm afraid that's I,' says Mr Optimist with a sigh.

'I'm afraid that's the great majority of us,' I hasten to add. 'The typical gambler withdraws from his savings deposit, say, 100 units and, betting 10 units at a time, considers himself reasonably safe from the danger of an adverse digression. Yet as the RATIO of 100/10 is 10 to 1, he's no better off than the millionaire – both have the same fifty–fifty chance of being ruined at the end of 267 throws.'

'As craps is one of my favorite games, I'll try to see that the lesson of Table 61 (p. 156) won't be lost on me!' exclaims Mr Optimist.

'But before we leave craps,' I interject, 'I want to point out another very typical and dangerous way many gamblers have of playing the game.'

'What's that?' asks our friend.

'If you watch a crap game very long, you'll soon observe some

158

player adopt the following strategy. First he bets, say, 1 unit on Pass – or 10, 20, 50, or 100 units – whatever he can afford. As soon as he wins, he hands his gain over to the dealer to put on one of the six Place bets, say, on 4 or 10. Then he bets another 1 unit on Pass. As soon as he wins, he makes a second Place bet, say, 5 or 9. For a third time he bets 1 unit on Pass. As soon as he wins, he bets a third Place bet, say, 6 or 8. Again he makes a Pass bet. Just for the sake of illustration let's say that the shooter throws all three points of the Place bets before sevening out. Just as the dealer is handing over each of the Place-bet gains to the gambler, the latter cries, "Press!" So the dealer lets all three winnings, one after another, ride on the three Place bets. Again the player bets 1 unit on Pass, all the while keeping his eye hopefully on the point numbers the shooter is throwing. Again for the sake of illustration let's say the shooter keeps throwing points without sevening out. Every time the shooter throws a point the player wins one of his three Place bets. Each time this happens, he hands his gain over to the dealer and cries, "Press!" Now, Mr Optimist, can you tell me what's so dangerous about this very common strategy at craps?' I ask.

'I bet I know!' exclaims Mr Optimist. 'In the long run the *average* PC of the three Place bets, which is $(6.67+4.00+1.52)/(3)=4.095$ per cent, is so large that, compared to the small 1.41 per cent on Pass, it wipes out the player!'

'Applied to the long run, I think your answer is correct,' I reply. 'But following the strategy just outlined, most players never reach the long run. *They're ruined in the short run*, and it's not through the larger PC of 4.095 per cent.'

'You mean we're back to Table 61 (p. 156)?' asks Mr Optimist.

'Not exactly, but it's a very related problem. Let's put it this way. The player's strategy requires him to bet *simultaneously* on *four different* and *independent* chances, each with a significantly different probability of success – Pass, and Place bets 4 or 10, 5 or 9, and 6 or 8. All the shooter has to do is throw ONE seven, and the player loses every single bet. The player knows this, but he likes his strategy, for it gives him lots of thrills, because it involves lots of "action",' I reply.

'Is that bad?' asks Mr Optimist, getting his back up.

'Well, let's put it this way, my friend. Which would you rather have, thrills or money?' I ask.

'Money!' asserts Mr Optimist promptly.

'Then *any* strategy which spreads your bets out over *more than*

159

*one* chance is poor,' I declare. 'The major reason for this is that you need an unusually large capital indeed to survive all the continually fluctuating ups and downs of your various independent wagers. Even betting simultaneously on just *two* different chances forces you to *spread your capital too thinly*. There is a way, however, of combining at least some thrills or "action", as gamblers call it, with a reasonable chance to win money.'

'What do I do?' asks Mr Optimist, about to get up and put on his coat.

'Wait a minute – I didn't say you'd *necessarily* win money. I said only that there is a much better way at craps – or at any game – than spreading your capital or winnings out recklessly all over the gaming table, which assures financial "sudden death" through a quick adverse digression. The strategy I recommend is very simple, but that's frequently the case for relatively successful strategies.

At craps what a gambler should do is *first* bet only on *one* chance at a time. The chance with the smallest PC is Take the Odds, so bet that – IF the fact of having to double your flat stake isn't dangerous from the standpoint of the ratio of bet size to capital – consult Table 61 (p. 156) for a rough estimate of this danger. And *second*, if a gambler wants to try to parlay his winnings rather than put them conservatively back into his pocket, he should adopt some sort of *pro* progression, in which he increases his bet after a win though not necessarily after every win. Of all the systems we examined in Chapters IX and X I think the simple paroli is the best.'

Blackjack

# CHAPTER XIV

# Blackjack

'I never know whether to stand or draw at blackjack,' declares Mr Optimist.

'Well, in a few moments I'm going to outline to you two black-jack strategies that are immeasurably superior to the "intuitive", "hunch", or "inspirational" approaches used by 99 per cent of blackjack players, who, let's be honest, do very badly at the game. They just lose, lose, lose. In the first of the two strategies the casino has a very small PC of 1.62 per cent against us, while in the second the casino has a PC of 0 per cent, i.e. they have no percentage advantage against us at all! But first let's set down the rules for blackjack used by most casinos,' I reply.

'A dealer stands behind a semi-circular table covered by a green felt layout. Opposite him there are chairs for 6 or 7 players. After shuffling an ordinary deck of 52 cards, which are then cut by one of the players, the dealer *burns* the top card, i.e. places it face up on the bottom of the deck. During this time each player has placed a bet before himself within a rectangle, slightly larger than a playing card, printed on the layout.

'Starting with the player on his left, the dealer deals one card face down to each player. Then he deals a card face up to himself. Then he deals a second card face down to each player. Then he deals a last card face down to himself. Thus except for the dealer's last or *up* card all the cards are face down and are called *hole* cards.

'The value of the cards in blackjack is as follows. Each card from 2 through 10 is worth its pip value. Face cards are worth 10. An ace is worth either 1 or 11, as one will. The suits are meaningless.

'The player's goal is to obtain a total larger than that of the dealer, yet which does not exceed 21.

'If a given player's first two cards total 21 (an ace and a 10-value card, called a *natural* or *blackjack*), the player always turns both hole cards face up. After peeking at his own hole card to see whether he also has 21, the dealer pays the player 1.5 times the amount of his bet, i.e. at 3 to 2 odds, unless the dealer also has 21, in which case the hand is a *standoff* or *tie*, and the player neither wins nor loses.

'If a given player's first two cards total less than 21, then the player may stand or draw additional cards in his proper turn.

'Whichever he does, he wins the amount of his bet if his total is more than the dealer's, yet doesn't exceed 21. He also wins the amount of his bet if his total doesn't exceed 21 but the dealer's total does exceed 21.

'On the other hand he loses his bet if his total is less than the dealer's, yet doesn't exceed 21. He loses his bet if his total exceeds 21.

'The player neither wins nor loses if his total is the same as the dealer's, yet doesn't exceed 21.

'If a given player's first two cards are identical, the player may immediately turn them face up, place his original bet on either card, and then place an equal amount on the other. This strategy is called *splitting a pair*, and the player plays each hand just like an ordinary one, standing or drawing as he will. If the player's first two cards are aces, however, he may draw only one card to each. If after splitting any pair of cards the player's final total for either hand is 21, this hand must be considered an ordinary 21, paid off at 1-to-1 odds, rather than a natural or blackjack. A player may usually never split anything but his original pair of hole cards.

'After having looked at his first two cards, a given player may elect to double his bet, turn both hole cards face up, and draw but a single card face down. This strategy is called *doubling down*. After having split any pair except aces and having received a single card on each hole card, a player may double down on either or both of his new hands.

'If the dealer's up card is an ace, a given player may *insure* against the dealer's hole card being a 10-value card by placing beside his regular bet another equal to one half the amount. If the dealer does have 21, he pays the player double the amount of his side bet. But if the dealer doesn't have 21, the player loses his side bet. The disposition of the player's regular bet is decided independently of the insurance bet. A player is advised never to make

162

the insurance bet, for against it there is an average PC of 5.09 per cent.

'As for the dealer's own strategy, it is simple and invariable. After each player either stands or draws a card, the dealer turns up his hole card. If his total is 16 or less, he must draw until it is 17 or more, at which point he must stand. If he has drawn an ace, and counting it as 11 would bring his total to 17 or more without exceeding 21, he must count the ace as 11 and stand. A player is advised not to mimick the dealer's strategy, i.e. draw to 16 or less, stand on 17 or more, never double down or split pairs, because against this strategy the PC is 5.73 per cent.

'So much for the rules of blackjack,' I conclude. 'Now, Mr Optimist, are they really very difficult?'

'No, I confess they aren't,' replies our friend. 'But what are the two strategies you promised me?'

'The first strategy, the simpler one, we'll call here the *Baldwin* strategy, as it was originally calculated in 1957 by four American statisticians, Messrs Roger R. Baldwin, Wilbert E. Cantey, James P. McDermott, and Herbert Maisel. Here are the three simple rules.

'(1) When the dealer's face-up card is 7 or higher or an ace, draw on 16 or less and stand on 17 or more. When the dealer's face-up card is 6 or less, draw on 11 or less and stand on 12 or more. If you get an ace, always count it as 1 unless counting it as 11 will make your total 18, 19, 20, or 21.

'(2) Always double down on 10 and 11 but never double down on any other totals.

'(3) Always split aces and 8's, but never split any other pairs.

'So much for the Baldwin rules. Remember, Mr Optimist, if you follow this very simple strategy the casino's PC against you will be only 1.62 per cent – only 0.21 per cent larger than the 1.41 per cent for the regular Pass bet at craps,' I conclude.

'Wonderful! And I especially like the great simplicity of the Baldwin rules,' comments Mr Optimist. 'There are only three steps to memorize.'

'Yes, that's true. As a matter of fact, Mr Optimist, in actual play at the blackjack table it's much *easier* to use the Baldwin strategy rather than the "intuitive", "hunch", or "inspirational" approaches, because we may play mechanically much faster and in a relaxed manner rather than having to stop and ponder our decision at every new hand.'

163

## TABLE 63

**P L A Y E R' S   H A N D**

Dealer's Draw or Stand (Hard)

| Up-card: | 2 | 3 | 4 | 5 | 6 | 7 | 8 | 9 | 10 | A |
|---|---|---|---|---|---|---|---|---|---|---|
| 17 | | | | | | S | S | S | S | S |
| 16 | | | | | | Note: 1 | | | | |
| 15 | | | | | | | | | | |
| 14 | | | | | | Note: 2 | | | | |
| 13 | S | S | | | | | | | | |
| 12 | | | S | S | S | | | | | |

Dealer's Draw or Stand (Soft)

| Up-card: | 2 | 3 | 4 | 5 | 6 | 7 | 8 | 9 | 10 | A |
|---|---|---|---|---|---|---|---|---|---|---|
| 19 | | | | | | | | S | S | |
| 18 | S | S | S | S | S | S | | | | S |

Dealer's Double Down (Hard)

| Up-card: | 2 | 3 | 4 | 5 | 6 | 7 | 8 | 9 | 10 | A |
|---|---|---|---|---|---|---|---|---|---|---|
| 11 | X | X | X | X | X | X | X | X | X | X |
| 10 | X | X | X | X | X | X | X | X | | |
| 9 | X | X | X | X | X | | | | | |
| Note;3  8 | | | | X | X | | | | | |

Dealer's Double Down (Soft)

| Up-card: | 2 | 3 | 4 | 5 | 6 | 7 | 8 | 9 | 10 | A |
|---|---|---|---|---|---|---|---|---|---|---|
| 18 | | X | X | X | X | | | | | |
| 17 | X | X | X | X | | | | | | |
| 13 to 16 | | | X | X | X | | | | | |

Dealer's Splitting Pairs

| Up-card: | 2 | 3 | 4 | 5 | 6 | 7 | 8 | 9 | 10 | A |
|---|---|---|---|---|---|---|---|---|---|---|
| A/8 | Z | Z | Z | Z | Z | Z | Z | Z | Z | Z |
| 9 | Z | Z | Z | Z | Z | | Z | Z | | |
| 7 | Z | Z | Z | Z | Z | Z | | | | |
| 6 | Z | Z | Z | Z | Z | | | | | |
| 10/5 | | | | | | | | | | |
| 4 | | | | Z | | | | | | |
| 3/2 | Z | Z | Z | Z | Z | | | | | |

Note: 1 Except when holding 3 or more cards.
Note: 2 Only when holding 2 7's against dealer's 10 in any combination of cards.
Note: 3 Except when holding the combination 6–2.

'Besides, playing a system is always much more fun, and that's a good part of what gambling should be,' adds Mr Optimist.

'I certainly agree. Now let's go on to the Thorp strategy, so called after its inventor, Professor Edward O. Thorp, who published it in his brilliant book, *Beat the Dealer* (N.Y., 1962, 1966). Although there have been numerous attempts to improve on Thorp's basic strategy, none has succeeded in doing so. Indeed, any gambler who wants the most comprehensive study of blackjack should definitely purchase *Beat the Dealer*,'

'Is the Thorp strategy more difficult than the Baldwin?' asks Mr Optimist.

'Essentially, the Thorp strategy is an extension of the Baldwin,' I reply. 'So as the Thorp strategy is based on the Baldwin, it's extremely easy to pass from the first to the second. And remember, Mr Optimist, for the Thorp strategy the casino's PC against you is 0 per cent, i.e. *they have no percentage advantage at all!*'

'Magnificent!' cries our friend. 'Lead on!'

'Table 63 (p. 164) summarizes the Thorp basic strategy and is divided into three self-explanatory sections.

'In the first section the letter *S* signifies *stand*. Otherwise we always *draw*.

'In the second section the letter *X* signifies *double down*.

'In the third section the letter *Z* signifies split the pair.

'In addition we note that the first two sections consist of hard and soft strategies. A hard total is one that contains no ace. A soft total is one that contains one ace.

'Furthermore, we should always adhere to the following order of precedence. Thus whenever the choice presents itself, we should always split a pair rather than double down. And similarly we should always double down rather than stand,' I conclude.[1]

'How long would you say it takes to learn Professor Thorp's basic strategy?' asks Mr Optimist.

'If you study and practice dealing out hands of cards at home, it shouldn't take you more than a few weeks,' I reply. 'Always remember, however, that in an actual casino the environment is often very distracting and inhibits successful concentration. So do your homework well!'

'I'm off already!' cries Mr Optimist enthusiastically.

---

[1] If the dealer's rules require his *taking all ties* or *pushes* (as in most Charity or Las Vegas Nights), his PC becomes an unacceptably large 9 per cent! Hence play another game, e.g. Craps or Nevada Baccarat.

# CHAPTER XV

# Nevada Baccarat

'I have a confession to make,' declares Mr Optimist. 'I've never played Nevada baccarat. First, they set the game apart – it's roped off in its own elegant area, and I don't know the qualifications allowing me to enter and play. Second, I don't know what the rules are. Third, the dealers pay off in large denomination chips, and I admit candidly I'm not a millionaire. And lastly, I don't know what the Bank's percentage or PC is against me at every bet.'

'The whole matter may be cleared up very quickly,' I reply, 'and Nevada baccarat is really one of the best games the casinos have to offer.

'First, as to the casino's setting the game apart, they do this only to keep out the merely curious tourists. If a visitor wants to gamble, all he has to do is enter the roped-off area and sit down if there is a vacant seat. But to gamble he must occupy a seat. He can't crowd in and wager standing up as at craps or roulette. Don't be frightened because rich players like betting in large denomination chips – you can bet as "little" as twenty dollars a hand. The minimum bet at the game is twenty dollars. The maximum wager is commonly two thousand dollars.

'Second, the rules are very simple and fall into two categories – first, where we place our bets, second, the procedure for dealing and receiving cards from the wooden shoe and when we stand and draw.

'At Nevada baccarat there are 12 chairs, half at one end of the oval layout, half at the other end. On the layout before each chair is the occupant's private betting number – 1, 2, 3, 4 ... 12. Each number is situated in a printed rectangle, where the gambler keeps his reserve of cash for betting purposes.

'There are only *two* types of bets that may be made, one that the

166

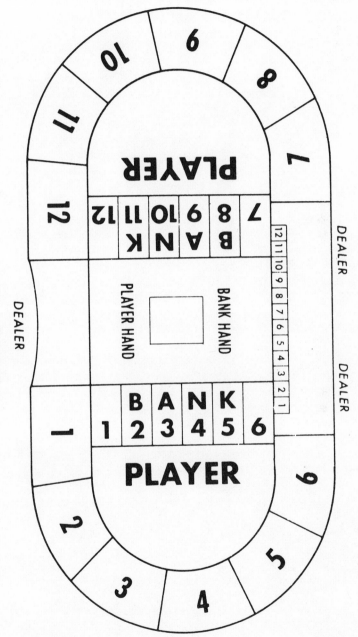

*Nevada Baccarat*

*Banker* will win the next hand, the other that his mathematical opponent the *Player* will win the next hand. Except for the casino's percentage or PC against each type of wager, they are related complementarily to each other as Heads is to Tails, at roulette as the red is to black, or at craps as Pass is to Don't Pass, etc. At each end of the oval layout is a large semi-circle containing the word *Player*. If a gambler wants to wager on the Player's success, he bets within this semi-circle. On the other hand if a gambler wants to wager on the Banker's success, he puts his pile of chips into the rectangle, also at either end of the layout, marked *Bank*. Adjacent to one or the other Player semi-circles, the Bank rectangle at one end is subdivided into squares marked 1, 2, 3, 4, 5, and 6 for the convenience of the gamblers seated at those numbered seats, and at the other end is subdivided into squares marked 7, 8, 9, 10, 11, and 12 for the convenience of the gamblers seated at the latter numbered seats.

'As most players know how to play Nevada baccarat before taking a seat and gambling, the game is usually conducted in almost total silence. On the other hand, if a gambler tells the nearest dealer he doesn't understand the procedure for dealing or receiving cards from the shoe, the dealer will politely direct the gambler in either role. It must be emphasized that this procedure *doesn't alter* in the slightest the mathematical chances for either the Banker bet or Player bet. Just as in craps the casino could have a machine throw the dice, so in baccarat they could have one dealing and turning over cards. But for gamblers to do this gives them a gratifying sense of participation.

'Either 8 or 6 decks are shuffled by the dealers, and then cut by one of the players. Then a dealer inserts a colored "cut card" between the last deck and the first decks, for the last deck is never dealt out.

'The shoe is then pushed over the felt layout to the gambler at seat #1. Let's assume this gambler is a novice at baccarat and has declared this to the nearest dealer. Holding the shoe with his left hand and dealing the cards out with the tip of his right forefinger, the dealer will illustrate in pantomime how the cards are dealt from the shoe always to that player, out of courtesy, who has the largest bet on *Player*. Then the dealer gives the shoe to the gambler at seat #1, who is called banker. Remember that the latter may have bet against himself by wagering on Player just as at craps the shooter may bet on Don't Pass, and that if this be so, it doesn't alter in the

167

slightest the chances for or against either the Banker or Player bets winning.

'"Release the cards, please," the dealer declares to the banker, indicating the first card goes to the player with the largest bet on *Player*. "One card to him, then one card to yourself. Then again one card to him, another card to yourself," the dealer instructs the banker, whose first two face down cards are usually tucked under the lip of the shoe. "Please look at your hand," the dealer says to the player. "Now face your cards, please," he tells the banker, and then puts face up the latter's two cards in the center of the table within a square marked *Banker Hand*. Then the dealer tells the player, "Face your cards, please," and puts face up the latter's two cards in the center of the table within a square marked *Player Hand*. If the rules call for the player's receiving a third and last card, the dealer instructs the banker, "Please deal one more card face down to the player." Then the dealer says to the latter, "Turn your card face up, please." Whatever the card, the dealer places it face up alongside the player's first two cards in the *Player Hand* square. If the rules call for the banker's receiving a third and last card, the dealer similarly instructs the banker, whose card is placed face up alongside his first two cards in the *Banker Hand* square.

'Then the dealer says either, "Banker wins" or "Player wins", and the two other dealers pay off the bets in the appropriate square by counting chips next to each gambler's bet.

'So much for the procedure of the game, Mr Optimist,' I conclude. 'Table 64 (p. 169) gives the invariable rules the banker and player must follow for dealing and receiving cards. By following these rules of standing and drawing each of the two gamblers hopes to gain a total as close to 9 as possible.'

'Tell me,' asks Mr Optimist, 'do I have to memorize Table 64 (p. 169) like Table 63 (p. 164), the Thorp strategy for blackjack?'

'Not at all, because at every casino where they play Nevada baccarat, the dealers will provide you with Table 64 (p. 169) on a small card, On the other hand you might be better off memorizing Table 64 (p. 169), because for inexplicable reasons, the casino's tables are defective,' I reply.

'In what way?' asks our friend.

'They leave out the letter $n$ in the banker's stand-draw rules, and when a gambler takes the banker's role, it's absolutely necessary, of course, for him to know whether he should or should not deal a third card to himself when the player stands,' I add.

168

TABLE 64

Rules for Nevada Baccarat
(Tens and face cards signify 0)

*Player*

| Having | |
|--------|--|
| 0–1–2–3–4–5 | Draws a card |
| 6–7 | Stands |
| 8–9 | Natural – turns cards over |

- - - - - - - - - - - - - - - - - - - - - - - - - - - - - - - - -

*Banker*
(n stands for 'no card at all')

| Having 0–1–2 | Draws | |
|-------|-------|--|
| | Draws after dealing | Stands after dealing |
| 3 | n–0–1–2–3–4–5–6–7–9 | 8 |
| 4 | n–2–3–4–5–6–7 | 0–1–8–9 |
| 5 | n–4–5–6–7 | 0–1–2–3–8–9 |
| 6 | 6–7 | n–0–1–2–3–4–5–8–9 |

- - - - - - - - - - - - - - - - - - - - - - - - - - - - - - - - -

| | |
|--|--|
| 7 | Stands |
| 8–9 | Natural – turns cards over |

'Do the dealers pay off both *Banker* and *Player* bets at the same 1-to-1 odds,' asks Mr Optimist.

'No, they don't,' I reply. 'They pay off the *Banker* bet at odds of 19 units to 20 units, or put another way, the dealers collect 5 per cent of the *winnings* of each *Banker* bet. On the other hand they pay off the *Player* bet at straight 1-to-1 odds.'

'Then from the standpoint of the Bank's percentage or PC is it advantageous for me always to make a *Player* bet?' asks Mr Optimist.

'Both in theory and practice it makes not the slightest difference, because as each of the bets wins and loses 50 per cent of the time, or in alternation, as it were, then any slight advantage lying with either bet is quickly nullified,' I reply regretfully.

169

'Then what is the PC against each bet?' asks Mr Optimist.

'For both the *Banker* and *Player* bets the PC is 1,2671 = 1.27 per cent,' I conclude.

'Why that's better than the 1.62 per cent PC at blackjack using the Baldwin strategy!' exclaims Mr Optimist.

'True enough, but you'll do even a little better, you'll recall, on the Pass Line at craps or the red at Monte-Carlo roulette, where the PC in both cases is only 1.41 per cent,' I conclude.

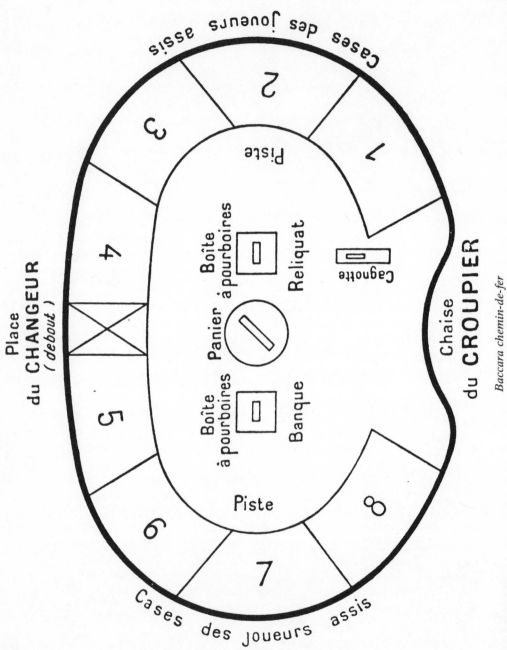

Baccara chemin-de-fer

# CHAPTER XVI

# Baccara chemin-de-fer

'How does this game differ from Nevada baccarat?' asks Mr Optimist.

'The procedure of the game, conducted in French, is more complicated, the stand–draw rules for the player allow him the option of standing or drawing if his first two-card total is 5, and the Bank's percentage or PC is slightly smaller,' I reply. 'But these three matters aside, the two games are basically the same.

'Although both layouts are oval, that for Nevada baccarat is considerably longer. For the gamblers the 12 seats of Nevada baccarat are reduced to 8 seats. All the semi-circular, rectangular, and square compartments and their printed words and numbers within the center of the oval of Nevada baccarat don't exist, being replaced by four slots, only one of which we have to know about, called the *cagnotte*, a space before it marked *reliquat*, and a space to its left marked *banque*.

'Into that slot marked *cagnotte* the seated croupier deposits chips equaling the casino's 5 per cent commission from the *winnings* of each banker bet. Before each hand is played, on to the space marked *reliquat* the croupier places that fraction of the banker's bet which is more than the total of all the other players' bets. And before each hand is played, on to the space marked *banque* the croupier places the banker's bet, which the latter hands to him.

'Six ordinary decks of cards are shuffled by the croupier, cut by a player, and then placed by the croupier into the oblong dealing box, the *sabot* or shoe. He passes the shoe to the first player on his right at seat #1, who becomes the *banquier* or banker. Each gambler will in turn become the banker, the role passing from the first player to the second, from the second to the third, etc., counter-clockwise around the table. As the banker must relinquish

171

his role on *losing* a hand, which occurs on an average every other hand, the privilege circles the table equably just as in Nevada baccarat. Whenever offered the banker's role, however, no player is obligated to accept it. Hence if the first player refuses the shoe, the croupier offers its accompanying role to the second player, and so on around the table. As in Nevada baccarat, should a banker wish to relinquish his role after any hand, he has merely to announce his wish. In baccara chemin-de-fer he says *la main passe* – "the deal passes". The banker always bets against all the other players as a group, and vice versa.

'After the first player has received the shoe, he passes to the croupier a sum of money, in the form of chips, which the croupier places, as mentioned, in the space marked *banque*. With the banker's consent another player, seated or standing, may add to the *banque* an amount equal to the banker's own wager. In other words unlike at Nevada baccarat, at baccara chemin-de-fer standing players may also gamble. By so doing, this player becomes the banker's *associé* or partner. Should the banker commit subsequently any errors in dealing, intentional or otherwise, he may be penalized by losing the amount of his bet, and his partner must share in the penalty.

'Now the croupier asks if any player wishes to call *banco*. To call *banco* signifies one's willingness to be the only player betting against the banker, and one must bet an amount equal to the latter's wager – or his wager plus that of his partner. If a seated and standing player call *banco* more or less simultaneously, the seated player is accorded the privilege. And if several seated players call *banco* more or less simultaneously, the player nearest the banker's right is accorded the privilege. If a player calls *banco* and subsequently loses the hand, then for the next hand he is reaccorded the privilege, called *banco suivi*, over all other players. With the consent of the player calling *banco*, another player, seated or standing, may become his *associé* or partner, sharing in the amount of the stake. This has the effect of diminishing the gain or loss of the player who called *banco*. Should the latter commit subsequently any errors in the deal, intentional or otherwise, the croupier will rectify the errors by reconstructing the hands of the deal.

'If no player calls *banco*, then any player may say *avec la table* or, more usually, simply *avec* – meaning "with the table" – signifying his willingness to bet an amount equal to at least *one half* the banker's wager – or the latter plus that of his partner. The other

172

players will then make up the difference with their own bets. If several players, seated or standing, say *avec la table* more or less simultaneously, the privilege is awarded on the same basis as that for *banco* itself. Should any player change his mind and call *banco* after another player has said *avec la table*, then the player calling *banco* is accorded the privilege.

'If no player says either *banco* or *avec la table*, the second player makes his bet, placing it on the thither side of his numbered section, followed in like manner by the third player, then by the fourth, and so on around the table until the sum of all the players' bets equals the banker's wager – or his wager plus that of his partner. If a player places a chip on the line dividing his section from the center of the table, this signifies he is betting *one half* the value of the chip. Should the sum of all the players' bets be less than the banker's wager – or his wager plus that of his partner, the croupier withdraws the difference from the *banque* and places it in the *reliquat*, whence it is restored to the banker after the latter passes the shoe. Should the sum of all the players' bets be more than the banker's wager – or his wager plus that of his partner, the croupier returns the superfluous sum to the appropriate player or players before the hand is played.

'Once the amount of the *banque* has been matched by all the wagers of the players considered together, the croupier designates as the *ponte* or punter that player who has called *banco* or that seated player who has contributed the largest sum to the collective wager matching that in the *banque*. The role of the punter is to receive the two or three cards dealt by the banker from the shoe. As the punter represents all the other players, he is held responsible for committing any errors. If the punter has called *banco* and doesn't have a partner, and then commits an error in the deal, he may or may not lose the hand depending on particular circumstances. On the other hand, if the punter has called *banco* and does have a partner, or has said *avec la table*, or has merely bet the largest amount of any player, then the croupier will rectify the error by reconstructing the hands of the deal.

'Once the punter has been designated by the croupier, and the banker holds the shoe in readiness to deal, the croupier announces *rien ne va plus* – "no more bets" – signaling that the deal should commence.

'If either banker or punter receives a two-card total of 8 or 9, he must say *huit* or *neuf* – "eight" or "nine", as appropriate – and

173

immediately turn his first two cards face up, and the other player must do likewise, regardless of his total. The player with the higher total wins, and if the totals are equal, the hand is a standoff or tie.

"If neither player has a two-card total of 8 or 9, then the punter faces three possible situations. If his two-card total is 0, 1, 2, 3, or 4, he must say *carte* – "draw", i.e. request a third card from the banker, who deals it to him *face up*. If his two-card total is 6 or 7, he must say *non* – "stand", i.e. request no third card. On the other hand the last possibility is the only one in which the punter's strategy at baccara chemin-de-fer differs from his counterpart's at Nevada baccarat as specified in the upper part of Table 64 (p. 169), which indicates that the player *must* draw a third card if his two-card total is 5. If his two-card total is 5, the punter may say either *carte* – "draw" – or *non* – "stand" – depending on his own voluntary inclination.

"On his part, however, the banker must follow invariably the stand–draw strategy of Nevada baccarat as specified in the lower part of Table 64 (p. 169). In baccara chemin-de-fer when standing or drawing, the banker *says* nothing.

"As at Nevada baccarat, so at baccara chemin-de-fer the goal of the banker and punter is to gain a total as close to 9 as possible.

"After a losing hand for the banker, using his *palette* or thin serving paddle, the croupier distributes to each player that share of the sum in *banque* which is his due.

'After a winning hand for the banker, if the latter wants to *pass* the deal, he declares so as mentioned. Using his *palette*, the croupier first delivers to the banker all the losing bets from in front of the players' sections. Second, he removes from the *banque* the banker's original bet and delivers it to him. And third, if there are any chips in the *reliquat*, the croupier delivers those too to the banker.

'On the other hand, after a winning hand for the banker, if the latter wants to *keep* the deal, he doesn't *say* anything, and with his palette the croupier picks up all the players' losing bets and places them next to the banker's original wager in the *banque*.

'Remember that the banker *may not remove* either his bet or his winnings until either he *loses* the hand owing to bad luck, as it were, or decides to *pass* the deal and announces this intention as mentioned.

'If the banker remains silent and thereby indicates he will *keep* the deal, the croupier declares to the players, say, "Un banco de

174

390 louis" – "A bank worth 390 louis" – and the players again begin betting individually before themselves any amount from the minimum of the table and the maximum of 390 louis. Note that the croupier announces the worth of the bank in the old legal tender, no longer in general circulation, of a "louis", which for gambling purposes is always worth 20 francs apiece. Out of courtesy for the players who can't multiply 20 times 390 to get 7,800 francs, the croupier does this for them, saying, "Un banco de 390 louis, 7,800 francs."'

\* \* \* \*

'Before stating the PC of baccara chemin-de-fer, Mr Optimist, what big difference in the rules for the banker may make the game for *him* very dangerous unless he passes the deal after every hand?' I ask.

'Well, according to the rule,' replies Mr Optimist, 'every time the banker keeps the bank, as he can't withdraw either his original bet or his winnings, then for the next hand he must bet whatever amount the players collectively wish to gamble – and using your example, in this case it could be anything up to 390 louis.'

'Precisely. In other words, forgetting the matter of the croupier's necessarily deducting 5 per cent for the casino from the banker's winnings, if the banker wants to keep the bank for one hand after another, presuming he keeps winning each hand he is forced by the rule to keep *doubling his bet*,' I add.

'In other words, the rule forces him to play the simple paroli staking system,' declares Mr Optimist.

'That's right, and it's a good system *if* the banker can afford it,' I continue. 'But, of course, if he wants to remove his wager and winnings after *any* hand, all he has to do is say, "la main passe" – "the deal passes" as I mentioned.'

'Tell me,' asks Mr Optimist, 'does the 5 per cent commission taken from the banker's winnings make it mathematically more favorable for a gambler always to remain in a player's role?'

'Not in the slightest – no more than it does in Nevada baccarat,' I reply, 'because as the banker and player each win and lose half the time, any advantage or disadvantage of being either banker or player is evened out.'

'How about the punter's option to *draw* or *stand* on a two-card total of 5?' asks our friend. 'Is one strategy more favorable than the other?'

175

'No, not in the slightest,' I reply. 'So the punter might as well always follow the strategy of the upper part of Table 64 (p. 169) and invariably *draw* to a total of 5. This way he may avoid useless mental frustration.'

'And now the ultimate question,' declares Mr Optimist. 'What is the Bank's percentage or PC at baccara chemin-de-fer?'

'For either the banker, the punter, or any gambler whosoever in the game, the Bank's percentage or PC at baccara chemin-de-fer is always 1.15 per cent at every hand or trial.'

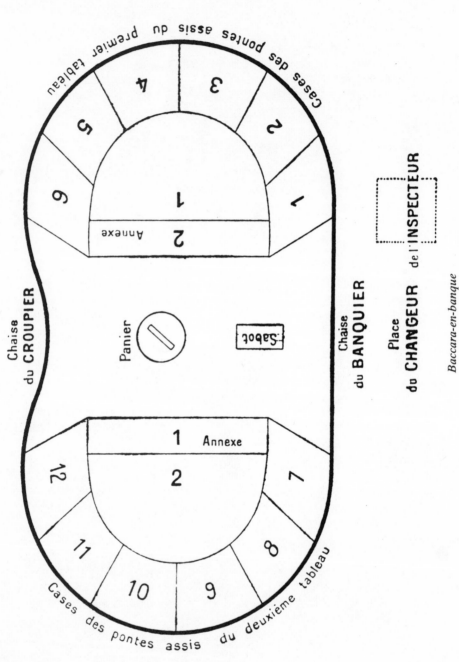

*Baccara-en-banque*

# CHAPTER XVII

# Baccara-en-banque

'Once I visited Monte Carlo and watched baccara-en-banque,' declares Mr Optimist. 'Do you know how much the minimum wager was?'

'No,' I reply.

'A hundred dollars!' exclaims our friend. 'So I just watched.'

'After we finish with the rules of the game,' I continue, 'we'll deal with the matter of the small Bank's percentage or PC against each player. Then perhaps next time you'll want to play.

'Just as at Nevada baccarat, so at baccara-en-banque there are 12 seats for players although the casino may squeeze extra chairs between the regular ones. But if at Nevada baccarat the 12 seats and their corresponding numbered sections go around the oval layout entirely counter-clockwise, at baccara-en-banque the right-hand half of the layout, called *tableau* #1, has 6 seats and their numbered sections going around also counter-clockwise, but the lefthand half of the layout, called tableau #2, has 6 seats and their numbered sections going around clockwise.

'Standing players may also make wagers – except between seats #1 and #7, where the casino's *banquier* or banker has his permanent seat and permanent shoe, and between seats #6 and #12, where the casino's croupier, with his *palette*, has his permanent high chair.

'It's helpful to point out some differences between baccara chemin-de-fer and the big game of baccara-en-banque.

'Thus at baccara-en-banque the dealing shoe, and its small mathematical advantage functioning as the PC, remains constantly in front of the banker, a higher echelon representative of the casino. During the game the banker, who must frequently do arithmetical calculations in his head pertinent to whether he stands

177

or draws, never *says* anything. It's the croupier who does *all* the talking – announcing the winning and losing totals of the three hands always dealt, and whether the banker or 1st or 2nd tableau wins, loses, or breaks even on any particular hand. There is no 5 per cent *cagnotte* charge for any player and consequently no *cagnotte* slot in the table. Unlike every other casino table game it is prohibited to tip the casino personnel, i.e. the banker or croupier. No player may wager in conjunction with an *associé* or partner. No player may call *banco* or announce *avec la table*. The players must at every hand bet against the banker, i.e. it's impossible for them to bet that the banker will win. No player is ever required by a rule to play the simple paroli, i.e. to bet anything more than the minimum wager of the table as set by the casino.

'Both from the standpoint of procedure and mathematics the banker is playing a game of baccara chemin-de-fer simultaneously, on the one hand, with the 6 players of the 1st *tableau*, and on the other, with the 6 players of the 2nd *tableau*. Whether he stands or draws a third card is dictated by whether so doing will enable him to beat the hand of the 1st rather than the 2nd *tableau*, or vice versa.

'On the thither side of their individually numbered sections the players place their wagers. To the banker's right is the 1st *tableau*, identified by a number 1 printed in its middle. Should the 6 players of this *tableau* wish to bet on the outcome of the 2nd *tableau* they have only to reach a little farther – or have their chips transferred by the croupier's *palette* – and put their bets in a strip, contiguous to the 1st *tableau*, marked by the number 2. Similarly, to the banker's left is the 2nd *tableau*, identified by a number 2 printed in its middle. Should the 6 players of this *tableau* wish to bet on the outcome of the 1st *tableau* they too have only to reach a little farther – or have their chips transferred by the croupier's *palette* – and put their bets in a strip, contiguous to the 2nd *tableau*, marked by the number 1.

'After six ordinary decks of cards are shuffled by the croupier, cut by a player, and then inserted into the regular oblong shoe facing the banker, the croupier announces, "Messieurs, faites vos jeux" – "Ladies and gentlemen, place your bets."

'A chip placed within the semi-circular border of either *tableau* is being bet for its *full* value. A chip placed on the line dividing a gambler's section from his immediate tableau is bet for *one half* its value. A chip placed on the line dividing either *tableau* from

178

the contiguous strip representing the other *tableau* is being bet simultaneously *half* for one *tableau*, *half* for the other.

'After all the bets have been placed, the croupier says, "Rien ne va plus" – "No more bets" – and the banker begins dealing out cards from the shoe, all face down.

'First the banker deals one card to the 1st tableau, another to the 2nd, and a third to himself. Then he repeats this so that all three hands are composed of two face-down cards. For the first hand the privilege of being the *ponte* or punter goes respectively to the players behind sections 1 and 7. Each punter must continue his role until he loses a hand. Then the privilege rotates counter-clockwise around the 1st *tableau* and clockwise around the 2nd. On his *palette* the croupier passes the cards from the banker to punters when necessary. Should an error in a deal be committed by either the banker, two punters, or croupier, the hand will be reconstructed if possible and, if not, then annulled.

'For both punters the procedure and rule for standing or drawing a third card are identical with those of baccara chemin-de-fer. Thus both punters follow the upper part of Table 64 (p. 169) although with a two-card total of 5 they may optionally stand or draw.

'As at Nevada baccarat and baccara chemin-de-fer, so at baccara-en-banque the goal of the banker and punters is to gain a total as close to 9 as possible. In all three games a face card or ten signifies zero – *baccara*.

'For the banker the rule for standing or drawing a third card is radically different from that of Nevada baccarat or baccara chemin-de-fer. In baccara-en-banque the banker's strategy only approximates that of the lower part of Table 64 (p. 169). As none of the players in baccara-en-banque may ever become banker, so far as actual gambling goes the details of his strategy are completely indifferent to them.

'We may make only one positive suggestion to any punter or player. So far as reducing the PC against you is concerned, you may on rare occasion reduce by a very small amount the PC against you by invariably betting on that *tableau* with the smallest collective wager.

'And now, Mr Optimist, as to the matter of the theoretical Bank's percentage or PC against a player at any hand. Remember that the banker is essentially tossing a coin Heads or Tails, first with the 1st *tableau*, second with the 2nd *tableau*. Hence whether he wins, loses, or breaks even at any hand with either tableau is independent of the outcome of the other tableau. Be this as it may, at any hand the Bank's percentage or PC against any gambler runs from a low of 0.84 per cent to a high of 1.27 per cent. In Table 12 (p. 21) for baccara-en-banque I cited 0.00917 or (0.00917) (100)=0.92 per cent as being perhaps typical in some way or other. It isn't possible to be more exact with an *à priori* value.

'The reason I suggested that a player bet on that *tableau* with the smallest collective wager is that the banker *tends* – but *not always* – to try to stand or draw a third card in order to beat that *tableau* weighted with the larger collective wager.

'In Table 65 (p. 180) I have listed, in the righthand column, the casino's PC against that *tableau* weighted with the *larger* collective bet. As we may observe in the lefthand column, the larger the ratio grows from the ordinary fifty–fifty or 1-to-1, the larger the casino's PC grows against the more collectively weighted *tableau*. Hence it behooves the players to bet collectively an equal amount on each *tableau* to prevent the banker's playing off the collectively larger bet of one *tableau* against the collectively smaller bet of the other one. But as the players are usually strangers to one another and wish anyway to follow their individual "intuition", in practice such co-operation is impossible. Hence I conclude that a PC of 0.92 per cent is typical.'

TABLE 65

| Bet ratio | Casino's PC against the tableau bearing the larger collective wager |
|---|---|
| 1:1 | 0.8400 % |
| 2:1 | 0.8576 % |
| 3:1 | 0.9600 % |
| 10:1 | 1.1648 % |
| Maximum:0 | 1.2799 % |

# CHAPTER XVIII

# Slot Machines

'You know, whenever I play a slot machine,' declares Mr Optimist, 'I always wonder what the casino's PC is against me on that particular machine. To do this I count the number of symbols on the three reels as they turn to a halt. But as this takes such an expensive length of time, and as I can see only nine symbols at once, I'm frankly rather discouraged about the whole process.'

'Well, you should feel discouraged, because it isn't possible to calculate the Bank's percentage by counting the few symbols that come to a halt after every time you've pulled the lever,' I reply. 'The only way to calculate the PC is to open an actual machine, remove the reels, and count the symbols at our leisure. That's exactly what I've done, and you'll find the results of the three reels listed in Table 66 (p. 182).

'As you can see, Mr Optimist, on each of the three reels there are a total of 20 symbols, most of them the traditional fruits. In Table 67 (p. 182) I have listed the total of each symbol, and in Table 68 (p. 183) I have listed all the information needed to calculate not only the Bank's percentage but to explain all the probabilities and how a slot machine actually works from a mechanical standpoint.

'Let's analyse the significance of the figures of the columns of Table 68 (p. 183). The digits of the top row are respectively 2, 2, and 3, signifying that there are 2 Bars on the first reel, 2 on the second, and 3 on the third. Table 67 (p. 182) shows there is a total of 20 symbols on each reel. Thus the digits 2, 2, and 3 are actually the numerators of the fractions 2/20, 2/20, and 3/20, whose product gives us the final favorable probability of 3 Bars – the Jack Pot – which is ...

$$(2/20)\ (2/20)\ (3/20)=12/8000$$

### TABLE 66

| Reel 1 | Reel 2 | Reel 3 |
|--------|--------|--------|
| Bell | Bell | Bell |
| Bar | Plum | Orange |
| Cherry | Cherry | Plum |
| Bell | Bar | Bell |
| Orange | Orange | Bar |
| Cherry | Bell | Plum |
| Lemon | Cherry | Orange |
| Cherry | Orange | Bell |
| Plum | Plum | Lemon |
| Orange | Bell | Orange |
| Cherry | Cherry | Plum |
| Bell | Plum | Bar |
| Orange | Orange | Lemon |
| Plum | Bell | Orange |
| Cherry | Cherry | Plum |
| Bell | Orange | Bell |
| Bar | Bar | Orange |
| Orange | Bell | Plum |
| Cherry | Cherry | Lemon |
| Plum | Orange | Bar |

### TABLE 67

| Reel 1 | | Reel 2 | | Reel 3 | |
|--------|---|--------|---|--------|---|
| Bar | 2 | Bar | 2 | Bar | 3 |
| Bell | 4 | Bell | 5 | Bell | 4 |
| Cherry | 6 | Cherry | 5 | Cherry | 0 |
| Lemon | 1 | Lemon | 0 | Lemon | 3 |
| Orange | 4 | Orange | 5 | Orange | 5 |
| Plum | $\frac{3}{20}$ | Plum | $\frac{3}{20}$ | Plum | $\frac{5}{20}$ |

'The numerator of this fraction is at the top of the $p$ column of Table 68 (p. 183). When we "hit the Jack Pot", we receive 120 units – the pay-off listed under $b$ at the top of the next column. As ever, our positive or winning expectation, signified by $pb$, is the product of the favorable probability and the Bank's pay-off in units. In this case we have consequently ...

$$(12/8000) \ (120) = 1440/8000$$

TABLE 68

| Winning combinations | Reel 1 | | Reel 2 | | Reel 3 | | p | | b | | Total | |
|---|---|---|---|---|---|---|---|---|---|---|---|---|
| 3 Bars (Jack Pot) | 2 | × | 2 | × | 3 | = | 12 × | 120 = | | | 1440 | units |
| 3 Bells | 4 | × | 5 | × | 4 | = | 80 × | 16 = | | | 1280 | units |
| 2 Bells    1 Bar | 4 | × | 5 | × | 3 | = | 60 × | 16 = | | | 960 | units |
| 3 Plums | 3 | × | 3 | × | 5 | = | 45 × | 12 = | | | 540 | units |
| 2 Plums    1 Bar | 3 | × | 3 | × | 3 | = | 27 × | 12 = | | | 324 | units |
| 3 Oranges | 4 | × | 5 | × | 5 | = | 100 × | 8 = | | | 800 | units |
| 2 Oranges 1 Bar | 4 | × | 5 | × | 3 | = | 60 × | 8 = | | | 480 | units |
| 2 Cherries 1 Lemon | 6 | × | 5 | × | 3 | = | 90 × | 4 = | | | 360 | units |
| 2 Cherries 1 Bell | 6 | × | 5 | × | 4 | = | 120 × | 4 = | | | 480 | units |
| 2 Cherries and anything (except a Lemon or a Bell) | 6 | × | 5 | × | 13 | = | 390 × | 2 = | | | 780 | units |
| | | | | | | | 984 | | | | 7444 | units |

'And in Table 68 (p. 183) this fraction is the total in the right-hand column, from which the denominator has been omitted simply for concision.

'Thus at any given pull of the handle – that is, at any given trial – our positive or winning expectation for 3 Bars – the Jack Pot – is 1440/8000. In other words 12 times out of every 8,000 pulls of the handle we shall win 120 units or 1,440 units all told. Hence at any given pull, for 3 Bars – the Jack Pot – our favorable probability $p$ is ...

$$12/8000 = 1/667$$

to win 120 units.'

'And our unfavorable or losing probability $q$ is $(1-p) = 666/667$ to lose 1 unit or whatever the value of the coin we insert. For the remaining 9 Winning Combinations listed in Table 68 (p. 183) we may thus compute any and all positive or winning expectations and favorable and unfavorable probabilities. Thus for 3 Bells the positive or winning expectation is 1280/8000. Or in other words 80 times out of every 8,000 pulls of the handle we shall win 16 units, or 1,280 units all told. Hence at any given pull or trial, for 3 Bells the favorable probability $p$ is $80/8000 = 1/100$, and the unfavorable or losing probability $q$ is $(1-p) = 99/100$.

'It follows that the sum at the bottom of the righthand column of Table 68 (p. 183), which is 7444/8000, is our total positive or winning expectation for *all* pay-offs *at any given trial*. And as 7444/8000 = 0.9305, this means that the actual slot machine that

183

we've taken apart returns on an average about 93 units – or coins – for every 100 units – or coins – we insert into the slot.

'And as 100 units minus 93 units leaves 7 units that the machine retains, then for this particular machine the Bank's percentage is about 7.00 per cent.

'It should also be noted, Mr Optimist, that the sum at the bottom of the $p$ column of Table 68 (p. 183), which is 984/8000, is the fraction signifying our total favorable probability at any given trial. In other words $p = (984/8000) = 0.123$, and $q = (1-p) = 0.877$. Thus if we pull the handle 1,000 times, we'll win *something* – from 2 to 120 units – on an average 123 times and lose our coin 877 times.'

'Now I know all about how a slot machine works,' declares Mr Optimist.

'Just about,' I reply.

'Tell me, I know that if I toss a coin for Heads or Tails the outcome of the *last* toss in no way affects the outcome of the *next* toss. The two tosses – or any tosses, for that matter – are *absolutely independent* of one another physically and – therefore – *mathematically too*,' asserts Mr Optimist.

'Absolutely. As the saying goes, "a coin has no memory",' I reply.

'Can we claim the same independence of the pulls or trials of a slot machine?' asks Mr Optimist.

'Again, absolutely,' I reply.

'In other words a slot machine has no ability to "store up the potentiality" for, say, a Jack Pot,' asks our friend.

'Absolutely none whatsoever. Thus if we got a Jack Pot from the *last* pull or trial, it in *no way* affects the outcome, *win* or *lose*, of the *next* pull or trial,' I emphasize. 'In the case of the particular slot machine we took apart we found that *at every trial* there is one chance out of 667 of the occurrence of the Jack Pot. As a matter of fact the Jack Pot, furthermore, has the following chances of occurring . . . :

| | 10 per cent chance at least once *before* the | 71st pull. |
|---|---|---|
| | 25 | 192nd |
| | 50 | 462nd |
| | 75 | 925th |
| | 90 | 1536th |
| | 95 | 1998th |
| | 99 | 3108th |

'And naturally when it does occur, we'll win the Jack Pot of 120 units,' I conclude.[1]

'In other words the Jack Pot is like a swaying pendulum,' adds Mr Optimist. 'But I see that it doesn't sway symmetrically – why is that?'

'The reason for that we'll have to postpone until the *Conclusion*,' I reply.

[1] For method of calculation see Appendix p. 221.

## CHAPTER XIX

# Bingo

'Isn't bingo really a lottery?' asks Mr Optimist.

'Yes, that's what bingo is essentially, so that people who like lotteries like bingo,' I reply.

'Then my chance of winning,' continues our friend, 'depends on the number of other gamblers I'm competing against at the bingo session?'

'Not exactly,' I reply. 'Your chance of winning depends on the number of *cards* bought by both you and your competitors. But first let's set down the very simple rules.

'Before any game each player buys 1 *or more* bingo cards like that illustrated in Table 69 (p. 186) and obtains also a quantity of pellets with which to cover the numbers printed on the card or cards. There are no duplicate cards. Any given card contains 24 different numbers plus a central space marked *Free*. The 24 numbers may be anywhere from 1 through 75. Custom ordains that under each of the five columns headed by the letters B-I-N-G-O only certain letters may be listed. Thus under *B* come only numbers 1 through 15. Under *I* come only numbers 16 through 30. And similarly under *N* come only numbers 31 through 45, under *G* come only numbers 46 through 60, and finally under *O* come only numbers 61 through 75. This distribution helps a player to determine quickly whether a particular card has or has not a number as soon as it has been announced.

TABLE 69

| B | I | N | G | O |
|----|----|------|----|----|
| 13 | 23 | 37 | 51 | 65 |
| 5 | 16 | 32 | 53 | 64 |
| 8 | 30 | Free | 52 | 73 |
| 9 | 17 | 41 | 54 | 62 |
| 12 | 18 | 34 | 48 | 71 |

'Into a clear plastic globe the *caller* places 75 plastic balls, each marked with a number plus a letter from the word *bingo*. A ball marked *A* may bear a number from only 1 through 15. A ball marked *B* may bear a number from only 16 through 30. And so forth, following the identical distribution just mentioned for the card itself.

'Before any ball is removed from the globe the *caller*, the game's announcer, randomly mixes the 75 balls within the globe by the mechanical means of a constant, vertical flow of air. Thus the subsequent selection of every ball is purely on the basis of chance.

'After the players have seated themselves at tables, placed their cards before themselves and their pellets close-by, the caller removes a ball from the globe, announces its letter and number over a loud-speaker, and then places the ball into a discard tray containing 75 receptacles marked in direct correspondence to the balls themselves. This last action mechanically illuminates the proper number in an electric board on a wall in full view of all the players. Hence players may observe at any time during the game exactly which of the 75 numbers have been called. On hearing a number called the players scrutinize their cards hopefully and, if any of the latter bears the announced number, cover it with a pellet. As the *Free* space in the center counts for any number, most players cover the *Free* space with a pellet before the game even begins.

'For each player the purpose of the bingo game is to cover 5 spaces in any horizontal, vertical, or diagonal line before any other player achieves the same result. On so covering 5 spaces a player shouts "bingo!" After an employee of the casino, the *floor man*, verifies the player's result in co-operation with the caller, the player wins a predesignated prize, and the game ends. If 2 or more players shout "bingo!" simultaneously, the casino awards 2 or more prizes.

'A typical bingo parlour operates a three-hour bingo session for 20 games, of which 18 are regular games and 2 are cover-all – a type we'll learn about in a moment.

'A typical bingo parlour charges 50 cents for one bingo card, $1.00 for 3 cards, and another $1.00 for a Master Card – the latter good for the whole session. A player may buy as many cards as he wants, and it's not unusual for a single player to keep his or her eye on as many as 27 cards in one game!

'A typical prize for a regular game runs anywhere from $12.00 to $60.00, while that for a cover-all game runs anywhere from

187

$100.00 to $500.00, which are called Jack Pots. Some Jack Pots may run into thousands of dollars.

'Although, as mentioned, the purpose of a regular game is for a player to cover 5 spaces in any horizontal, vertical, or diagonal line, the pre-announced purpose of some regular games is to cover spaces in the form of the letters E, H, X, Y, and Z, or the number 7, or just the one number at each of the four corners of a card.

'And lastly, the purpose of a *cover-all* game is for a player to cover *all 24* spaces on a given card before another player achieves the same result.

'What is our chance of winning either a regular or cover-all game? The solution is extremely simple. All we have to do is count the number of cards the casino or bingo parlour sells for any given game. The sum of the number of cards is our *denominator*. The number of cards we ourselves buy is our *numerator*. The *fraction* itself is the *probability of our winning* any given game.

'Thus if the casino sells 400 cards for a game and we buy 4 cards, the probability of our winning the game is (4/400)=1/100.

'If the casino sells 200 cards for a game and we buy 1 card, the probability of our winning the game is 1/200.

'Let's say, for example, that the prize for a particular bingo game is $75.00 and the casino sells 200 cards at $1.00 a piece. Would it be worth our buying *all 200* cards, paying ($1.00) (200)=$200.00 to have a certainty of winning $75.00? Obviously not.

'Of much greater mathematical interest is to know the probability of our winning *any* game if we play *continuously* one game after another. Let's say that just as a spin at roulette, a throw of the dice at craps, a hand at blackjack, a hand at chemin-de-fer or baccara, or a pull of a slot machine handle may each be considered a *trial*, so we may consider a *trial* a *single* game at bingo.

'Let us assume furthermore that the probability of $p$ of our winning such a bingo game at any given trial is 1/200.

'And let's say that the Jack Pot for any given game is $75.00, and that a card at each game costs $1.00.

'If we play this game continuously, one game after another, what is the *probability P* of our winning the $75.00 prize *at least* once *before the nth* game? The answers for various values of $n$ comprises the righthand column of Table 70 (p. 189), while the corresponding percentage values of $P$ comprise the lefthand column.

'Thus by the 21st game we have spent $21.00 for 21 cards for 21 games, and our chance for winning the $75.00 prize is only 10 per

Table 70

| P | n |
|---|---|
| 0.10 % | 21 |
| 0.25 % | 57 |
| 0.50 % | 138 |
| 0.75 % | 277 |
| 0.90 % | 459 |
| 0.95 % | 597 |
| 0.99 % | 923 |

cent. If we continue playing 57 games and spend $57.00 for cards, our chance of winning the $75.00 prize increases to only 25 per cent. We don't get a fifty–fifty chance of winning the $75.00 until playing 138 games. And even after playing 923 games and expending $923.00 for cards, there is still once chance out of a hundred that we shan't have won at least one game.[1]

'Some casinos and bingo parlours offer the following addition to the cover-all game.

'If any player can win a cover-all game in either 51, 52, 53, 54 or 55 *or fewer* numbers, he wins respectively $5,000.00, $2,500.00, $2,000.00, $1,500.00, or $1,000.00. What is the chance for any player at all to win one of these large sums?

'Table 71 (p. 189) lists the various probabilities from 46 *or fewer* numbers to all 75 *or fewer* numbers.

Table 71

| 46 | 0.0000003061 | 56 | 0.0001689 | 66 | 0.02422 |
|---|---|---|---|---|---|
| 47 | 0.0000006255 | 57 | 0.0002918 | 67 | 0.03774 |
| 48 | 0.000001251 | 58 | 0.0004978 | 68 | 0.05833 |
| 49 | 0.000002452 | 59 | 0.0008391 | 69 | 0.08944 |
| 50 | 0.000004715 | 60 | 0.001399 | 70 | 0.1361 |
| 51 | 0.000008906 | 61 | 0.002306 | 71 | 0.2056 |
| 52 | 0.00001654 | 62 | 0.003762 | 72 | 0.3084 |
| 53 | 0.00003023 | 63 | 0.006077 | 73 | 0.4595 |
| 54 | 0.00005441 | 64 | 0.009723 | 74 | 0.6800 |
| 55 | 0.00009654 | 65 | 0.01541 | 75 | 1.0000 |

'As we observe at the bottom of the lefthand column, the number 55 has been italicized, because the casino doesn't award us a Jack Pot prize if we win the cover-all game in *more than* 55

[1] For method of calculation see Appendix p. 221.

numbers drawn. For completeness, however, I've listed all the probabilities for numbers 56 through 75.

'It is self-evident that by the 75th number called *some* player *must* cry "bingo!" as the 75th ball is the last in the globe. Hence the probability of any player's covering his entire card within 75 numbers is certainty, signified by the numeral 1.

'What is the probability of some player's covering his card within 51 or fewer numbers? It is only 0.000,008,906. In other words, at any given game there are only about 8 chances in 1,000,000 that the casino will have to pay out the $5,000 Jack Pot prize.

'And by the same token there is a probability of only 0.000,096,540 or about 1 chance in 10,000 that the casino will have to pay out even the $1,000 Jack Pot prize for anyone's being able to cover his whole card by 55 or fewer numbers.

'But when a casino or bingo parlour advertises on its marquee these enormous prizes – *without* their attendant probabilities, of course – it certainly helps to bring in the crowds!' I conclude.

'Well, all I can say,' adds Mr Optimist, 'you might find me in a gambling casino – but never playing bingo!'

| 1 | 2 | 3 | 4 | 5 | 6 | 7 | 8 | 9 | 10 |
|---|---|---|---|---|---|---|---|---|---|
| 11 | 12 | 13 | 14 | 15 | 16 | 17 | 18 | 19 | 20 |
| 21 | 22 | 23 | 24 | 25 | 26 | 27 | 28 | 29 | 30 |
| 31 | 32 | 33 | 34 | 35 | 36 | 37 | 38 | 39 | 40 |

| 41 | 42 | 43 | 44 | 45 | 46 | 47 | 48 | 49 | 50 |
|---|---|---|---|---|---|---|---|---|---|
| 51 | 52 | 53 | 54 | 55 | 56 | 57 | 58 | 59 | 60 |
| 61 | 62 | 63 | 64 | 65 | 66 | 67 | 68 | 69 | 70 |
| 71 | 72 | 73 | 74 | 75 | 76 | 77 | 78 | 79 | 80 |

*Keno Ticket*

# CHAPTER XX

# Keno

'Like bingo, Mr Optimist, keno is a kind of lottery,' I declare.

'Are the Bank's percentages, the casino's pay-offs, and the player's probabilities of winning more favorable than those at bingo?' asks our friend.

'In a minute we'll see. The rules for keno are very simple. A new keno game starts about once every 10 minutes. Before it begins, a seated player marks an *outside ticket*, a rectangle containing 80 numbers from 1 through 80. For any game a player may buy as many tickets as he wants. Using a brush dipped into an inkwell, he marks with a blotch either 1, 2, 3, 4 ... or at most 15 numbers or "spots" as they're called. As to which among the 80 possible numbers are marked, evidently most players follow nothing more than "whim" or "intuition". In addition, on the right side of his paper ticket a player must inscribe two figures – the total number of blotches and the sum of money he is betting. For most casinos the standard betting amounts vary from a minimum of 70 cents to a maximum of $3.75. Next, the player surrenders his ticket to an employee standing behind the keno counter, where the ticket is duplicated. The original of this *inside ticket* is kept and filed by the employee, while a copy is given to the player. If the player wins, he presents his copy after the game at the counter and is paid off at odds predesignated by the casino in little folders it hands out to the players. Although the pay-off odds themselves never vary, the amount a player receives is naturally in proportion to the amount he decides to bet, i.e. pay for his ticket. Remember that the price of a winning ticket is never refunded. In this respect keno differs from craps, blackjack, roulette, etc., where the amount bet is always returned to the player along with the pay-off itself. Hence before a game even begins we've lost our 70 cents or $3.75.

'The drawing of a keno game is similar to that of a bingo game. A clear plastic globe contains 80 plastic balls numbered 1 through 80. Both before and during the actual drawing the 80 balls are randomly mixed in the globe by an interior vertical current of air. A keno drawing lasts about 2 minutes. The drawing itself consists of the employee's removing a random ball, announcing the number over a loud-speaker, and then placing the ball on a perforated tray, which automatically illuminates the corresponding number in an electric board on a wall in full view of all the players. After having withdrawn exactly 20 balls out of the 80 in the globe, the employee always stops, and the game has ended. During the drawing the players scrutinize hopefully the copies of their keno tickets. Depending on the number of blotches on his ticket corresponding to numbers called, a player will win some predesignated amount.

'In Table 72 (p. 192) I've itemized the Bank's percentages, pay-offs, and favorable probabilities pertinent to all 15 possible keno tickets.

TABLE 72

*Keno Tickets*

1-Spot: PC – 25.00 %

| Guess | Pay-off | Chance p |
|-------|---------|----------|
| 1     | 2.10    | 1/4      |

2-Spot: PC – 26.98 %

| Guess | Pay-off | Chance p |
|-------|---------|----------|
| 2     | 8.50    | 1/17     |

3-Spot: PC – 26.66 %

| Guess | Pay-off | Chance p |
|-------|---------|----------|
| 2     | 0.70    | 1/7      |
| 3     | 30.00   | 1/72     |

4-Spot: PC – 27.05 %

| Guess | Pay-off | Chance p |
|-------|---------|----------|
| 2     | 0.70    | 1/5      |
| 3     | 2.70    | 1/23     |
| 4     | 80.00   | 1/326    |

### 5-Spot: PC – 28.37%

| Guess | Pay-off | Chance p |
|-------|---------|----------|
| 3 | 1.20 | 1/13 |
| 4 | 15.00 | 1/83 |
| 5 | 340.00 | 1/1551 |

### 6-Spot: PC – 28.60%

| Guess | Pay-off | Chance p |
|-------|---------|----------|
| 3 | 0.60 | 1/9 |
| 4 | 3.30 | 1/36 |
| 5 | 60.00 | 1/324 |
| 6 | 1,100.00 | 1/7908 |

### 7-Spot: PC – 28.79%

| Guess | Pay-off | Chance p |
|-------|---------|----------|
| 3 | 0.30 | 1/7 |
| 4 | 1.20 | 1/20 |
| 5 | 15.00 | 1/117 |
| 6 | 230.00 | 1/1367 |
| 7 | 3,500.00 | 1/4086 |

### 8-Spot: PC – 29.90%

| Guess | Pay-off | Chance p |
|-------|---------|----------|
| 5 | 6.00 | 1/55 |
| 6 | 60.00 | 1/423 |
| 7 | 1,150.00 | 1/6233 |
| 8 | 12,500.00 | 1/230115 |

### 9-Spot: PC – 28.63%

| Guess | Pay-off | Chance p |
|-------|---------|----------|
| 4 | 0.30 | 1/10 |
| 5 | 2.30 | 1/32 |
| 6 | 30.00 | 1/176 |
| 7 | 200.00 | 1/1691 |
| 8 | 2,800.00 | 1/30683 |
| 9 | 12,500.00 | 1/1380689 |

### 10-Spot: PC – 28.11 %

| Guess | Pay-off | Chance p |
|-------|---------|----------|
| 5 | 1.40 | 1/20 |
| 6 | 14.00 | 1/88 |
| 7 | 98.00 | 1/621 |
| 8 | 700.00 | 1/7385 |
| 9 | 2,662.00 | 1/163182 |
| 10 | 12,500.00 | 1/8911712 |

### 11-Spot: PC – 29.84 %

| Guess | Pay-off | Chance p |
|-------|---------|----------|
| 5 | 0.60 | 1/14 |
| 6 | 6.00 | 1/50 |
| 7 | 50.00 | 1/278 |
| 8 | 250.00 | 1/2431 |
| 9 | 1,200.00 | 1/35245 |
| 10 | 7,500.00 | 1/945190 |
| 11 | 12,500.00 | 1/62322441 |

### 12-Spot: PC – 29.40 %

| Guess | Pay-off | Chance p |
|-------|---------|----------|
| 5 | 0.60 | 1/11 |
| 6 | 3.00 | 1/32 |
| 7 | 20.00 | 1/143 |
| 8 | 150.00 | 1/981 |
| 9 | 400.00 | 1/10483 |
| 10 | 1,000.00 | 1/184224 |
| 11 | 5,000.00 | 1/5978273 |
| 12 | 25,000.00 | 1/478261834 |

### 13-Spot: PC – 27.72 %

| Guess | Pay-off | Chance p |
|-------|---------|----------|
| 6 | 1.20 | 1/21 |
| 7 | 12.00 | 1/81 |
| 8 | 50.00 | 1/458 |
| 9 | 475.00 | 1/3848 |
| 10 | 2,500.00 | 1/49845 |
| 11 | 4,500.00 | 1/1060033 |
| 12 | 10,000.00 | 1/41694621 |
| 13 | 25,000.00 | 1/4065225580 |

## 14-Spot: PC – 29.52 %

| Guess | Pay-off | Chance p |
|-------|---------|----------|
| 6 | 2.20 | 1/15 |
| 7 | 5.50 | 1/50 |
| 8 | 22.00 | 1/239 |
| 9 | 175.00 | 1/1644 |
| 10 | 500.00 | 1/16740 |
| 11 | 2,000.00 | 1/262397 |
| 12 | 7,500.00 | 1/6764018 |
| 13 | 15,000.00 | 1/324250135 |
| 14 | 25,000.00 | 1/38910016200 |

## 15-Spot: PC – 30.00 %

| Guess | Pay-off | Chance p |
|-------|---------|----------|
| 6 | 1.00 | 1/12 |
| 7 | 5.00 | 1/33 |
| 8 | 15.00 | 1/136 |
| 9 | 75.00 | 1/789 |
| 10 | 200.00 | 1/6576 |
| 11 | 1,500.00 | 1/81021 |
| 12 | 5,000.00 | 1/15393973 |
| 13 | 15,000.00 | 1/483627321 |
| 14 | 20,000.00 | 1/28534011940 |
| 15 | 25,000.00 | 1/4280101791000 |

'The first of 1-Spot Ticket is the easiest to understand. Before the drawing we obtain a ticket, a paper rectangle of the 80 numbers and mark any 1 number. Let's assume we bet the minimum of 70 cents. If whatever number we mark is among the 20 drawn by the employee, then according to Table 72 (p. 192) we win $2.10 – for which our probability $p$ is 1/4 or 1 chance out of 4.

'Let's say we pay 70 cents for a 3-Spot Ticket and mark any 3 numbers out of the 80. If 2 of our numbers are among the 20 drawn by the employee, then we get paid back 70 cents. If all 3 of our members are among the 20 drawn by the employee, then we get paid $30.00.

'A parallel explanation may be applied to all the figures of the 13 other keno tickets.

'As for the Bank's percentage at keno, if we take the average of all 15 keno tickets, an average varying little, we note, from ticket to ticket, we find it's a whopping 28.31 per cent!

195

'Although the 10-Spot ticket is the most popular keno ticket, we note that its PC of 28.11 per cent is very close to the common average.

'And although the 12-, 13-, 14-, and 15-Spot Tickets offer the very large prize of $25,000.00, for any given player, as Table 72 (p. 192) shows, the probabilities of winning this sum at any keno game are respectively one chance out of 478,261,834, one chance out of 4,065,225,580, one chance out of 38,910,016,200, and lastly one chance out of 4,280,101,791,000.

'Now, Mr Optimist, after learning these facts do you have any desire to go and play keno?' I conclude.

'Forget it!' exclaims our friend, throwing up his hands.

# TRENTE ET QUARANTE TABLE

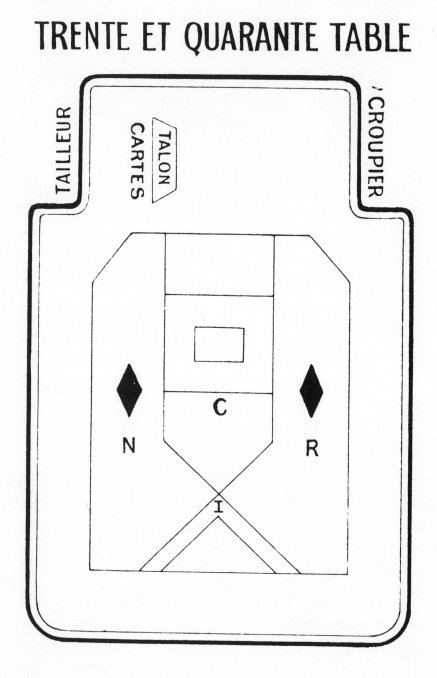

# CHAPTER XXI

# Trente-et-Quarante

'On my trip to Monte Carlo,' declares Mr Optimist, 'I saw this game played, but I didn't play it myself. What do the words mean?'

'The name of the game, *Trente-et-Quarante*, means simply "Thirty-and-Forty", and it's a game much older than roulette,' I reply. 'Trente-et-Quarante has two pairs of even-money chances, each pair being, *for all gambling purposes*, both mathematically and practically independent of each other. The first pair is the *red* and *black*, which are complementary to each other and, *excluding the matter of the PC*, are identical to the red and black at American or Monte-Carlo roulette. The second pair is *color* and *inverse*, which are complementary to each other and, *again excluding the matter of the PC*, are identical to, say, odd and even at American or Monte-Carlo roulette. The relationship between the two pairs of bets at Trente-et-Quarante is identical to that between the two *Tableaux* at baccara-en-banque. In each game there are two *completely independent* coin-tossing games simultaneously in progress at each hand.

'Trente-et-Quarante is played with 6 ordinary decks of cards, which are shuffled by an attendant croupier and then cut by any one of the players. Then they are placed by the *tailleur* or dealer about 2 feet in front of himself on the green felt layout. Their backs are toward him, and all 6 decks, faces outwards, lean against a dark marble block.

'Then the dealer puts face down into his left hand a number of the top cards sufficient for at least one hand or trial. After the players have placed their bets on either red, black, color, or inverse, the dealer announces the traditional, *rien ne va plus*, or "no more bets".

'Now, on the layout the dealer begins to deal the cards one by one face up in a row a short distance away, silently adding the pips

197

of the cards as he deals from left to right. Face cards and tens count 10, aces count 1, and the other cards according to their pip value.

'By definition this first row of cards represents *black*, and it is ended just as soon as its total exceeds 30, i.e. is either 31, 32, ... or 40. Whatever the total the dealer announces it by proclaiming only its last digit – thus *deux* for 32, *trois* for 33, etc. The exception is the total 40, which is given its full pronunciation, *quarante*.

'Then the dealer immediately deals the second row of cards between himself and the first or black row. By definition this second row represents red, and he ends it just as soon as its total exceeds 30.

'Unless the total of both rows be identical, that row is the winner whose total is *nearer 30*. Thus if the sum of the black row is 33 and that of the red 37, then black wins the hand. If the sum of the black row is 35 and that of the red 31, then red wins, and so forth.

'As for *color* and *inverse*, whether the one or the other wins depends entirely on the color of the *first card* of the *black row*. If this first card is the same color as the winning row, then *color* wins. On the other hand, if this first card is the opposite color of the winning row, then *inverse* wins.

'In announcing the result of a hand, custom disallows the dealer from using the two words *black* and *inverse*.

'Thus excluding ties, the dealer announces the 4 possible outcomes as follows:

'1. If both red and color win, the dealer says, *rouge gagne et couleur*, or "red wins, and color too".

'2. If red wins and color loses – that is, inverse wins – he says, *rouge gagne, couleur perd*, or "red wins, color loses".

'3. If red loses – that is, black wins – and color wins, he says, *rouge perd, couleur gagne*, or "red loses, color wins".

'4. If both red and color lose – that is, black and inverse win, he says, *rouge perd, et couleur*, or "red loses, and color too".

'On the other hand, if the total of both rows is identical, the hand is an *après*, a stand-off or tie for *all* 4 chances.

'If the tie is either 32–32, 33–33, 34–34 ... 40–40, the hand doesn't count. The gamblers may take away their old bets, put down new bets, or shift their old bets from one of the four chances to another. Then a new hand is dealt.

'If the total of both rows is 31–31, however, the hand is a special tie called *un après*, from which the Bank derives its *cagnotte* or PC.

'On the occurrence of the *un après* all uninsured bets go "into prison" just as they do on the occurrence of zero on the even-money chances at Monte-Carlo roulette.

'On the layout wagers on red and black are pushed by the croupier on to the red- and black-colored diamonds. Wagers on color are pushed into the small central square. And wagers on inverse are pushed inside the lines delimiting its triangular space.

'Should the next hand be a win, the bets are released from "prison" and pulled back to their original areas. Should it be a loss, the bets are raked in permanently by the croupier.

'This "in-prison" rule reduces the player's rate of loss by almost 1/2 – from a PC of what would have been about 1/42 to one of only 1/80.

'Given the "in-prison" rule, therefore, at Trente-et-Quarante the player has against him a PC of 1.25 per cent.

'On the other hand, all casinos allow the player to reduce even further the PC of 1/80 by *insuring* his wager for 1.00 per cent of its value. Before each hand the player pays this premium to the croupier, who in return places next to the stake a small white rectangular *contrat* or marker, saying *assurance payée*, or "insurance paid". The premium must be repaid after *every* hand, including after an *un après*, but excluding the ordinary *après* or tie. Hence the only amount the player loses is the cumulative sum paid for his insurance.

'A player is warned against paying a premium which, multiplied by 100, equals anything more than exactly the amount of the stake itself. To do otherwise is to pay witlessly too much insurance for the benefit received, i.e. we increase the PC unnecessarily. Thus although it's advantageous to pay a 5-unit premium for a 500-unit wager – the product of 5 and 100 being exactly 500 – it becomes increasingly disadvantageous to pay a 5-unit premium for, say, a 400-, 300-, 200-, or 100-unit wager, or a 10-unit premium for, say, a 900-, 800-, 700-, or 600-unit wager, etc.

'Given a stake properly insured for 1.00 per cent before every hand, therefore, at Trente-et-Quarante a player has against him a PC of 1.00 per cent.

'Combining a simple layout, procedure, rapidity of deals, and the relatively low PC's of either 1.25 per cent or 1.00 per cent, I think Trente-et-Quarante is quite a favorable game. What do you think Mr Optimist?' I conclude.

'I agree!' exclaims Mr Optimist.

199

# CHAPTER XXII

# Boule

'When I made my trip to Europe,' declares Mr Optimist, 'I had to buy a ticket to get into the gaming rooms to play roulette, baccara chemin-de-fer, baccara-en-banque, blackjack, craps, or Trente-et-Quarante. But I didn't have to buy a ticket to play *boule*, which is always located outside the main gaming rooms and open to the general public. I didn't play boule very much though.'

'The game of boule,' I comment, 'is superficially quite similar to roulette. Instead of a small plastic ball circling a wheel marked with 37 or 38 numbers, however, we have a larger rubber ball first circling then rolling at random over and around a low metal dome set in the center of a moderately shallow wooden basin. The surface of the dome is pocked with 18 cavities, into one of which the ball soon comes to rest. As the cavities are shallow and concave, the ball always rolls first rapidly then slowly into and out of several of them, following a sinuous, erratic path before lodging at random in one particular cavity. Although there are 18 cavities, there are actually only 9 different numbers represented, ranging from 1 through 9, each repeated twice.

'At American roulette there are 38 numbers, but all the pay-offs are based on only 36. At European roulette there are 37 numbers, but all the pay-offs are again based on only 36. At boule there are 9 numbers, but all the pay-offs are based on only 8. Thus at boule if we bet on a single number, on the green-felt layout, and win, we're paid off at odds of 7 to 1 – whereas 8 to 1 would be mathematically fair, If we bet on one of the 6 even-money chances and win, we're paid off at odds of 1 to 1 – whereas 5 to 4 would be mathematically fair.

'Thus the Bank makes a profit of 1/9 or 0.1111 ..., or a percentage or PC of 11.11 per cent on *all chances* on the layout.

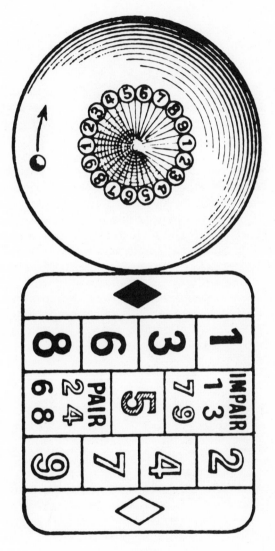

*Boule*

'At boule the 6 even-money chances are identical to those at Monte-Carlo roulette – *rouge*, *noir*, *pair*, *impair*, *passe*, and *manque*, i.e. red, black, even, odd, high, and low. The red numbers are 2, 4, 7, and 9, while the black ones are 1, 3, 6, and 8.

'The number 5 is *yellow* and is neither even, odd, high, or low. The number 5 functions at boule exactly like zero at American or Monte-Carlo roulette, being that extra number that makes the game mathematically unfair to the player.

'That's about all there is to say about boule,' I conclude.

'It seems foolish to play boule,' declares Mr Optimist, 'when its PC is as large as 11.11 per cent. Such a Bank's percentage is identical to the crap bets of Hardway 4 or 10, Any Craps, or the Field. It's obviously much less expensive to buy a ticket, for a small sum, for the main gaming rooms of the casino, where almost all the games have bets with much smaller PC's against a player.'

'Mr Optimist,' I add, 'I couldn't agree with you more!'

CHAPTER XXIII

# Conclusion

'I've read elsewhere,' declares Mr Optimist, 'that *all else being equal* a casino gambler's best strategy should be to bet only on that bet at that game with the smallest PC against him.'

'Yes, I've read that overly simple piece of advice many times myself,' I reply. 'The trouble is that *all else is never equal.* Consequently let's examine the matters which show the other facts – and therefore choices – a casino gambler must take into consideration.

'First, you'll recall your own statement, Mr Optimist, that when you visited the Monte-Carlo Casino you found that the minimum wager at the big game of baccara-en-banque was $100.00.'

'Yes, that's what I said,' responds our friend. 'As a matter of fact that's why I didn't play the game. I'm not a rich man, and I just can't afford that high a minimum.'

'I think you did absolutely the right thing. On the other hand had you followed that advice of the sole guide being the smallest PC you would have bet at baccara-en-banque, because as you'll recall, its PC of only 0.84 per cent is smaller than at any other game, blackjack aside. But let's add another factor which we must always consider, and which we may always calculate easily in our head. What we do is simply multiply the minimum wager by the PC of the bet at one game, multiply the minimum wager by the PC of the bet at another game, and compare the two products. The *smaller* product should serve as our guide. Let's take, for example, two games at the Monte-Carlo Casino. We recall that at baccara-en-banque the PC is 0.84 per cent, and that on any of the 6 even-money chances at roulette, say, red, the PC is 1.41 per cent. Let's say that for the first game the minimum, as you say, is $100.00, while for the second game it's $5.00. Hence if we multiply

202

0.84 per cent by $100 we get 84 cents, and if we multiply 1.41 per cent by $5.00 we get only 7 cents, so naturally *even though it has a higher PC*, the red at roulette is a much more favourable bet.

'In American casinos we follow exactly the same procedure. Thus if the minimum at, say, roulette is $5.00 and its PC is 5.26 per cent, then we multiply 5.26 per cent by $5.00 and get 26 cents. On the other hand, at craps on the Pass the minimum is, say, double or $10.00 and its PC is 1.41 per cent. Then we multiply $10.00 by 1.41 per cent and get 14 cents,' I conclude.

'In which case it's much better to shoot craps,' says Mr Optimist.

'Exactly,' I reply.

'By the way, how about a player's trying to win,' asks our friend, 'based on astrology, the occult, soothsayers, or parapsychology rather than on mathematics?'

'I think that may be answered very simply,' I reply. 'Which does the casino use – astrology, the occult, soothsayers, parapsychology – or mathematics?'

'Mathematics,' concedes Mr Optimist.

'Then presumably you've answered your own question,' I reply. 'But there's another point I want to bring up about the PC. Sometimes you'll read that if the casino has a bet with *no* PC then the casino and the player will just keep breaking even. This is ridiculous. First, let's take the following example. Let's say, Mr Optimist, that I'm the casino and you're the player. Let's say that your only capital is 1 unit and that my only capital is 1 unit. Let's say that we flip a coin once, Heads or Tails, you betting on Heads to win, I betting on Tails. Let's say the coin is flipped and lands Tails up.'

'Then I've lost all my capital and am ruined,' declares Mr Optimist somewhat sadly.

'Yes – and *yet the PC against you was zero*!' I affirm. 'What I'm talking about here is exactly what I was talking about in our discussion of craps. Do you remember the implications of Table 61 (p. 156)?'

'That Table showed,' recalls our friend, 'that even if there is *no* PC, owing to the ordinary fluctuations of *losing* digressions we'll go broke if our capital is inadequate.'

'Correct. And you know, Mr Optimist, there is a correct mathematical theorem which some people misapply. The theorem says that, all else being equal, the bettor with the larger capital will eventually beat the bettor with the smaller capital, and in proportion to the ratio of the larger to the smaller capital. Again, let's

203

say I'm the casino and you're the player. Let's say that my capital is 10 units and yours 1 unit. Let's say we're flipping a coin again and betting 1 unit a flip. Then the odds are 10 to 1 in my favor that you'll go broke before I do. Let's take a second example. Let's say my capital is 3 units and yours 2 units. Then the odds are 3 to 2 in my favor that again you'll go broke before I do.'

'But as the general public has not only millions but billions of dollars in capital compared to the capital of a casino, why doesn't the casino go broke? Is it because in actuality the casino has the PC in its favor?' asks Mr Optimist.

'No, a casino doesn't win because it has the PC in its favor,' I reply. 'The PC only *contributes* to the casino's winnings, which stem largely from ordinary *adverse digressions* that set in against a player, as indicated by Table 61 (p. 156). You see, you're entirely correct that the general public's capital is many times larger than the casino's. Let's say the public's capital is only a billion dollars, and that the casino's is 20 million dollars.'

'Then using the formula,' continues Mr Optimist, 'the odds that the casino will go broke before the public does are as large as 1,000,000,000 to 20,000,000, or 51 to 1 – yet I've never heard of a casino going broke!'

'Indeed you haven't,' I concede. 'But, you see, Mr Optimist, because of the casino's *maximum bet* – which, let's say, is 5,000 dollars – the public can't *collectively*, or an individual *singly*, wager more than 5,000 dollars out of the enormous billion dollars. Naturally every casino puts on a maximum to avoid ruin, which, without the maximum, would be inevitable.

'On the other hand, we mustn't forget entirely the matter of the casino's PC,' I add. 'In other words, any individual should always be guided by Table 12 (p. 21), which compares the various PC's on the even-money chances. And naturally he should be sure he has made the mentioned adjustment of multiplying the PC by the amount of the minimum bet.

'In addition, I want to stress again,' I continue, 'the results of the Hartman sample on the even-money chance of red at Monte-Carlo roulette, which you'll recall are listed in 100-spin games for 500 games in Table 27 (p. 59). You'll also recall that *at the end* of these 500 games 40 result in a return to equilibrium, 187 result in a plus digression, and 273 result in a minus digression.'

'What would be the results if we were betting flat stakes?' asks Mr Optimist.

204

'First we should subtract from the 500 games the 40 resulting in a return to equilibrium, because *at the end* of these we only break even – as we know. This leaves us with 460 games, of which 273 end in a minus digression and 187 in a plus digression, for a final net loss of $273-187=86$ games or units,' I conclude.

'If we use a *pro* staking system like the simple paroli,' asks Mr Optimist, 'can't we improve our performance?'

'No, and for two reasons,' I reply. 'The first reason is that any staking system inevitably raises the average amount we must stake. Let's say we adopt the simple paroli of doubling up our bet after every 4 winning trials. This increases our average wager from 1 unit to 2.133 units as indicated by Table 39 (p. 97). Thus in theory *at the end* of 50,000 spins instead of losing any$=(1)(50,000)(0.0141)=705$ units we'll lose any$=(2.133)(50,000)(0.0141)=1504$ units. The second reason is that although any staking system does well if a game *ends* in *winning* trials the same staking system does very badly if a game *ends* in *losing* trials. I discussed this important fact in the introduction to Chapter X (p. 112), the second chapter on staking systems. But the fact can't be repeated too often. Hence a staking system would win much more for us on the 187 games which *end* in a *plus* digression but lose much more for us on the 273 games which *end* in a *minus* digression.'

'And if a staking system inevitably wins more for us on *half* the 40 games ending in a return to equilibrium, because these 20 games *end* in *winning* trials,' adds Mr Optimist, 'then by the same unfortunate token the same staking system inevitably loses more for us on *half* the 40 games ending in a return to equilibrium, because these 20 games *end* in *losing* trials.'

'I'm afraid so,' I reply, 'and as indicated by Table 43 (p. 103), this gain exactly cancels out the loss.'

'So in the long run we'd do much better by playing flat stakes rather than any staking system whatsoever!' affirms Mr Optimist.

'Not necessarily,' I continue, 'This is what I meant a moment ago when I said every casino gambler must make choices – but so far as I'm concerned, the choices are oftentimes arbitrary. Let's take the following example. There are two crap tables with two Pass bets, whose PC is 1.41 per cent as we know. Which would you rather choose, Mr Optimist – to bet 1 unit on two Pass lines or 2 units on one Pass line? Remember the loss from the PC is identical in both cases – $(2.00)(1.41$ per cent$)=2.82$ units.

205

'As I remember your advising me at craps not to spread my capital thinly over more than one bet, I think I'd prefer to bet my 2 units on one Pass line,' answers Mr Optimist.

'I think I'd do the same thing,' I add, 'but it's true that we see some casino gamblers running from table to table placing bets on all of them – or placing a lot of different bets on one table, which amounts to the same thing. But as you say, it spreads out a gambler's capital thinly, which leads him to his ruin more quickly.

'And now, Mr Optimist, there is another matter a gambler must take into account when making up his mind about choice of bets. No author on gambling has ever pointed out that using a staking system on an even-money chance like red at roulette – a *short shot* – is an unconscious attempt by a player to turn the moderate *plus* and *minus* digressions of both *during* and *at the end* of n spins into the more violent ones of a bet like a single number at roulette – a *long shot*.

'To illustrate what I mean let's compare a simple paroli of 4 (or more) wins on red, where, let's say, $p=1/2$, to a 1-unit bet on a single number, say, zero, where $p=1/37$. As we learned in Chapter VIII (p. 84), the first of two chapters on the theory of runs, the probability at any trial of a run of 4 (or more) wins on red is $(1/2)^{4+1}=(1/2)^5=1/32$, which is roughly close to the probability at any trial of the occurrence of a single number, like zero, which is $p=1/37$. In other words the player "succeeds", if that's the right word, in changing the moderate *plus* and *minus* digressions of, say, those of the 4th and 5th columns of Table 27 (p. 59), to the much more violent *plus* and *minus* digressions of, say, those of Table 36 (p. 86) or those of Table 21 (p. 42),' I conclude.

'And as we also learned just now,' adds Mr Optimist, getting into the intellectual swim, 'the use of the simple paroli raises our average bet so that *at the end* of, say, 10,000 spins we lose any=(2.133) (10,000) (0.0141)=*300* units, whereas on a single number we lose only any=(1) (10,000) (0.027027)=*270* units. So by adopting the simple paroli we unwittingly erase our smaller loss from the flat-stake PC of only 1.41 per cent and increase it to *more than* that of the larger single-number PC of 2.70 per cent!

'And now, in ending our discussion on choices and strategies, Mr Optimist, there is one more matter which almost no author on gambling has ever explained, and it's indeed one of the most important mathematical facts a gambler must know!' I affirm.

'What matter is that?' asks Mr Optimist.

'It's the probability of a given event occurring *at least once* during *r* trials versus *not at all* during the same *r* trials.

'First, let's select an event – say one number at roulette, like zero, whose probability of occurrence at any given trial is $p=1/37$, and whose probability of not occurring at any given trial is $q=36/37$, as we know.

'Now *during the very next r* trials the probability of $Q^r$ of a *losing run*, i.e. that zero will *not occur* at all is ...

$$Q^r$$

'And *during the very next r* trials the probability $(1-Q^r)=P$ that zero will occur *at least once* is ...

$$(1-Q^r)=P$$

'Table 73 (p. 207) shows, in the lefthand column, the probability of zero's occurring *at least once during r* spins, while, in the right-hand column, the probability of zero's occurring *not at all* during *r* spins (a *losing run*).

TABLE 73

| at least once | not at all | during r spins |
|---|---|---|
| 25 % | 75 % | 10 spins |
| 50 % | 50 % | 25 ,, |
| 75 % | 25 % | 50 ,, |
| 90 % | 10 % | 83 ,, |
| 95 % | 5 % | 108 ,, |
| 99 % | 1 % | 169 ,, |
| 999 % | 0.001 % | 253 ,, |
| 9,999 % | 0.000,1 % | 336 ,, |
| 99,999 % | 0.000,01 % | 417 ,, |
| 999,999 % | 0.000,0001 % | 500 ,, |

'For a gambler the righthand column of percentages is perhaps the most instructive. Thus the probability of zero's not occurring at all during 10 spins is 75 per cent, during 25 spins is 50 per cent, during 50 spins is 25 per cent, and the probability of a losing run as long as 253 spins is as small as 0.001 per cent – yet it DOES occur.

'If we look back at Table 21 (p. 42), giving the length *r* of all the *losing runs during* the 46,080 spins of the Hartman sample, we'll find that the 6th *losing run* is as long as 159 spins. Yet how many gamblers would say that there "must be something wrong with the roulette wheel" if their number doesn't occur *during* 159 spins?

'And if we look back at Table 22 (p. 48), giving the length $r$ of the longest *losing run during* all 45 sessions, each 1,024 spins long, we find that the longest *losing run*, occurring *during* the 17th session, is as long as 268 spins. Again, how many gamblers would be "very suspicious" of the roulette wheel? Yet groundlessly so!

'Now remember, Mr Optimist, what I've said before – even though I may be talking about roulette, I'm also talking – by extension – of all the other games found in a gambling casino.

'Let's say a player buys the usual "stack" of chips or checks to play roulette, i.e. a stack of 20 chips each $1.00 apiece. Let's say he begins betting $1.00 a spin on, say, zero. Let's say zero doesn't occur even once *during* the first 25 spins. As we note from the righthand column of Table 73 (p. 207), there is as much as a 50 per cent probability that this will occur every time a player sits down and begins betting. Yet having bought the standard "stack" of 20 chips, our imaginary player has lost his entire capital by only the 20th spin!

'Let's say zero doesn't occur even once *during* the first 83 spins. Again, as we note from the righthand column of Table 73 (p. 207), there is as much as a 10 per cent probability that this will occur every time a player sits down and begins betting. Yet having bought as many as *four* standard "stacks" of 20 chips each, our imaginary player has lost *all four* stacks by the 80th spin. If we imagine 10 players betting at 10 different roulette wheels, this will happen on an average to one of them. Yet will this unfortunate soul complain to the management that "there is something wrong" with the roulette wheel? Or perhaps he'll only think so and not favor anyone else with his "suspicions".

'In sum we may generalize by saying that if the probability of the occurrence of an event is only slightly small gamblers *should not be the least surprised* that *losing runs* will occur *during r* trials.

'Let's take, for example, the system called the simple paroli. As we learned in Chapter VIII (p. 84), the first of two chapters on the theory of runs, the probability at any trial of a run of 4 (or more) wins on red is $(1/2)^{4+1}=(1/2)^5=1/32$, and that the probability of its not occurring at any given trial is consequently $1-(1/32)=31/32$. Hence if we make out for the simple paroli of 4 (or more) wins Table 74 (p. 209) corresponding to Table 73 (p. 207), we have ...

TABLE 74

| at least once | not at all | during r trials |
|---|---|---|
| 25 % | 75 % | 9 trials |
| 50 % | 50 % | 22 ,, |
| 75 % | 25 % | 43 ,, |
| 90 % | 10 % | 72 ,, |
| 95 % | 5 % | 93 ,, |
| 99 % | 1 % | 145 ,, |
| 999 % | 0.001 % | 218 ,, |

'Or in other words, a gambler playing the simple paroli or 4 (or more) wins should expect a *losing run* 22 trials long 50 per cent of the time, a *losing run* 43 trials long 25 per cent of the time, a losing run 72 trials long 10 per cent of the time . . . and a *losing run* as long as 218 trials as often as 0.001 per cent of the time.' I conclude.

'I notice that if a run of 4 (or more) wins should occur on an average once every 32 trials,' comments Mr Optimist, 'and if half of 32 is 16, yet the fifty–fifty point comes significantly *after* 16 trials. In the simple paroli of 4 (or more) wins, for instance, I note that the fifty–fifty point occurs not at the 16th trial but at the 22nd trial. In other words, I must remember that the probability of occurrence of a *losing run* is *asymmetrical*.'

'Indeed it is asymmetrical as you put it. At roulette any number should occur on an average once every 37 spins,' I continue, 'and if half of 37 is 19, yet the fifty–fifty point comes *after* 19 spins as we note in Table 73 (p. 207), which gives 25 spins.'

'Now I understand more why the fifty–fifty point for a slot-machine Jack Pot is also *asymmetrical*,' declares Mr Optimist. 'Although in the slot machine we examined, the probability at any pull or trial was 1/667, the fifty–fifty point didn't occur at the (667/2)=334th pull but at the 462nd pull as shown by the figures at the end of Chapter XVIII (p. 181).'

'Yes, and the same thing may be said of winning the bingo prize.' I add. 'Although the probability of our imaginary bingo prize was 1/200, the fifty–fifty point didn't occur at the (200/2)=100th game but at the 138th game as shown by Table 70 (p. 189).

'In general, to calculate the fifty–fifty point of occurrence of any event we multiply the odds-to-1 against its occurrence in a single trial by the fraction 7/10 or 0.7. It's a little number you can keep in your pocket, Mr Optimist,' I conclude.

'And now, Mr Optimist, as I can think of no more helpful points

209

to tell you, I'm afraid my conclusion discussing choices and strategies must come to an end. I hope that nothing I've told you either in this chapter or earlier ones has in any way discouraged you,' I say finally.

'Oh, you haven't discouraged me one bit!' announces Mr Optimist, getting up to go to the casino.

'Wait a minute, Mr Optimist,' I exclaim, 'you've got on your shoes, spats, striped trousers, cutaway, yellow-flowered vest, velvet coat, white boutonnière, and top hat – why aren't you wearing your shirt?'

'Oh, I lost that last night! Good-bye!' he cries back.

# Bibliography

Bachelier, Louis (1870–1946), *Traité sur le Calcul des Probabilités*, Paris, 1912.

*Le Jeu, la Chance, et le Hasard*, Paris, 1914.

Baldwin, Cantey, Maisel, and McDermott, *Playing Blackjack to Win*, New York, 1957.

Epstein, Richard A., *The Theory of Gambling and Statistical Logic*, New York, 1967.

Feller, William (1906–1970), *An Introduction to Probability Theory and its Applications*, New York, 1950, 1968.

Gall, Martin (Arnous de Rivière, Jules), *La Roulette et le Trente-et-Quarante*, Paris, 1882.

Hartman, Hans, *Roulette Expert*, Berlin, 1934.

Hopkins, Marsh, *Chance and Error*, New York, 1923.

Humble, Lancelot, *Blackjack Gold*, Toronto, 1976.

Thorp, Edward O., *Beat the Dealer*, New York, 1962, 1966.

Whitworth, William A., *Choice and Chance*, New York, 1951.

Wiley, Dean, *Understanding Gambling Systems*, Las Vegas, 1975.

Wilson, Allan N., *The Casino Gambler's Guide*, New York, 1965.

211

# Appendix

(1) Table 1 (p. 2). Formulas: (a) mathematically fair pay-off odds to 1: $(q/p)$ *to 1*. *(b)* conversion of $z$ units into $x$: $x$ is number of wins more or less from $pn$; $a$ is average number of units bet; hence: $(ax/p)=z$. (c) average plus or minus digression $x$ *at the end* of $n$ trials: $x=0.7978\sqrt{npq}$.

(2) Table 2 (p. 2). Formula: (a) probability of a return to equilibrium *at the end* of $n$ trials: $eq=0.3989/\sqrt{npq}$.

(3) Table 3 (p. 3). Formula: (a) just add consecutively values of (2) above, viz. $0.5000+0.37500=0.8750$, etc. (b) or use $0.7978\sqrt{n-1}$.

(4) Table 4 (p. 4). Formula: (a) for such small values see Pascal's figurate triangle, as in Bibliography – Gall, Martin, pp. 147, 306 and 331.

(5) Table 5A and 5B. Formulas: (a) probability $P$ of $z$ *or fewer* returns to equilibrium *during n* trials – just add consecutively the values of (4) above, viz. $0.176+0.176+0.167=0.519$, etc. (b) or $t=(z+1)\,(0.7071)/\sqrt{n-z}$, yields $P$, and $1-P=Q$; $t$ signifies *theta* function (with 2 under the radical) and appropriate table is in Bibliography – Hopkins, Marsh, his Appendix, p. 214 *et seq*.

(6) Table 6 (p. 6). Formula: see (5) (b) above.

(7) Table 7 (p. 7). See Bibliography – Feller, William, 3rd ed., p. 87.

(8) Table 8 (p. 11). Formula: see (5) (b) above.

(9) Table 9 (p. 13). Formula: $T=(x+0.5)/\sqrt{2npq}$; given $z$, whence $x$, what is $P$? and $Q=1-P$. Again $t$ signifies *theta* function,

and appropriate table is in Bibliography – Hopkins, Marsh, his Appendix, p. 214 *et seq*.

(10)  Table 10 (p. 15). Formulas: (a) for values in 1st column of $z$ see (1) above. (b) for values in 2nd column of $z$ just multiply those in (a) by the factor 1.625; (c) or $z = (ax/p)$, and $x = 1.31\sqrt{npq}$, value of average digression *during n* trials.

(11)  Table 12 (p. 21). For calculations and values of PC see subsequent notes on each game. Formula: $0.04/y^2$: $0.4\sqrt{npq} = ny$, and when $p = q = 1/2$, then $0.2\sqrt{n} = ny$, which gives $n = 0.04/y^2$.

(12)  Table 15. Formula: see (9) above.

(13)  Table 17 (p. 37). Formulas: (a) *at end* of $n$ trials theoretical number *winning* runs exactly $r$ trials long: $(np^rq^2)$; ditto *losing* runs: $(np^2q^r)$; (b) *winning* runs of $r$ (or more): $(nqp^r)$ ditto *losing* runs of $r$ (or more); (c) theoretical average number *winning* runs: $npq$; ditto losing runs; (d) winning trials: $np$; (e) ditto losing trials: $nq$. (f) *winning* runs of $r$ (or more): $r + (1/q)$; ditto *losing* runs of $r$ (or more): $r + (1/p)$.

(14)  Table 18 (p. 37). Formula: see (13) above.

(15)  Table 34 (p. 79): see (10) above. Although the theoretical values of both *at end* and *during* are both for fair game and should be for unfair one, I didn't want possibly to confuse readers with a third parameter; for unfair *during* see Bibliography, Bachelier, Louis, pp. 231–32, and examples, p. 230.

(16)  Chapter IV, p. 23: the value of $n$ must be adjusted to $n - (3n/74)$ owing to the 'in-prison' rule for the 6 even-money chances, like red, because 3 hidden ties in the game must be eliminated before the PC may be calculated.

The traditional value of the PC on any even-money chance at Monte-Carlo roulette is explained by Ballore, Montessus de, in *Calcul des Probabilites*, Paris, 1908, Chapter III, 'Avantage du Banquier à la Roulette', which goes as follows.

The probability of zero in a single trial is $p = 1/37$, that of either red or black 1/2. When zero occurs, a bet on red is put 'into prison', i.e. the croupier takes his rake and pulls the wager on to a yellow line printed on the rectangular area reserved for a red bet. If the *next* spin is red, the croupier 'frees' the bet by pushing it back to its original position. If the *next* spin is black, the croupier rakes in the red bet, which is permanently lost. As zero will be followed half the

213

time by a red and black alternately, then half the time after zero occurs it will be lost. Hence the PC of a bet on red is $(1/37)(1/2)=1/74=0.135135$ ... Both Bachelier, Louis (see Bibliography), Bertrand, Joseph, and Borel, Emile agree with Ballore's reasoning and arrive at the same PC.

Owing to the 3 hidden ties, my own reasoning is as follows.

The following equation represents the theoretical situation, with the 3 underlined quantities signifying the ties. The letter $R$ signifies red, $B$ black, and $Z$ zero:

$18R+18B+\underline{1Z}$ (into prison)$+1R$ (out of prison) $+17R+17B+\underline{1Z}$ (into prison)$+1B$ (permanently lost)$=74$ spins

Two cycles of 37 spins each, making one of 74, are required to get the bet into prison, out of it, and into it again, and then permanently lost. In each cycle there must be exactly $18R$ plus $18B$ plus $1Z$, no more, no less. Thus in the second cycle the main quantity of red is only $17R$ not $18R$, because $1R$ had to be expended getting the bet out of prison, into which it had gone in the first cycle. Likewise the main quantity of black is only $17B$, not $18B$, because $1B$ has to be conserved for use when the bet is permanently lost to the Bank on the last spin. As the bet on red is neither won nor lost by either the Bank or the player when it goes into or comes out of prison, the 3 underlined spins function as ties and must be subtracted, therefore, from the total number of 74 possibilities:

$$18R+18B+17R+1B=71R \ \& \ B,$$
$$\text{and } 35R+36B=71R \ \& \ B$$

Hence the final favorable probability of red (or of any of the 6 even-money chances) is 35/71, and the PC is 1/71 or 0.014084. ... On the numbers themselves the PC remains $1/37=0.027027027$ ...

(17) Table 35 (p. 84). Formula: when $p=q=1/2$, the average length of runs of $r$ (or more) Heads (Tails) is always $r+2$. Ditto average number of trials absorbed by Heads (Tails).

(18) Table 36 (p. 86). 6th column: $(11,918/47)=253.58$, etc.

(19) Table 55 (p. 136). Formula: see Bibliography – Whitworth, William A, Prop. LXVIII (p. 235), $P=w/(w+1)$, $Q=1-P$;

hence, $w=1$, 1 (letter) equals 10, then $P=1/(1+10)=0.91$, $Q=0.09$, etc. Although Mr Optimist remains enthusiastic about this progression, we note sadly that the fifty-fifty point comes as early as when a player's progression increases to as few as 3 units; after that the value of $P$ continues its precipitous decline to infinity; when the bet becomes 6, $Q=0.71$; when the bet becomes 10, $Q=0.83$; and when the bet becomes 20, $Q=0.91$, etc; and in an unfair game, of course, the value of $Q$ increases much more rapidly.

(20) Table 57 (p. 139). Formula: the figures of the righthand column are directly related to a diagonal of coefficients of Pascal's triangle; see (4) above.

(21) Table 59 (p. 143). Formula: see (9) above.

(22) Table 60 (p. 153). Formula: see (9) above.

(23) Table 61 (p. 156). Formula: $t=(x+0.5)/\sqrt{2npq}$, and $n= (x^2+x+0.25) / (t^2 2pq)$; hence the constant with which one multiplies the expression … $(x^x+x+0.25)/pq$ … (which equals $n$) … is always $1/(0.5/t^2)$. Hence when $Q=0.01$, the constant is 0.15; when $Q=0.05$, the constant is 0.26 … when $Q=0.50$, the constant is 2.21, etc. For the value of $t$, see (5) above.

(24) Table 63 (p. 164), See Bibliography – Thorp, Table 3.5, p. 30. Although I consider Professor Edward O. Thorp's *Beat the Dealer* still the best book on blackjack, the enthusiast should see also the appropriate entry in Bibliography – Wilson, Allan. Other books are: Humble, Lancelot, *Blackjack Gold*, Toronto (Ontario), Canada, 1976; 'Noir, Jacques', *Casino Holiday*, Berkeley, 1968, 1970; and Revere, Lawrence, *Playing Blackjack as a Business*, Las Vegas, 1970.

(25) For the mathematical information on Nevada baccarat, see the paper, *A Favorable Side Bet in Nevada Baccarat*, by Thorp, Edward O., and Walden, William E., *JASA*, June, 1966, Vol. 61, Part I, pp. 313–28.

For rules and general information, see: 'Nolan, Walter I' (Luckman, John), *The Facts of Baccarat*, Las Vegas, 1970.

(26) For the mathematical information on baccara chemin-de-fer, see:

(a) the book, *La Chance et les Jeux de Hasard*, by Boll,

Marcel, Paris, 1936, Chapter XV–Chapter XVII, pp. 205–39.

(b) the paper, *Statistical Aspects of the Legality of Gambling*, by Kendall, M. G., and Murchland, J. D., *JRSS*, A (1964), vol. 127, *Part 3*, pp. 359–91.

(c) the paper, *Banker's Games and the Gaming Act of 1968*, by Downton, F., and Holder, R. L., *JRSS*, A (1972), vol. 135, *Part 3*, pp. 336–64.

(d) the paper, *Calcul de l'Avantage du Banquier au Jeu de Baccara*, by Lafrogne (Admiral), Jules L. H., Paris, 1927.

27 For the mathematics of baccara-en-banque, see (26) (b)(c)(d) above.

I myself draw on my own unpublished paper, *Banker's Strategy at Baccara-en-Banque*, New York, 1974 (87 pp.), whence the following data:

For baccara chemin-de-fer the Banker's advantage (not the casino's PC of 1.15 per cent) is 1.28 per cent at every hand or trial. For this optimal advantage, regardless of the player's strategy, see (26)(c) (pp. 345–46) above.

There are 7 possible hands between the Banker and the 1 Player.

At baccara-en-banque there occur 11 possible hands between the Banker and the 2 Players (*tableaux* 1 and 2), of which 6 hands alone give the Banker his advantage. There occur about 38 hands in a 6-deck shoe (versus 59 hands at baccara chemin-de-fer).

For both baccara chemin-de-fer and baccara-en-banque, when the Banker's initial 2-card total is either 0, 1, 2, 7, 8, or 9, his advantage is zero, while if the total is either 3, 4, 5, or 6, his advantage is positive.

For baccara-en-banque, for purposes of analysis I divide the 11 hands into Non-conflicting Situations (NCS) or Conflicting Situations (CS). Definition of NCS: if the Banker must S (stand) or D (draw) because of the values of both Player's 3rd cards (or lack of them if the Players S) indicates S or D. Definition of CS: if the Banker must S because the value of one Player's 3rd card (or lack of it if the Player S) indicates S, while that of the other Player's 3rd card (or lack of it if the Player S) indicates D.

'When NCS occurs, which is 13.76 per cent of the 11 possible hands, if the Banker adopts the optimal strategy, his advantage, as mentioned, is invariably 1.28 per cent regardless of the differing

216

amounts bet by each Player (i.e. of the differing amounts of the collective wagers on both *tableaux*).

For a NCS the Banker follows his ordinary S-D strategy for baccara chemin-de-fer or Nevada baccarat, Table 64, lower part, p. 169.

When a CS occurs, which is 6.39 per cent of the 11 possible hands, the Banker's advantage extends from a low of 0.84 per cent, when both Players bet even money, to a high of 1.28 per cent, when one Player (*tableau*) bets nothing and the other (*tableau*) bets the maximum.

For a CS the Banker follows a different strategy if the Players' bets are *equal* or *unequal*.

If the Players' bets are *equal*, the Banker notes the values of the 3rd cards (or lack of them), that one indicates he should S, the other that he should D, compares their *q* multipliers, and S or D according to which *q* multiplier is *larger*. Thus the Banker easily turns a CS into a NCS. Table 75 (p. 217) consists of the *q* multipliers in a simplified version. The Banker must rigorously commit the table to memory.

TABLE 75

Banker's *q* Multipliers

| Banker's total | | Banker's giving | | | | | | | | | | |
|---|---|---|---|---|---|---|---|---|---|---|---|---|
| | | 0 | 1 | 2 | 3 | 4 | 5 | 6 | 7 | 8 | 9 | No |
| 3 | $q$ | 11 | 21 | 31 | 49 | 53 | 38 | 23 | 7 | **3** | 1 | 50 |
| 4 | $q$ | **15** | **4** | 6 | 16 | 33 | 38 | 23 | 7 | **9** | **18** | 50 |
| 5 | $q$ | **33** | **30** | **20** | **10** | 0.5 | 18 | 23 | 7 | **9** | **24** | 37 |
| 6 | $q$ | **39** | **49** | **46** | **35** | **25** | **15** | 3 | 7 | **9** | **24** | **8** |

Draw on light numbers. **Stand on dark numbers.**

On the other hand, if the Players' bets are *unequal*, then the Banker must use the *q* multipliers of Table 75 (p. 217) as follows.

Let *a* and *b* signify the amounts of the bets of Players 1 and 2 (*tableaux* 1 and 2) respectively at each hand. If *c* and *d* are considered the two *q* multipliers applying respectively to Players 1 and 2 (*tableaux* 1 and 2) at any hand, then when *ac* is *larger* than *bd* (or vice versa), to the Banker the advantage of Player 1 is larger than that of Player 2 (or vice versa). Thus the Banker will ignore the Player with the *smaller* advantage and, against the Player with the *larger* advantage, S or D according to the Banker's ordinary strategy for baccara chemin-de-fer found in the Nevada baccarat Table 64, lower part, p. 169.

Before the hand starts, i.e. before the croupier says, *rien ne va plus* or 'no more bets', the Banker should always add up the amounts of both *a* and *b* and remember them. The fact that the chips of different denominations are of different colors aids him in his addition. When the moment in the hand comes for the Banker either to S or D, if *ac* and *bd* are close to being equal and the Banker has forgotten the result of his addition, and accordingly doesn't know whether to S or D, he may announce to the croupier opposite him on his high chair, *faire compter* or 'please count the units on each tableau'. After the croupier does this aloud, the banker remultiplies *ac* and *bd*, and follows the strategy as indicated.

As for Table 65 (p. 180), we note that the casino's PC of 0.84 per cent to 1.28 per cent is identical to that of the Banker's PC. To calculate the percentages of Table 65 (p. 180) we take a ratio of, say, 2:1; $2/3 = 0.67$, and $(0.67)(0.0128) = 0.008576$. Ditto for the other ratios.

As my own casual observation of the baccara-en-banque game at the Monte-Carlo Casino has been that the ratio seldom exceeds 2:1, I have set down arbitrarily in Table 12 (p. 21) a 'typical' PC of 0.92 per cent.

There are typically two sessions a day at baccara-en-banque at Monte-Carlo, one between 5:30 p.m. and 7:30 p.m., the other between 11:00 p.m. and 1:00 a.m. The two sessions are divided into two deals, each about 45 minutes long. Each deal exhausts one 6-deck shoe of about 38 hands. The 6 decks are thoroughly shuffled or reshuffled by croupiers before every deal. During the 15-minute intermissions between deals the players may rise from their chairs and congregate socially. Although paid very well by the casino and consequently its employee, being on an equal par, as it were, with the other players in the game, in the casino the Banker may mix socially with the other players. But the croupier may not.

(28) Table 71 (p. 189). Formula: (a) There are 24 numbers on each bingo card and a total of 75 balls in the bingo blower. Hence substitute 75 for *n* and 24 for *r* in ...

$$n(n-1)\ (n-2)\ \dots\ (n-r+1)/r!$$

... for which see Bibliography – either Whitworth, William A., Prop. VIII (bis)., p. 62, or Feller, William, 'Substitutions and Partitions', p. 34 *et seq*.

Then (b) using above formula, substitute 50, 51, 52, etc. for $n$ and 24 for $r$.

Then for (c), divide (a) by (b) above.

(29) Table 72 (p. 192). Formula: Following (28)(a) above, substitute 80 for $n$ and the number of spots for $r$.

As new and even more unfavorable pay-offs for every ticket were introduced in Nevada in 1974, the results of prior calculations are naturally erroneous. The average old keno PC was about 21 per cent a ticket, while the average new PC is 28.31 per cent a ticket.

As the 10-Spot ticket is the most popular of the 15 tickets there follows the calculations for the 10-Spot ticket:

| Pay-offs | | | permutations | | ticket value |
|---|---|---|---|---|---|
| 5 | 1.40 | × | 84,675.3 | = | 118,545.42 |
| 6 | 14.00 | × | 18,900.7 | = | 264,609.80 |
| 7 | 98.00 | × | 2,652.7 | = | 259,964.60 |
| 8 | 700.00 | × | 223.0 | = | 156,100.00 |
| 9 | 2,660.00 | × | 10.1 | = | 26,866.00 |
| 10 | 12,500.00 | × | 0.2 | = | 2,500.00 |
| | | | | | 828,585.82 |

... and $(1,152,544.4-828,585.82)/(1,152,544.4)=0.281,081,2$ ..., and $(0.281,081,2 \dots)\ (100)=28.11$ per cent.

(30) Trente-et)Quarante, Chapter XXI (pp. 197–99): The first adequate calculations for this game were done in the paper, *Sur l'Avantage du Banquier au Jeu du Trente-et-Quarante*, Annales de Mathématiques, Vol. XVI, 1825–26, by Poisson, Denis, whose values for the probabilities of success at any given trial are:

0.021967 for the *un après* (31–31)
0.087830 for the ordinary *après* (32–32, 33–33 ... 40–40)
0.890250 for both red and black (or color and inverse)
1.000047

Subtraction of the *après* gives us 21,967 – 890,250=912,217 ostensibly significant hands from the standpoint of the PC. Then

219

following reasoning of (16) above, instead of a preliminary cycle of $2 \times 37 = 74$ spins and the final one of 71, for Trente-et-Quarante the preliminary cycle is $2 \times 912,127 = 1,824,434$ hands and the final one of 1,758,533. As before, $R$ stands for red, $B$ for black, but instead of $Z$ for zero we have $U$ for *un après*. Again, assuming we bet on red to win, we have the ties underlined and get ...

445,125R + 445,125B + 21,967U (into prison) + 21,967R (out of prison) + (445,125R − 21,967R) + (445,125B − 21,967B) + 21,967U (into prison) + 21,967B (lost) = 1,824,434

Again, as in roulette, some red and black quantities must be 'borrowed', others 'saved' in the second half of the equation so that the total number of reds and blacks of which it is composed will be no more or less numerous than those composing the first half. In roulette the quantities were $1R$ and $1B$, whereas here they are $21,967R$ and $21,967B$. After simplification and subtraction of all ties we have ...

445,125R + 445,125B + 423,158R + 423,158B + 21,967B = 868,283R + 890,250B = 1,758,533R & B

Hence the final favorable probability of red (black, color, inverse) is $868,283/1,758,533 = 0.493,754 \ldots$

And the Bank's percentage as a decimal fraction is $21,967/1,758,533 = 0.012492 \ldots$ (*uninsured*). With *insurance*, of course, the Bank's expectation is 0.0100. Hence it's better to take insurance *invariably*.

For further study consult the paper, *The Fundamental Theorem of Card Counting with Applications to Trente-et-Quarante and Baccarat*, by Thorp, Edward O., and Walden, William E., in *International Journal of Game Theory*, Vol. 2, No. 2, pp. 109–19 (1973).

From *The Fundamental Theorem* ... we learn that, for practical gambling purposes, it is not possible to sum consecutively the cards with any positive gambling result at either baccara chemin-de-fer or Trente-et-Quarante.

(31) Tables 73, 74, etc. (pp. 207–209). Formula: if $P$ signifies the probability of the occurrence of an event *at least once* and $Q$ *not at all*, both *during n* trials, then we have ... $P = 1 - Q^r$. To calculate $P$ we adopt the logarithmic formula ... $R = (\log P)/(\log Q)$.

Using $p = 1/37$, for a single number at roulette, one computes the following constants for $P$:

| P | constants |
|---|---|
| 0.10 | 0.106×36 (odds to 1 against) |
| 0.25 | 0.288 |
| 0.33 | 0.398 |
| 0.50 | 0.6944 ... =0.7 |
| 0.63 | 1.0277 |
| 0.67 | 1.1111 |
| 0.75 | 1.3888 |
| 0.875 | 2.0832 |
| 0.90 | 2.3056 |
| 0.95 | 3.0000 |
| 0.99 | 4.6667 |
| 0.999 | 7.0222 |
| 0.999,9 | 9.3333 |
| 0.999,99 | 11,5833 |
| 0.999,999 | 13.8888 |

Although the above constants may be used with relative safety when $p$ is smaller than $1/37$ (though the value of $r$ becomes too large), if $p$ is larger than $1/37$ the error increases rapidly, and the value of $r$ becomes much too small. Thus when $p=1/6$, $P=0.50$, and the constant is 4; $P=0.75$, and the constant is 8.

For a discussion of *losing* runs, see Bibliography – Feller, William, 3rd ed., Table 3 (p. 325); when $p=q=1/2$, his values are 3/4, 5/8, 8/16, 13/32, etc., i.e. to get the next value, for numerator, add last two numerators; for denominator, multiply last denominator by 2.

221